CAMBRIDGE LIBRARY COLLECTION

Books of enduring scholarly value

Polar Exploration

This series includes accounts, by eye-witnesses and contemporaries, of early expeditions to the Arctic and the Antarctic. Huge resources were invested in such endeavours, particularly the search for the North-West Passage, which, if successful, promised enormous strategic and commercial rewards. Cartographers and scientists travelled with many of the expeditions, and their work made important contributions to earth sciences, climatology, botany and zoology. They also brought back anthropological information about the indigenous peoples of the Arctic region and the southern fringes of the American continent. The series further includes dramatic and poignant accounts of the harsh realities of working in extreme conditions and utter isolation in bygone centuries.

A Voyage towards the North Pole

A friend of Sir Joseph Banks, and with scientific interests of his own, the naval officer Constantine John Phipps (1744–92) was appointed by the Admiralty in 1773 to command an Arctic expedition in search of a passage to the Pacific. Among the crew was a young Horatio Nelson and a freed slave, Olaudah Equiano, who became the first African to visit the Arctic. Although unsuccessful in its primary aim, the voyage is noteworthy for Phipps' description of the polar bear as a distinct species, and for being a naval voyage on which research was deemed as crucial as exploration. Following the publication of this account in 1774, the *Gentleman's Magazine* commented that 'there has not appeared a voyage in any language so replete with nautical information, nor in which the mariner and philosopher can find such liberal entertainment'. Illustrated throughout, the work includes a substantial appendix containing the scientific data.

Cambridge University Press has long been a pioneer in the reissuing of out-of-print titles from its own backlist, producing digital reprints of books that are still sought after by scholars and students but could not be reprinted economically using traditional technology. The Cambridge Library Collection extends this activity to a wider range of books which are still of importance to researchers and professionals, either for the source material they contain, or as landmarks in the history of their academic discipline.

Drawing from the world-renowned collections in the Cambridge University Library and other partner libraries, and guided by the advice of experts in each subject area, Cambridge University Press is using state-of-the-art scanning machines in its own Printing House to capture the content of each book selected for inclusion. The files are processed to give a consistently clear, crisp image, and the books finished to the high quality standard for which the Press is recognised around the world. The latest print-on-demand technology ensures that the books will remain available indefinitely, and that orders for single or multiple copies can quickly be supplied.

The Cambridge Library Collection brings back to life books of enduring scholarly value (including out-of-copyright works originally issued by other publishers) across a wide range of disciplines in the humanities and social sciences and in science and technology.

A Voyage towards the North Pole

Undertaken by His Majesty's Command 1773

CONSTANTINE JOHN PHIPPS

CAMBRIDGE
UNIVERSITY PRESS

CAMBRIDGE
UNIVERSITY PRESS

University Printing House, Cambridge, CB2 8BS, United Kingdom

Published in the United States of America by Cambridge University Press, New York

Cambridge University Press is part of the University of Cambridge.
It furthers the University's mission by disseminating knowledge in the pursuit of
education, learning and research at the highest international levels of excellence.

www.cambridge.org
Information on this title: www.cambridge.org/9781108069724

© in this compilation Cambridge University Press 2014

This edition first published 1774
This digitally printed version 2014

ISBN 978-1-108-06972-4 Paperback

A

VOYAGE

TOWARDS

THE NORTH POLE.

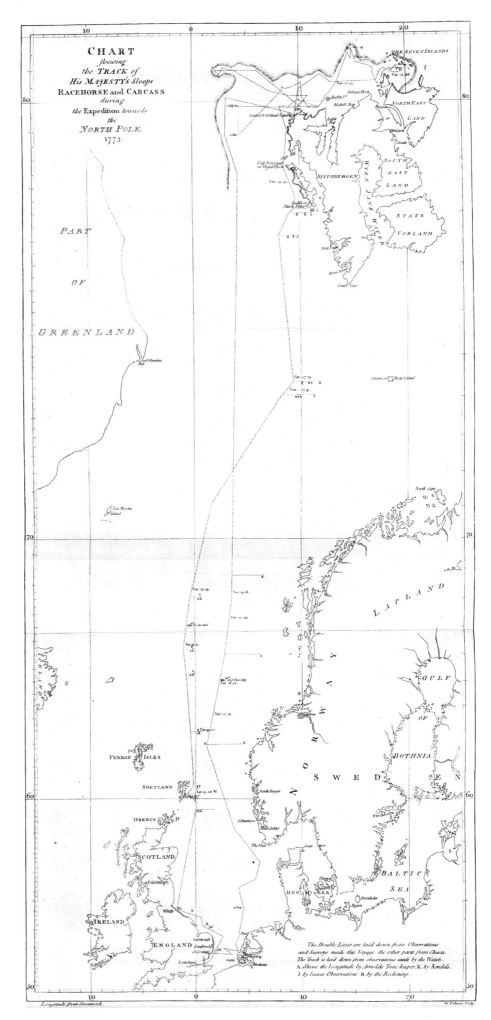

The material originally positioned here is too large for reproduction in this reissue. A PDF can be downloaded from the web address given on page iv of this book, by clicking on 'Resources Available'.

A

VOYAGE

TOWARDS

THE NORTH POLE

UNDERTAKEN

BY HIS MAJESTY'S COMMAND

1773

BY CONSTANTINE JOHN PHIPPS

LONDON;

PRINTED BY W. BOWYER AND J. NICHOLS,
FOR J. NOURSE, BOOKSELLER TO HIS MAJESTY,
IN THE STRAND.
MDCCLXXIV.

TO

THE KING.

SIRE,

AS a Sea Officer addreffing Your MAJESTY
on a profeffional fubject, I might juftly be
accufed of fingular ingratitude did I not avail
myfelf

myſelf of this opportunity of reminding the World, that the Voyage to explore how far Navigation was practicable towards the North Pole, was undertaken at a Period peculiarly diſtinguiſhed by Your MAJESTY's gracious Attention to Your Navy.

In a Time of profound Peace Your MAJESTY, by a liberal Addition to the Half Pay of the Captains, relieved the Neceſſities of many, and gratified the Ambition of all, at once demonſtrating Your MAJESTY's regard to their Welfare, and Remembrance of their Services.

The Armament which followed in a few Months, and Your MAJESTY's Review of that Armament which by the Diſpatch of its

Equipment

Equipment had prevented a War, afforded to Your Navy the moſt flattering and diſtinguiſhed Mark of Royal Favour, and to Your Majeſty an additional Proof of that Alacrity for Your Service which had ſo recently received both its Reward and Encouragement from Your MAJESTY's Protection.

Permit me, SIRE, to add, that Your MAJESTY's gracious Approbation of my Endeavours, and the Permiſſion I have been honoured with, of inſcribing the following Account of them to Your MAJESTY, are ſtrong Proofs of that Indulgence with which Your MAJESTY receives every Attempt to promote Your Service.—An Indulgence which, at the ſame Time that it cannot fail of animating the Zeal of others more worthy of

Your

Your MAJESTY's Notice, has added to the moſt devoted Attachment the warmeſt Gratitude of,

SIRE,

Your MAJESTY's moſt dutiful

Subject and Servant,

CONSTANTINE JOHN PHIPPS.

INTRODUCTION.

THE idea of a paffage to the Eaft Indies by the North Pole was fuggefted as early as the year 1527, by Robert Thorne, merchant, of Briftol, as appears from two papers preferved by Hackluit; the one addreffed to king Henry VIII; the other to Dr. Ley, the king's ambaffador to Charles V. In that addreffed to the king he fays, " I know it to be my bounden duty to manifeft this " fecret to your Grace, which hitherto, I fuppofe, has " been hid." This fecret appears to be the honour and advantage which would be derived from the difcovery of a paffage by the North Pole. He reprefents in the ftrongeft terms the glory which the kings of Spain and Portugal had obtained by their difcoveries Eaft and Weft, and exhorts the king to emulate their fame by undertaking difcoveries towards the North. He ftates in a very mafterly ftyle the reputation that muft attend the attempt, and the great benefits, fhould it be

B   crowned

crowned with fuccefs, likely to accrue to the fubjects of this country, from their advantageous fituation ; which, he obferves, feems to make the exploring this, the only hitherto undifcovered part, the King's peculiar duty.

To remove any objection to the undertaking which might be drawn from the fuppofed danger, he infifts upon " the great advantages of conftant day-light in feas, " that, men fay, without great danger, difficulty, and peril, " yea, rather, it is impoffible to pafs; for they being paft " this little way which they named fo dangerous (which " may be two or three leagues before they come to the " Pole, and as much more after they pafs the Pole), it is " clear from thenceforth the feas and lands are as tem- " perate as in thefe parts."

In the paper addreffed to Dr. Ley he enters more minutely into the advantages and practicability of the undertaking. Amongft many other arguments to prove the value of the difcovery, he urges, that by fail-ing northward and paffing the Pole, the navigation from England to the Spice Iflands would be fhorter, by more than two thoufand leagues, than either from Spain by the Straits of Magellan, or Portugal by the Cape of Good Hope ; and to fhew the likelihood of fuccefs in the enter-prize he fays, it is as probable that the cofmographers fhould be miftaken in the opinion they entertain of the

polar

polar regions being impaſſable from extreme cold, as, it has been found, they were, in ſuppoſing the countries under the Line to be uninhabitable from exceſſive heat. With all the ſpirit of a man convinced of the glory to be gained, and the probability of ſucceſs in the undertaking, he adds,—" God knoweth, that though by it I ſhould " have no great intereſt, yet I have had, and ſtill have, no " little mind of this buſineſs: ſo that if I had faculty to " my will, it ſhould be the firſt thing that I would un- " derſtand, even to attempt, *if our ſeas Northward be* " *navigable to the Pole or no.*" Notwithſtanding the many good arguments, with which he ſupported his pro- poſition, and the offer of his own ſervices, it does not appear that he prevailed ſo far as to procure an attempt to be made.

Borne, in his *Regiment of the Sea*, written about the year 1577, mentions this as one of the five ways to Cathay, and dwells chiefly on the mildneſs of climate which he imagines muſt be found near the Pole, from the conſtant preſence of the ſun during the ſummer. Theſe arguments, however, were ſoon after controverted by Blundeville, in his Treatiſe on Univerſal Maps.

In 1578, George Beſt, a gentleman who had been with Sir Martin Frobiſher in all his voyages for the diſ- covery of the North Weſt paſſage, wrote a very ingenious diſcourſe, to prove all parts of the world habitable.

No voyage, however, appears to have been undertaken to explore the circumpolar feas, till the year 1607, when " Henry Hudfon was fet forth, at the charge of certain " worfhipful merchants of London, to difcover a paffage " by the North Pole to Japan and China." He failed from Gravefend on the firft of May, in a fhip called the Hopewell, having with him ten men and a boy. I have taken great pains to find his original journal, as well as thofe of fome others of the adventurers who followed him; but without fuccefs : the only account I have feen is an imperfect abridgement in Purchas, by which it is not poffible to lay down his track; from which, however, I have drawn the following particulars :—He fell in with the land to the Weftward in latitude 73°, on the twenty-firft of June, which he named Hold-with-Hope. The twenty-feventh, he fell in with Spitfbergen, and met with much ice; he got to eighty degrees twenty-three minutes, which was the Northernmoft latitude he obferved in. Giving an account of the conclufion of his difcoveries, he fays, " On the fixteenth of " Auguft I faw land, by reafon of the clearnefs of the " weather, *ftretching far into eighty-two degrees*, and, by " the bowing and fhewing of the fky, much farther; " which when I firft faw, I hoped to have had a free fea " between the land and the ice, and meant to have com- " paffed this land by the North; but now finding it was " impoffible, by means of the abundance of ice com- " paffing us about by the North, and joining to the " land;

" land ; and feeing God did blefs us with a wind, we re-
" turned, bearing up the helm." He afterwards adds :
" And this I can affure at this prefent, that between
" feventy-eight degrees and an half, and eighty-two de-
" grees, by this way there is no paffage."—In confequence
of this opinion, he was the next year employed on the
North Eaft difcovery.

In March 1609, old ftyle, " A voyage was fet forth by the
" right worfhipful Sir Thomas Smith, and the reft of the
" Mufcovy Company, to Cherry Ifland, and for a further
" difcovery to be made towards the North Pole, for the like-
" lihood of a trade or a paffage that way, in the fhip called
" the Amity, of burthen feventy tuns, in which Jonas
" Poole was mafter, having fourteen men and one boy."—
He weighed from Blackwall, March the firft, old ftyle ; and
after great feverity of weather, and much difficulty from
the ice, he made the South part of Spitfbergen on the
16th of May. He failed along and founded the coaft,
giving names to feveral places, and making many very
accurate obfervations. On the 26th, being near Fair
Foreland, he fent his mate on fhore ;—and fpeaking of
the account he gave at his return, fays, " Moreover, I was
" certified that all the ponds and lakes were unfrozen, they
" being frefh water ; which putteth me in hope of a mild
" fummer here, after fo fharp a beginning as I have had ;
" and my opinion is fuch, and I affure myfelf it is fo, that
" a paffage may be as foon attained this way by the Pole,

" as

" as any unknown way whatfoever, by reafon the fun doth
" give a great heat in this climate, and the ice (I mean
" that freezeth here) is nothing fo huge as I have feen in
" feventy-three degrees."

Thefe hopes, however, he was foon obliged to relinquifh
for that year, having twice attempted in vain to get beyond
79° 50. On the 21ft of June, he ftood to the Southward,
to get a loading of fifh, and arrived in London the laft of
Auguft. He was employed the following year (1611) in a
fmall bark called the Elizabeth, of 50 tuns. The inftructions for this voyage, which may be found at length in Purchas, are excellently drawn up: They direct him, after
having attended the fifhery for fome time, to attempt difcoveries to the North Pole as long as the feafon will permit;
with a difcretionary claufe, to act in unforefeen cafes as fhall
appear to him moft for the advancement of the difcovery,
and intereft of his employers. This however proved an unfor-
tunate voyage: for having ftaid in Crofs Road till the 16th of
June, on account of the bad weather, and great quantity
of ice, he failed from thence on that day, and fteered
W b N fourteen leagues, where he found a bank of ice:
he returned to Crofs Road; from whence when he failed,
he found the ice to lie clofe to the land about the latitude of 80°, and that it was impoffible to pafs that way;
and the ftrong tides making it dangerous to deal with the
ice, he determined to ftand along it to the Southward, to
try if he could find the fea more open that way, and fo

get

get to the Weſtward, and proceed on his voyage. He found the ice to lie neareſt S W and S W b S and ran along it about an hundred and twenty leagues. He had no ground near the ice at 160, 180, or 200 fathoms: perceiving the ice ſtill to trend to the ſouthward, he determined to return to Spitsbergen for the fiſhery, where he loſt his ſhip.

In the year 1614, another voyage was undertaken, in which Baffin and Fotherby were employed. With much difficulty, and after repeated attempts in vain with the ſhip, they got with their boats to the firm ice, which joined to Red-Beach; they walked over the ice to that place, in hopes of finding whale-fins, &c. in which they were diſappointed. Fotherby adds, in his account: " Thus, " as we could not find what we deſired to ſee, ſo did we " behold that which we wiſhed had not been there to be " ſeen; which was great abundance of ice, that lay cloſe " to the ſhore, and alſo off at ſea as far as we could " diſcern." On the eleventh of Auguſt they ſailed from Fair-Haven, to try if the ice would let them paſs to the Northward, or Northeaſtward; they ſteered from Cape Barren, or Vogel Sang, N E b E eight leagues, where they met with the ice, which lay E b S and W b N The fifteenth of Auguſt they ſaw ice frozen in the ſea of above the thickneſs of an half-crown.

Fotherby

Fotherby was again fitted out the next year in a pinnace of twenty tons, called the Richard, with ten men. In this voyage he was prevented by the ice from getting farther than in his laſt. He refers to a chart, in which he had traced the ſhip's courſe on every traverſe, to ſhew how far the ſtate of that ſea was diſcovered between eighty and ſeventy-one degrees of latitude, and for twenty-ſix degrees of longitude from Hackluit's headland. He concludes the account of his voyage in the following manner:

" Now, if any demand my opinion concerning hope
" of a paſſage to be found in thoſe ſeas, I anſwer; that it
" is true, that I both hoped and much deſired to have
" paſſed further than I did, but was hindered with ice;
" wherein although I have not attained my deſire, yet
" foraſmuch as it appears not yet to the contrary, but
" that there is a ſpacious ſea betwixt Groinland and king
" James his new land [Spitsbergen] although much peſter-
" ed with ice; I will not ſeem to diſwade this worſhip-
" ful company from the yearly adventuring of 150 or 200
" pounds at the moſt, till ſome further diſcovery be made
" of the ſaid ſeas and lands adjacent." It appears that
the Ruſſia company, either ſatisfied with his endeavours
and deſpairing of further ſucceſs, or tired of the expence
of the undertaking, never employed any more ſhips on this
diſcovery.

All

All thefe voyages having been fitted out by private adventurers, for the double purpofe of difcovery and prefent
advantage; it was natural to fuppofe, that the attention
of the navigators had been diverted from purfuing the
more remote and lefs profitable objeƐt of the two, with
all the attention that could have been wifhed. I am
happy, however, in an opportunity of doing juftice to
the memory of thefe men; which, without having
traced their fteps, and experienced their difficulties,
it would have been impoffible to have done. They
appear to have encountered dangers, which at that
period muft have been particularly alarming from their
novelty, with the greateft fortitude and perfeverance; as
well as to have fhewn a degree of diligence and fkill, not
only in the ordinary and praƐtical, but more fcientific
parts of their profeffion, which might have done honour
to modern feamen, with all their advantages of later improvements. This, when compared with the accounts
given of the ftate of navigation, even within thefe forty
years, by the moft eminent foreign authors, affords the
moft flattering and fatisfaƐtory proof of the very early
exiftence of that decided fuperiority in naval affairs, which
has carried the power of this country to the height it has
now attained.

This great point of geography, perhaps the moft important in its confequences to a commercial nation and

C

maritime

maritime power, but the only one which had never yet been the object of royal attention, was fuffered to remain without further inveftigation, from the year 1615 till 1773, when the Earl of Sandwich, in confequence of an application which had been made to him by the Royal Society, laid before his Majefty, about the beginning of February, a propofal for an expedition to try how far navigation was practicable towards the North Pole; which his Majefty was pleafed to direct fhould be immediately undertaken, with every encouragement that could countenance fuch an enterprize, and every affiftance that could contribute to its fuccefs.

As foon as I heard of the defign, I offered myfelf, and had the honour of being entrufted with the conduct of this undertaking. The nature of the voyage requiring particular care in the choice and equipment of the fhips, the Racehorfe and Carcafs bombs were fixed upon as the ftrongeft, and therefore propereft for the purpofe. The probability that fuch an expedition could not be carried on without meeting with much ice, made fome additional ftrengthening neceffary: they were therefore immediately taken into dock, and fitted in the moft compleat manner for the fervice. The complement for the Racehorfe was fixed at ninety men, and the ordinary eftablifhment departed from, by appointing an additional number of officers, and entering effective men inftead of the ufual number of boys.

I was

I was allowed to recommend the officers; and was very happy to find, during the courfe of the voyage, by the great affiftance I received on many occafions from their abilities and experience, that I had not been miftaken in the characters of thofe upon whom fo much depended in the performance of this fervice. Two mafters of Greenlandmen were employed as pilots for each fhip. The Racehorfe was alfo furnifhed with the new chain-pumps made by Mr. Cole according to Captain Bentinck's improvements, which were found to anfwer perfectly well. We alfo made ufe of Dr. Irving's apparatus for diftilling frefh water from the fea, with the greateft fuccefs. Some fmall but ufeful alterations were made in the fpecies of provifions ufually fupplied in the navy; an additional quantity of fpirits was allowed for each fhip, to be iffued at the difcretion of the commanders, when extraordinary fatigue or feverity of weather might make it expedient. A quantity of wine was alfo allotted for the ufe of the fick. Additional clothing, adapted to that rigor of climate, which from the relations of former navigators we were taught to expect, was ordered to be put on board, to be given to the feamen when we arrived in the high latitudes. It was forefeen that one or both of the fhips might be facrificed in the profecution of this undertaking; the boats for each fhip were therefore calculated, in number and fize, to be fit, on any emergency, to

C 2   tranfport

tranfport the whole crew. In fhort, every thing which
could tend to promote the fuccefs of the undertaking, or
contribute to the fecurity, health, and convenience of the
fhips' companies, was granted.

The Board of Longitude agreed with Mr. Ifrael Lyons
to embark in this voyage, to make aftronomical obfervations. His reputation for mathematical knowledge was
too well eftablifhed to receive any addition from the few
opportunities which a voyage in fuch unfavourable
climates could afford. The fame Board fupplied him with
fuch inftruments as they imagined might be ufeful for
making obfervations and experiments. The Royal Society favoured me with fuch information as they judged
might ferve to direct my enquiries, whenever the circumftances of the voyage fhould afford me leifure and opportunity for making obfervations. Befides, thefe learned bodies,
I was obliged to many individuals for hints; amongft
whom it is with pleafure I mention Monfieur D'Alembert,
who communicated to me a fhort paper, which, from the
concifenefs and elegance with which it was drawn up, as
well as from the number of interefting objects that it recommended to my attention, would have done honour to
any perfon whofe reputation was not already eftablifhed
upon fo folid a foundation as that learned philofopher's.
To Mr. Banks I was indebted for very full inftructions in
the branch of natural hiftory, as I have fince been for his

affiftance

affiftance in drawing up the account of the productions of that country; which I acknowledge with particular fatis-faction, as inftances of a very long friendfhip which I am happy in an opportunity of mentioning.

As a voyage of this kind would probably afford many opportunities of making experiments and obfervations in matters relative to navigation, I took care to provide my-felf with all the beft inftruments hitherto in ufe, as well as others which had been imperfectly, or never, tried.

The length of the Second Pendulum in fo high a lati-tude as I was likely to reach, appearing to me an experi-ment too interefting to be neglected, I defired Mr. Cum-ming to make me fuch an inftrument as he thought would beft anfwer the purpofe. That modefty and candour which always attend real merit, induced him to lend me the identical pendulum with which Mr. Graham had made his experiments, rather than furnifh me with one of his own conftruction; but the judgment as well as fkill with which the apparatus joined to it was contrived and exe-cuted, notwithftanding the fhortnefs of the time, will, I am fure, do him credit.

The Board of Longitude fent two watch machines for keeping the longitude by difference of time; one con-ftructed by Mr. Kendal, on Mr. Harrifon's principles;

the

the other by Mr. Arnold. I had alfo a pocket watch conftructed by Mr. Arnold, by which I kept the longitude to a degree of exactitude much beyond what I could have expected; the watch having varied from its rate of going only 2′ 40″ in 128 days.

In the Journal which follows, I mean to confine myfelf to the occurrences of the voyage as they fucceeded in order of time; which, for the convenience of the generality of readers, I have reduced from the nautical to the civil computation: to this I fhall add, by way of Appendix, an account of all the experiments and obfervations under their refpective heads, that thofe who intereft themfelves in any particular branch, may find whatever they want, unmixed with foreign matters; while thofe who may wifh only to trace the whole progrefs of the voyage, as well as thofe who may be fatiffied with the general refults of the experiments, will find the account unincumbered with that detail which I wifh to fubmit to others, who may chufe to examine more minutely, and compare the facts with the conclufions.

A voyage of a few months to an uninhabited extremity of the world, the great object of which was to afcertain a very interefting point in geography, cannot be fuppofed to afford much matter for the gratification of

mere

mere curiofity. The experiments and obfervations may poffibly from their novelty, and the peculiar circumftances of the climate in which they were made, afford fome entertainment to philofophers ; and might perhaps have been more numerous and fatisfactory, if the purfuit of the great object of the voyage had not rendered them, however interefting in themfelves, but a fecondary confideration.

J O U R N A L.

D

J O U R N A L.

APRIL 19th, 1773, I received my commiſſion for the Racehorſe, with an order to get her fitted with the greateſt diſpatch for a voyage of diſcovery towards the North Pole, and to proceed to the Nore for further orders.

23d. The ſhip was hauled out of dock.

May 21ſt. The ſhip being manned and rigged, and having got in all the proviſions and ſtores, except the Gunner's, we fell down to Galleons.

22d. We received on board the powder, with eight ſix-pounders, and all the gunner's ſtores. Lord Sandwich gave us the laſt mark of the obliging attention he had ſhewn during the whole progreſs of the equipment, by coming on board to ſatisfy himſelf, before our departure, that the whole had been compleated to the wiſh of thoſe who were embarked in the expedition. The Eaſterly

D 2   winds

winds prevented our going down the river till the 26th, when I received my inſtructions for the voyage, dated the 25th; directing me to fall down to the Nore in the Racehorſe, and there taking under my command the Carcaſs, to make the beſt of my way to the Northward, and proceed up to the North Pole, or as far towards it as poſſible, and as nearly upon a meridian as the ice or other obſtructions might admit; and, during the courſe of the voyage, to make ſuch obſervations of every kind as might be uſeful to navigation, or tend to the promotion of natural knowledge: in caſe of arriving at the Pole, and even finding free navigation on the oppoſite meridian, not to proceed any farther; and at all events to ſecure my return to the Nore before the winter ſhould ſet in. There was alſo a clauſe authorizing me to proceed, in unforeſeen caſes, according to my own diſcretion; and another clauſe directing me to proſecute the voyage on board the Carcaſs, in caſe the Racehorſe ſhould be loſt or diſabled.

27th. I anchored at the Nore, and was joined by Captain Lutwidge, in the Carcaſs, on the 30th: her equipment was to have been in all reſpects the ſame as that of the Racehorſe, but when fitted, Captain Lutwidge finding her too deep in the water to proceed to ſea with ſafety, obtained leave of the Admiralty to put ſix more guns on ſhore, to reduce the complement to eighty men, and return a quantity of proviſions proportionable to that re-

duction.

duction. The officers were recommended by Captain Lutwidge, and did juftice to his penetration by their conduct in the courfe of the voyage. During our ftay here, Mr. Lyons landed with the aftronomical quadrant at Sheernefs fort, and found the latitude to be 51° 31′ 30″, longitude 0° 30′ Eaft. The Eafterly winds prevented our moving this day and the following.

June 2d. Having the wind to the Weftward of North, at five in the morning I made the fignal to weigh ; but in lefs than half an hour, the wind fhifting to the Eaftward and blowing frefh, I furled the topfails. The wind came in the afternoon to N b E ; we weighed, but did not get far, the tide of flood making againft us.

3d. The wind blowing frefh all day Eafterly, we did not move.

4th. The wind coming round to the Weftward at fix in the morning, I weighed immediately, and fent the boat for Captain Lutwidge, to deliver him his orders. At 10 A. M. longitude by the watch 56′ E. At noon the latitude obferved was 51° 37′ 36″ N. At eight in the evening we had got as far as Balfey Cliff, between Orford and Harwich. Little wind at night.

5th. Anchored in Hofeley Bay at half paft feven in the evening, in five and an half fathom water. Orford Caftle N E b N.   Angle

Angle between Aldborough Church and Orford
Light Houfe. }   7° 38′

Light Houfe and Orford Church,   - -   18 16

Orford Church and Caftle,   - -   2 20

Caftle and Hofeley Church,   - - -   100 59

Hofeley and Balfey Church,   - - -   35 27

6th. At five in the morning, the wind at S S W, weighed, and ftood out to fea, finding I might lofe two tides by going through Yarmouth Roads. Examined the log line, which was marked forty-nine feet; the glafs was found, by comparing it with the time-keeper, to run thirty feconds: at noon latitude obferved 52° 16′ 54″, longitude by the watch 1° 30′ 15″ E.

Angle between Southwold and Walderfwick,   10° 39′

Walderfwick and Dunwich,   - - -   20 21

Dunwich and Aldborough,   - - -   46 53

Southwold N W ½ N, fuppofed diftance three leagues. We concluded the latitude of Southwold to be 52° 22′, and longitude 1° 18′ 15″ E. The dip was 73° 22′.

7th. The wind was Northerly all day, and blew frefh in the morning. We had ftood far out in the night and the day before, to clear the Lemon and Ower.

8th. Little wind moft part of the day, with a very heavy fwell. Stood in for the land. At half paft ten longitude by the watch 0° 41′ 15″ E. At noon the latitude

was

was 53° 38′ 37″· We saw the high land near the Spurn, in the evening.

9th. About noon Flamborough Head bore N W b N distant about six miles: we were by observation in latitude 54° 4′ 54″, longitude 0° 27′ 15″ E; which makes Flamborough Head, in latitude 54° 9′, longitude 0° 19′ 15″ E. In the afternoon we were off Scarborough. Almost calm in the evening.

10th. Anchored in the morning for the tide in Robin Hood's Bay, with little wind at N W: worked up to Whitby Road next tide, and anchored there at four in the afternoon, in fifteen fathom, with very little wind.

11th. Calm in the morning; compleated our water, live stock and vegetables. At nine in the morning longitude observed by the watch 1° 55′ 30″ W; Whitby Abbey bore S ¼ W. Weighed with the wind at S E, and steered N E b N to get so far into the mid-channel as to make the wind fair Easterly or Westerly, without being too near either shore, before we were clear of Shetland and the coast of Norway.

12th. The wind at S E, and the ship well advanced, I ordered the allowance of liquor to be altered, serving the ship's company one-fourth of their allowance in beer, and the other three-fourths in brandy; by which means the

beer

JOURNAL.

beer was made to laſt the whole voyage, and the water confiderably faved. One half of this allowance was ſerved immediately after dinner, and the other half in the evening. It was now light enough all night to read upon deck.

13th. The weather ſtill fine, but confiderably leſs wind than the day before, and in the afternoon more Northerly. The longitude at ten in the morning was found by my watch 0° 6′ W. We took three obſervations of the moon and fun for the longitude; the extremes differed from one another near two degrees: the mean of the three gave the longitude 1° 37′ E. At noon the latitude obſerved was 59° 32′ 31″. We found a difference of 36′ between the latitude by dead reckoning and obſervation, the ſhip being ſo much more Northerly than the reckoning. The diſtance by this log was too ſhort by forty-three miles. A log marked forty-five feet, according to the old method, would have agreed with the obſervation within two miles in the two days' run. The circumſtance of ſteering upon a meridian, which afforded me ſuch frequent opportunities of detecting the errors of the log, induced me to obſerve with care the comparative accuracy of the different methods of dividing the line, recommended by mathematicians, or practiſed by ſeamen. In the afternoon I went on board the Carcaſs to compare the time-keepers by my watch. At fix in the evening the longitude by my watch 0° 4′ E. This evening the fun

fet

fet at twenty-four minutes paft nine, and bore about N N W by the compafs. The clouds made a beautiful appearance long after to the Northward, from the reflection of the fun below the horizon. It was quite light all night: the Carcafs made the fignal for feeing the land in the evening.

14th. Little wind, or calm, all day; but very clear and fine weather. Made feveral different obfervations for the longitude by the fun and moon, and by my watch. The longitude of the fhip was found by my watch, at ten in the morning, to be 1° 11′ 45″ W. The longitude by the lunar obfervations differed near two degrees from one another. By the mean of them the fhip was in longitude 2° 57′ 45″ W. Some Shetland boats came on board with fifh. At noon the latitude by obfervation was 60° 16′ 45″. At one in the afternoon the dip was obferved to be 73° 30′; and at eight, 75° 18′: the evening calm, and very fine; the appearance of the fky to the Northward very beautiful. Variation, by the mean of feveral obfervations, 22° 25′ W.

15th. By an obfervation at eight in the morning, the longitude of the fhip was by the watch 0° 39′ W: Dip 74° 52′. At half paft ten in the morning, the longitude, from feveral obfervations of the fun and moon, was 0° 17′ W; at noon being in latitude 60° 19′ 8″, by obfervation, I took the diftance between the two fhips by

E   the

the Megameter; and from that bafe determined the pofition of Hangcliff, which had never before been afcertained, though it is a very remarkable point, and frequently made by fhips. According to thefe obfervations
it is in latitude 60° 9′, and longitude 0° 56′ 30″ W. In
the Appendix I fhall give an account of the manner of
taking furveys by this inftrument, which I believe never
to have been practifed before. At one, obferved the dip
to be 75°. A thick fog came on in the afternoon,
with a flat calm; we could not fee the Carcafs, but
heard her anfwer the fignals for keeping company.
Variation, from the mean of feveral obfervations,
25° 1′ W.

16th. A very thick fog in the morning; latitude obferved at noon 60° 29′ 17″: the dip was obferved at
nine in the evening to be 76° 45′. In the afternoon, the
weather clear, and the wind fair, fteered N N E: fent
Captain Lutwidge his further orders and places of rendezvous.

17th. Wind fair, and blowing frefh at S S W, continued the courfe N N E: ordered the people a part of
the additional clothing: faw an Englifh floop, but had
no opportunity of fending letters on board, the fea running high. At ten in the morning, longitude by the
watch 0° 19′ 45″ W: at noon, the latitude obferved
was 62° 59′ 27″. The fhip had out-run the reckoning

eleven

eleven miles.   I tried Bouguer's log twice this day, and found it give more than the common log.   Variation 19° 22′ W.

18th.   Little wind all day, but fair, from S S W to S E: ſtill ſteering N N E: latitude obſerved at noon 65° 18′ 17″.   At three in the afternoon, ſounded with 300 fathom of line, but got no ground.   Longitude by the watch 1° 0′ 30″ W.

19th.   Wind to the N W.   Took the meridian obſervation at midnight for the firſt time: the ſun's lower limb 0° 37′ 30″ above the horizon; from which the latitude was found 66° 54′ 39″ N: at four in the afternoon, longitude by the watch 0° 58′ 45″ W: at ſix the variation 19° 11′ W.

20th.   Almoſt calm all day.   The water being perfectly ſmooth, I took this opportunity of trying to get ſoundings at much greater depths than I believe had ever been attempted before.   I ſounded with a very heavy lead the depth of 780 fathom, without getting ground; and by a thermometer invented by lord Charles Cavendiſh for this purpoſe, found the temperature of the water at that depth to be 26° of Fahrenheit's thermometer; the temperature of the air being 48° ½.

We

We began this day to make ufe of Doctor Irving's apparatus for diftilling frefh water from the fea: repeated trials gave us the moft fatisfactory proof of its utility: the water produced from it was perfectly free from falt, and wholefome, being ufed for boiling the fhip's provifions; which convenience would alone be a defirable object in all voyages, independent of the benefit of fo ufeful a refource in cafe of diftrefs for water. The quantity produced every day varied from accidental circumftances, but was generally from thirty-four to forty gallons, without any great addition of fuel. Twice indeed the quantity produced was only twenty-three gallons on each diftillation; this amounts to more than a quart for each man, which, though not a plentiful allowance, is much more than what is neceffary for fubfiftence. In cafes of real neceffity I have no reafon to doubt that a much greater quantity might be produced without an inconvenient expence of fuel.

21ft. A frefh gale at S E all day; fteered N N E. At four in the morning we fpoke with a fnow from the feal fifhery, bound to Hamburg, by which we fent fome letters. At fix in the morning the variation, by the mean of feveral obfervations, was 23° 18′ W. Longitude by the watch at nine was 0° 34′ 30″ W. Latitude obferved at noon 68° 5′.

22d.

22d. Calm moſt part of the day; rainy and rather cold in the evening. At noon obſerved the dip to be 77° 52′.

23d. Very foggy all day; the wind fair; altered the courſe and ſteered N E and E N E, to get more into the mid channel, and to avoid falling in with the Weſtern ice, which, from the increaſing coldneſs of the weather, we concluded to be near. At ſeven o'clock in the morning, being by our reckoning to the Northward of 72°, we ſaw a piece of drift wood, and a ſmall bird called a Red-poll. Dip obſerved at nine in the evening to be 81° 30′.

24th. Very foggy all the morning; the wind came round to the Northward. The dip obſerved at noon was 80° 35′. In the afternoon, the air much colder than we had hitherto felt it; the thermometer at 34°. A fire made in the cabin for the firſt time, in latitude 73° 40′.

25th. Wind Northerly, with a great ſwell; ſome ſnow, but in general clear. At eight in the morning, the longitude obſerved by the watch was 7° 15′ E. Made ſeveral obſervations on the variation, which we found, by thoſe taken at ſeven in the morning, to be 17° 9′ W; by others at three in the afternoon, only 7° 47′ W. I could not account for this very ſudden and extraordinary

decreaſe,

decreafe, as there were feveral different obfervations taken both in the morning and evening, which agreed perfectly well with each other, without any apparent caufe which could produce an error affecting all the obfervations of either fet. At eight in the evening the longitude by the moon was 12° 57′ 30″ E, which differed 2° 35′ from that by the watch. Little wind at night.

26th. Little wind all day; the weather very fine and moderate. The latitude obferved at noon was 74° 25′. The thermometer expofed to the fun, which fhone very bright, rofe from 41° to 61° in twenty minutes. By each of two lunar obfervations which I took with a fextant of four inches radius, at half paft one, the longitude was 9° 57′ 30″ E; which agreed within thirty-feven minutes with an obfervation made by the watch at half an hour after three, when the longitude was 8° 52′ 30″ E. Dip 79° 22′.

27th. At midnight the latitude obferved was 74° 26′. The wind came to the S W, and continued fo all day, with a little rain and fnow. The cold did not increafe. We fteered N b E. At feven in the morning the variation, by a mean of feveral obfervations, was found to be 20° 38′ W. We were in the evening, by all our reckonings, in the latitude of the South part of Spitfbergen, without any appearance of ice or fight of land, and with a fair wind.

28th.

28th. Lefs wind in the morning than the day before, with rain and fleet: continued fteering to the Northward. At five in the afternoon picked up a piece of drift wood, which was fir, and not worm-eaten: founded in 290 fathom; no ground. At fix the longitude by the watch was 7° 50′ E: between ten and eleven at night, faw the land to the Eaftward at ten or twelve leagues diftance. At midnight, dip 81° 7′.

29th. The wind Northerly; ftood clofe in with the land. The coaft appeared to be neither habitable nor acceffible; it was formed by high, barren, black rocks, without the leaft marks of vegetation; in many places bare and pointed, in other parts covered with fnow, appearing even above the clouds: the vallies between the high cliffs were filled with fnow or ice. This profpect would have fuggefted the idea of perpetual winter, had not the mildnefs of the weather, the fmooth water, bright funfhine, and conftant day-light, given a chearfulnefs and novelty to the whole of this ftriking and romantick fcene.

I had an opportunity of making many obfervations near the Black Point. Latitude obferved at noon 77° 59′ 11″. The difference of latitude, from the laft obfervation on the 27th at midnight to this day at noon, would according to the old method of marking the log have been

two

two hundred and thirteen miles; which agrees exactly with the obfervation. At three in the afternoon, brought to and founded 110 fathom; foft muddy ground: hoifted out the boat and tried the ftream; found it, both by the common and Bouguer's log (which agreed exactly) to run half a knot North; Black Point bearing E N E. At four the longitude by the watch was 9° 31′ E: at eight the variation, by the mean of nineteen obfervations, 11° 53′ W. I could not account from any apparent caufe for this great change in the variation: the weather was fine, the water fmooth, and every precaution we could think of ufed to make the obfervations accurate. The dip was 80° 26′. Plying to the Northward.

30th. At midnight the latitude by obfervation was 78° 0′ 50″. At four in the morning, by Lord Charles Cavendifh's thermometer the temperature of the water at the depth of 118 fathoms was 31° of Fahrenheit's; that of the air was at the fame time 40°½. At nine in the morning we faw a fhip in the N W, ftanding in for the land. Having little wind this morning, and that Northerly, I ftood in for the land, with an intention to have watered the fhip, and got out immediately, but was prevented by the calm which followed. At noon the latitude obferved was 78° 8′; the dip 79° 30′. At two in the afternoon we founded in 115 fathom; muddy bottom: at the fame time we fent down Lord Charles Cavendfh's thermometer, by which we found the

temperature

temperature of the water at that depth to be 33°; that of the water at the furface was at the fame time 40°, and in the air 44° ¼. Fahrenheit's thermometer plunged in water brought up from the fame depth, ftood at 38° ½. This evening the mafter of a Greenland Ship came on board, who told me, that he was juft come out of the ice which lay to the Weftward about fixteen leagues off, and that three fhips had been loft this year, two Englifh, and one Dutch. The weather fine, and rather warm. At fix in the evening the longitude by my watch was 9° 28′ 45″ E.

July 1ft. Little wind Northerly, or calm, all day: the weather very fine, and fo warm that we fat without a fire, and with one of the ports open in the cabin. At noon the latitude obferved was 78° 13′ 36″; Black Point bearing S 78° E; which makes the latitude of that point nearly the fame as that of the fhip, and agrees very well with the chart of this coaft in Purchas.

2d. Little wind, and calms, all day; the weather very fine. At fix in the morning five fail of Greenlandmen in fight. At noon the latitude obferved was 78° 22′ 41″. I took a furvey of the coaft, as far as we could fee: I took alfo with the megameter the altitudes of feveral of the mountains: but as there is nothing particularly in-terefting to navigators in this part of the coaft, I fhall only mention the height of one mountain, which was

F

fifteen

fifteen hundred and three yards. This may ferve to give fome idea of the appearance and fcale of the coaft. At half paft fix the longitude by the watch was 9° 8′ 30″ E: Variation 14° 55′ W.

3d. Latitude at midnight 78° 23′ 46″: Dip 80° 45′. The weather fine, and the wind fair all day. Running along by the coaft of Spitfbergen all day: feveral Greenlandmen in fight. Between nine and ten in the evening we were abreaft of the North Foreland, bearing E b S ¼ S, diftance 1 ¼ mile. Sounded in twenty fathom; rocky ground.

4th. Very little wind in the morning. At noon the latitude by obfervation was 79° 31′. Magdalena Hook bore N 39° E diftant about four miles; which gives the latitude of that place 79° 34′; the fame as Fotherby obferved it to be in 1614. Stood in to a fmall bay to the Southward of Magdalena and Hamburgher's Bay: anchored with the ftream anchor, and fent the boat for water. About three in the afternoon, when the boat was fent on fhore, it appeared to be high water, and ebbed about three feet. This makes high water full and change at half an hour paft one, or with a S S W moon; which agrees exactly with Baffin's obfervation in 1613. The flood comes from the Southward. Went afhore with the aftronomer, and inftruments, to obferve the variation. A thick fog came on before we had completed the obfervations.

The

The ſhip driving, I weighed and ſtood out to ſea under an eaſy ſail, firing guns frequently to ſhew the Carcaſs where we were; and in leſs than two hours joined her. Soon after (about four in the morning of the 5th) the Rockingham Greenland Ship ran under our ſtern, and the maſter told me he had juſt ſpoke with ſome ſhips from which he learnt, that the ice was within ten leagues of Hacluyt's Head Land, to the North Weſt. In conſequence of this intelligence, I gave orders for ſteering in towards the Head Land; and if it ſhould clear up, to ſteer directly for it; intending to go North from thence, till ſome circumſtance ſhould oblige me to alter my courſe.

5th. At five the officer informed me, that we were very near ſome iſlands off Dane's Gat, and that the pilot wiſhed to ſtand farther out; I ordered the ſhip to be kept N b W, and hauled farther in, when clear of the iſlands. At noon I ſteered North, ſeeing nothing of the land; ſoon after I was told that they ſaw the ice: I went upon deck, and perceived ſomething white upon the bow, and heard a noiſe like the ſurf upon the ſhore; I hauled down the ſtudding ſails, and hailed the Carcaſs to let them know that I ſhould ſtand for it to make what it was, having all hands upon deck ready to haul up at a moment's warning: I deſired that they would keep cloſe to us, the fog being ſo thick, and have every body up ready to follow our motions inſtantaneouſly, determining to ſtand on under ſuch ſail as ſhould enable us to keep

F 2 the

the fhips under command, and not rifk parting company. Soon after two fmall pieces of ice not above three feet fquare paffed us, which we fuppofed to have floated from the fhore. It was not long before we faw fomething on the bow, part black and part covered with fnow, which from the appearance we took to be iflands, and thought that we had not ftood far enough out; I hauled up immediately to the N N W and was foon undeceived, finding it to be ice which we could not clear upon that tack; we tacked immediately, but the wind and fea both fetting directly upon it, we neared it very faft, and were within little more than a cable's length of the ice, whilft in ftays. The wind blowing frefh, the fhips would have been in danger on the lee ice, had not the officers and men been very alert in working the fhip. The ice, as far as we could then fee, lay nearly E b N and W b S. At half paft feven in the evening, the fhip running entirely to the Southward, and the weather clearing a little, I tacked, and ftood for the ice. When I faw it, I bore down to make it plain; at ten the ice lay from N W to Eaft, and no opening. Very foggy, and little wind, all day; but not cold. At eleven came on a thick fog. At half paft midnight, heard the furge of the ice, and hauled the wind to the Eaftward.

6th. Clear weather all day, and the wind Eafterly off the ice. In the morning I ftood in to make the land plain. At fix, was within four miles of the ice, which

bore

bore from E N E to W N W: at ten near Vogel Sang: at noon, latitude obferved 79° 56′ 39″; wind Eafterly. Continued plying to windward between the land and the ice: was within a quarter of a mile of the ice, which lay from E N E to N N W, when I tacked at two in the afternoon; and within half a cable's length at midnight: the Carcafs was a great way aftern and to leeward all day. Being fo near the laft rendezvous, I did not chufe to bring to for her, but was very anxious to avail myfelf of this favourable opportunity, having the wind off the ice and clear weather, to fee whether there was any opening to the N E of the Head Land. By all the accounts from the Greenlandmen this year, and particularly the laft account from the Rockingham, as well as from what we had feen ourfelves, the ice appeared to be quite clofe to the N W. We had feen it from E S E to W N W. It was probable that the fea, if open any where, would be fo to the Eaftward, where the Greenlandmen do not often venture, for fear of being prevented from returning by the ice joining to Spitfbergen. I determined therefore, fhould the wind continue in the fame quarter next day, to find whether the ice joined to the land, or was fo detached as to afford me an opportunity of paffing to the Eaftward. In cafe of the ice being faft I could, with the wind Eafterly, range clofe along the edge of it to the Weftward. The weather exceedingly fine. At fix in the afternoon, the longitude by the watch was 9° 43′ 30″ E.

7th.

7th. At five in the morning the wind was Northerly, and the weather remarkably clear. Being near the ice I ranged along it. It appeared to be clofe all round; but I was in hopes that fome opening might be found to get through to a clear fea to the Northward. I ran in amongft the fmall ice, and kept as clofe as poffible to the main body, not to mifs any opening. At noon, Cloven Cliff W ½ S feven leagues. At one in the afternoon, being ftill amongft the loofe ice, I fent the boat to one of the large pieces to fill water. At four we fhoaled the water very fuddenly to fourteen fathom: the outer part of Cloven Cliff bore W ½ N: Redcliff, S ¼ E. The loofe ice being open to the E N E, we hauled up, and immediately deepened our water to twenty-eight fathom; muddy ground, with fhells. At half paft four, the ice fetting very clofe, we ran between two pieces, and having little wind were ftopped. The Carcafs being very near, and not anfwering her helm well, was almoft on board of us. After getting clear of her, we ran to the Eaftward. Finding the pieces increafe in number and fize, and having got to a part lefs crowded with the drift ice, I brought to, at fix in the evening, to fee whether we could difcover the leaft appearance of an opening: but it being my own opinion, as well as that of the pilots and officers, that we could go no farther, nor even remain there without danger of being befet, I fent the boat on board the Carcafs for her pilots, to hear their opinion; they both

declared

declared that it appeared to them impracticable to proceed that way, and that it was probable we should soon be beset where we were, and detained there. The ice set so fast down, that before they got on board the Carcass we were fast. Captain Lutwidge hoisted our boat up, to prevent her being stove. We were obliged to heave the ship through for two hours, with ice anchors, from each quarter; nor were we quite out of the ice till midnight. This is about the place where most of the old discoverers were stopped. The people in both ships being much fatigued, and the Carcass not able to keep up with us, without carrying studding-sails, I shortened sail as soon as we were quite out, and left orders to stand to the Northward under an easy sail: I intended, having failed in this attempt, to range along the ice to the N W, in hopes of an opening that way, the wind being fair, and the weather clear; resolving, if I found it all solid, to return to the Eastward, where probably it might by that time be broken up, which the very mild weather encouraged me to expect.

8th. Little wind in the morning, and a swell setting on the ice, we were obliged to get the boats a-head, to tow the ship clear; which they effected with difficulty. A breeze springing up when we were within two cables lengths of the main body of the ice, stood in for the land, and tacked at two, to stand to the N W for the ice; but the weather coming thick between five and six, I

stood

stood in again for the land. It clearing up soon after, I bore away again N W for the ice. At ten, spoke with a Greenland Ship which had just left the ice all close to the N N W. Between eleven and twelve the wind came to the S W, with an heavy swell, and thick weather. Double-reefed the topsails, and tacked at twelve, to stand in for Hacluyt's Head Land, not thinking it proper to run in with the fast ice to leeward in thick weather, without even the probability of an opening; and proposing if that weather continued, to complete the ship's water, and be ready with the first wind, off or along the ice, to look out for an opening, and run in. To avoid any inconvenience which from the experience of the preceding day I perceived might happen, from too many running to one place on any sudden order, I divided the people into gangs under the midshipmen, and stationed them to the ice hooks, poles, crabs, and to go over upon the ice when wanted.

9th. Having a fair opportunity, and S W wind, stood to the Westward; intending, when the weather was clear, to make the ice to the Northward, and run along it. About twelve, clearer; saw the fast ice to the Northward, and the appearance of loose ice to the N W: stood directly for it, and got amongst it between two and three; steering as much to the Northward as the situation of the ice would permit. At six observed the dip 81° 52'. At half past seven, found the ice quite fast to the West, being

in

in longitude 2° 2′ E, by our reckoning, which was the fartheft to the Weftward of Spitfbergen that we got this voyage. At eight the fog was fo very thick, that we could neither fee which way to pufh for an opening, nor where the Carcafs was, though very near us. That we might not rifk parting company with her, I was obliged to ply to windward under the topfails, tacking every quarter of an hour to keep in the opening in which we were, and clear of the ice which furrounded us. At four in the afternoon we were in 80° 36′.

10th. We loft the Carcafs twice in the night, from the very thick fog, and were working all night amongft the ice, making very fhort tacks; the opening being fmall, and the floating ice very thick about the fhip. The fituation of the people from the very fatiguing work and wet weather, made the moft minute precautions neceffary for the prefervation of their health: we now found the advantage of the fpirits which had been allowed for extraordinary occafions; as well as the additional cloathing furnifhed by the Admiralty. Notwithftanding every attention, feveral of the men were confined with colds, which affected them with pains in their bones; but, from the careful attendance given them, few continued in the fick lift above two days at a time. At nine in the morning, when it cleared a little, we faw the Carcafs much to the Southward of us. I took the opportunity of the clear

G   weather

weather to run to the Weftward, and found the ice quite folid there; I then ftood through every opening to the Northward, but there alfo foon got to the edge of the folid ice. I was forced to haul up to weather a point which ran out from it. After I had weathered that, the ice clofing faft upon me, obliged me to fet the forefail, which, with the frefh wind and fmooth water, gave the fhip fuch way as to force through it with a violent ftroke. At one in the afternoon, immediately on getting out into the open fea, we found a heavy fwell fetting to the North-ward; though amongft the ice, the minute before, the water had been as fmooth as a mill pond. The wind blew ftrong at SSW. The ice, as far as we could fee from the maft head, lay ENE: we fteered that courfe clofe to it, to look for an opening to the Northward. I now began to conceive that the ice was one compact impene-trable body, having run along it from Eaft to Weft above ten degrees. I purpofed however to ftand over to the Eaftward, in order to afcertain whether the body of ice joined to Spitfbergen. This the quantity of loofe ice had before rendered impracticable; but thinking the Wefterly winds might probably by this time have packed it all that way, I flattered myfelf with the hopes of meeting with no obftruction till I fhould come to where it joined the land; and in cafe of an opening, however fmall, I was determined at all events to pufh through it. The weather clearer, and the land in fight.

11th.

11th. At half paſt four in the morning the longitude by the lunar obſervation was 9° 42′ E. And at the ſame time by my watch 9° 2′ E. Cloven Cliff S S E, diſtant eight miles. This would make the longitude of Cloven Cliff 9° 38′ E; which is within twenty minutes of what it was determined by the obſervations and ſurvey taken in Fair Haven. At noon the latitude obſerved was 80° 4′; Vogel Sang W S W. Little wind and a great ſwell in the morning. Calm moſt part of the day.

12th. Calm all day, with a great ſwell from the S W, and the weather remarkably mild. At eight in the evening longitude by the watch 10° 54′ 30″ E: Cloven Cliff S W b S. The Carcaſs drove with the current ſo near the main body of the ice, as to be obliged to anchor; ſhe came to in twenty-ſix fathom water.

13th. Calm till noon, the ſhip driving to the Weſt-ward with the current, which we obſerved to be very irre-gular, the Carcaſs being driven at the ſame time to the Eaſtward. Near the main body of the ice, the detached pieces probably affect the currents, and occaſion the great irregularity which we remarked. We had found an heavy ſwell from the S W theſe two days. At two in the afternoon it came on very ſuddenly to blow freſh from that quarter, with foggy weather: we worked into Vogel

G 2

Sang,

Sang, and anchored with the beſt bower in eleven fathom, ſoft clay.

The place where we anchored is a good road-ſtead, open from the N E to the N W. The Northeaſternmoſt point is the Cloven Cliff, a bare rock ſo called from the top of it reſembling a cloven hoof, which appearance it has always worn, having been named by ſome of the firſt Dutch navigators who frequented theſe ſeas. This rock being entirely detached from the other mountains, and joined to the reſt of the iſland by a low narrow iſthmus, preſerves in all ſituations the ſame form ; and being nearly perpendicular, it is never diſguiſed by ſnow. Theſe circumſtances render it one of the moſt remarkable points on the coaſt. The Northweſternmoſt land is an high bluff point, called by the Dutch, Vogel Sang. This ſound, though open to the Northward, is not liable to any inconvenience from that circumſtance, the main body of the ice lying ſo near as to prevent any great ſea ; nor are ſhips in any danger from the looſe ice ſetting in, as this road communicates with ſeveral others formed by different iſlands, between all which there are ſafe paſſages. To all the ſounds and harbours formed by this knot of iſlands, the old Engliſh navigators had given the general name of Fair Haven ; of which Fotherby took a *plat* in 1614 : that in which the Racehorſe and Carcaſs lay at this time they called the North Harbour ; the harbour of Smeerenberg, diſtant about eleven miles, (in which we anchored in Auguſt) they named

the

the South Harbour. Befides thefe, there are feveral others; particularly two, called, Cook's Hole, and the Norways, in both which feveral Dutch fhips were lying at this time. Here the fhore being fteep-to, we completed our water with great eafe, from the ftreams which fall in many places down the fides of the rocks, and are produced by the melting of the fnow. I fixed upon a fmall flat ifland, or rock, about three miles from the fhip, and almoft in the center of thofe iflands which form the many good roads here, as the propereft place for erecting a tent, and making obfervations. The foggy weather on the 14th prevented us from ufing the inftruments that day. I regretted this circumftance much, fearing it would deprive me of the only probable opportunity of making obfervations on fhore in thofe high latitudes, as our water was nearly recruited: however, having little wind, with the weather very fair from the 15th to the 18th in the morning, I made the beft ufe of that time. Even in the cleareft weather here, the fky was never free from clouds, which prevented our feeing the moon during the whole of our ftay, or even being fure of our folar obfervations, Mr. Lyons never having been able to get equal altitudes for fettling the rates of going of the time keepers. Once indeed we were fortunate enough to obferve a revolution of the fun, of which I availed myfelf to determine the going of the pendulum adjufted to vibrate feconds at London. During the courfe of this experiment, a particular and conftant attention was paid

to

to the ftate of the thermometer, which I was furprifed to find differ fo little about noon and midnight ; its greateft height was 58°½, at eleven in the forenoon ; at midnight it was 51°.

On the 16th, at noon, the weather was remarkably fine and clear. The thermometer in the fhade being at 49°, when expofed to the fun rofe in a few minutes to 89°½, and remained fo for fome time, till a fmall breeze fpringing up, made it fall 10° almoft inftantly. The weather at this time was rather hot ; fo that I imagine, if a thermometer was to be graduated according to the feelings of people in thefe latitudes, the point of temperature would be about the 44th degree of Fahrenheit's fcale. From this ifland I took a furvey, to afcertain the fituation of all the points and openings, and the height of the moft remarkable mountains : the longeft bafe the ifland would afford was only 618 feet, which I determined by a crofs bafe, as well as actual meafurement, and found the refults not to differ above three feet. To try how far the accuracy of this furvey might be depended upon, I took in a boat, with a fmall Hadley's fextant, the angles between feven objects, which interfected exactly when laid down upon the plan. I had a farther proof of its accuracy fome days after, by taking the bearings of Vogel Sang and Hacluyt's Head Land in one, which correfponded exactly with their pofition on my chart.

On

On the 17th, the weather being very clear, I went up one of the hills, from which I could fee feveral leagues to the N E: the ice appeared uniform and compact, as far as my view extended. During our ftay here, we found the latitude of the ifland on which the obfervations were made, to be 79° 50′; longitude 10° 2′ 30″ E; variation 20° 38′ W; dip 82° 7′: latitude of Cloven Cliff 79° 53′; longitude 9° 59′ 30″ E: Hacluyt's Head Land 79° 47′; longitude 9° 11′ 30″ E. The tide rofe about four feet, and flowed at half an hour after one, full and change. The tide fet irrregularly, from the number of iflands between which it paffed; but the flood appeared to come from the Southward.

18th. The calm weather fince the 14th had given us full time to finifh the obfervations, and complete our water: a breeze fpringing up in the morning, I went afhore to get the inftruments on board. Between one and two we weighed, with the wind Wefterly, and ftood to the Northward. Between eleven and twelve at night, having run about eight leagues, we were prevented by the ice from getting farther. We ftood along the edge of it to the Southward. At two in the morning, being embayed by the ice, I tacked, and left orders to ftand to the Eaftward along the edge of the ice, as foon as we could weather the point; hoping, if there fhould be no opening

between

between the land and the ice, that I fhould at leaft be able to afcertain where they joined, and perhaps to dif-cover from the land, whether there was any profpect of a paffage that way: At that time the ice was all folid as far as we could fee, without the leaft appearance of water to the Northward.

19th. At fix in the morning we had got to the Eaft-ward among the loofe ice which lay very thick in fhore, the main body to the Northward and Eaftward: the land near Deer Field not four miles off, and the water fhoaled to twenty fathoms. Here we found ourfelves nearly in the fame place where we had twice been ftopped, the ice fituated as before, locked with the land, without any paffage either to the Eaftward or Northward: I there-fore ftood back to the Weftward. At noon the Northern-moft part of Vogel Sang bore S W b S, diftant about feven leagues. The weather being very fine, and the wind to the Eaftward, we were enabled to coaft along the ice to the Weftward, hauling into all the bays, going round every point of ice in fearch of an opening, and ftanding clofe along by the main body all day, generally within a fhip's length.

20th. At half after three in the morning the land was out of fight, and we imagined ourfelves in rather more than eighty degrees and an half; fome of the openings being

near

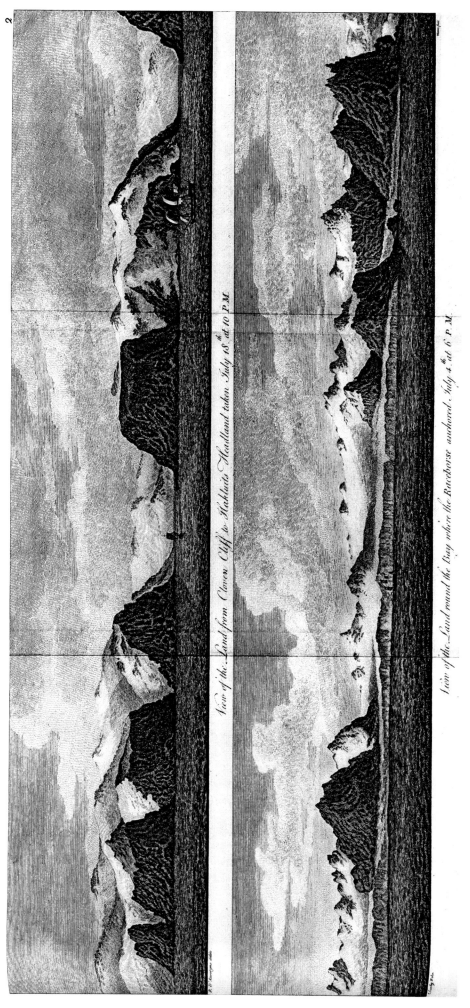

View of the Land from Cloven Cliff to Hathleets Headland taken July 18th at 10 P.M.

View of the Land round the Bay where the Racehorse anchored, July 4th at 6 P.M.

The material originally positioned here is too large for reproduction in this reissue. A PDF can be downloaded from the web address given on page iv of this book, by clicking on 'Resources Available'.

near two leagues deep, had flattered us with hopes of getting to the Northward; but thefe openings proved to be no more than bays in the main body of the ice. About one in the afternoon, we were by our reckoning in about 80° 34, nearly in the fame place where we had been on the 9th. About three we bore away for what appeared like an opening to the S W; we found the ice run far to the Southward.

21ft. We ftill continued to run along the edge of the ice, which trended to the Southward. At noon we were in the latitude of 79° 26′, by obfervation, which was twenty-five miles to the Southward of our reckoning. Finding that the direction of the ice led us to the Southward, and that the current fet the fame way, I ftood to the Northward and Weftward clofe along the ice, to try whether the fea was opened to the Northward by the wind from that quarter. At nine in the evening we had no ground with 200 fathom of line. At ten we got into a ftream of loofe ice. The weather fine, but cool all day, and fometimes foggy.

22d. At two in the morning we bore away to the N E, for the main body of the ice; the weather became foggy foon afterwards. At fix we faw the ice; and the weather being ftill foggy, we hauled up to the S S E, to avoid being embayed in it. The air very cold.

H   23d.

23d. At midnight, tacked for the body of the ice. Latitude obferved 80° 13′ 38″ Rainy in the morning; fair in the afternoon: ftill working up to the Northward and Eaftward, with the wind Eafterly. At fix in the evening, the Cloven Cliff bearing South about fix leagues, founded in 200 fathom, muddy ground; the lead appeared to have funk one third of its length in the mud. At two in the morning, with little wind, and a fwell from the South Weft, I ftood to the Northward amongft the loofe ice: at half paft two the main body of the ice a cable's length off, and the loofe ice fo clofe that we wore fhip, not having room or way enough to tack; ftruck very hard againft the ice in getting the fhip round, and got upon one piece, which lifted her in the water for near a minute, before her weight broke it. The fhips had been fo well ftrengthened, that they received no damage from thefe ftrokes; and I could with the more confidence pufh through the loofe ice, to try for openings. Hacluyt's Head Land bore S 50° W diftant about feven leagues.

24th. By this fituation of the ice we were difappointed of getting directly to the Northward, without any profpect after fo many fruitlefs attempts of being able to fucceed to the Weftward; nor indeed, could I with an Eafterly wind and heavy fwell attempt it, as the wind from that quarter would not only pack the loofe ice clofe to the Weftward, but by fetting the fea on it, make it as improper to be

approached

approached as a rocky lee fhore. To the Eaftward on the
contrary it would make fmooth water, and detach all the
loofe ice from the edges; perhaps break a ftream open, and
give us a fair trial to the Northward; at all events, with an
Eafterly wind we could run out again, if we did not find
it practicable to proceed. Finding the ice fo faft to the
Northward and Weftward, it became a defirable object to
afcertain how far it was poffible to get to the Eaftward,
and by that means purfue the voyage to the Northward.
Thefe confiderations determined me to ply to the Eaftward, and make another pufh to get through where I had
been three times repulfed. In working to the Eaftward,
we kept as near the body of the ice as poffible. At noon
the Cloven Cliff bore S W b S about feven leagues. At fix
we were working to the N E, and at nine we fteered to the
S E, the ice appearing more open that way : we had frefh
gales and cloudy weather. The fhip ftruck very hard in
endeavouring to force through the loofe ice. At midnight
the wind frefhened, and we double reefed the topfails.
It was probably owing to the frefh gales this day, as well
as to the fummer being more advanced, that we were
enabled to get farther than in any of our former attempts
this way. We continued coafting the ice, and at two in
the morning the north part of Vogel Sang and Hacluyt's
Head Land in one bore S 65° W ; Cloven Cliff S 52°
W ; the neareft part of the fhore about three leagues off.
When I left the deck, at four in the morning, we were
very near the fpot where the fhips had been faft in the ice

H 2   on

on the 7th in the evening, but rather farther to the Eaftward; we had paffed over the fame fhoal water we had
met with that day, and were now in twenty fathom,
rocky ground; ftill amongft loofe ice, but not fo clofe as
we had hitherto found it.

25th. At feven in the morning we had deepened our
water to fifty-five fathom, and were ftill amongft the loofe
ice. At noon we had deepened our water to feventy
fathom, with muddy bottom, at the diftance of about
three miles from the neareft land. By two in the afternoon we had paffed Deer Field, which we had fo often
before attempted without fuccefs; and finding the fea
open to the N E, had the moft flattering profpect of
getting to the Northward. From this part, all the way
to the Eaftward, the coaft wears a different face; the
mountains, though high, are neither fo fteep or fharp-
pointed, nor of fo black a colour as to the Weftward.
It was probably owing to this remarkable difference in the
appearance of the fhore, that the old navigators gave to
places hereabouts the names of *Red Beach*, *Red Hill*, and
Red Cliff. One of them, fpeaking of this part, has defcribed the whole country in a few words: " Here (fays
" he) I faw a more natural earth and clay than any that I
" have feen in all the country, but nothing growing
" thereupon more than in other places." At two in the
afternoon we had little wind, and were in fight of Moffen
Ifland, which is very low and flat.

The

The Carcafs being becalmed very near the ifland in the evening, Captain Lutwidge took that opportunity of obtaining the following exact account of its extent, which he communicated to me.

"At 10 P M, the body of Moffen Ifland bearing
" E b S diftant two miles; founded thirteen fathoms;
" rocky ground, with light brown mud, and broken fhells.
" Sent the mafter on fhore, who found the ifland to be
" nearly of a round form, about two miles in diameter,
" with a lake or large pond of water in the middle, all
" frozen over, except thirty or forty yards round the edge
" of it, which was water, with loofe pieces of broken ice,
" and fo fhallow they walked through it, and went over
" upon the firm folid ice. The ground between the fea
" and the pond is from half a cable's length to a quarter
" of a mile broad, and the whole ifland covered with
" gravel and fmall ftones, without the leaft verdure or
" vegetation of any kind. They faw only one piece of
" drift wood (about three fathom long, with a root on it,
" and as thick as the Carcafs's mizen maft) which had
" been thrown up over the high part of the land, and lay
" upon the declivity towards the pond. They faw three
" bears, and a number of wild ducks, geefe, and other
" fea fowls, with birds nefts all over the ifland. There
" was an infcription over the grave of a Dutchman, who
" was buried there in July 1771. It was low water at eleven
" o'clock when the boat landed, and the tide appeared to
" flow eight or nine feet; at that time we found a current

2	" carrying

" carrying the Ship to the N W from the ifland, which
" before carried us to the S.E (at the rate of a mile an
" hour) towards it. On the Weft fide is a fine white
" fandy bottom, from two fathoms, at a fhip's length
" from the beach, to five fathoms, at half a mile's
" diftance off."

The foundings all about this ifland, and to the
Eaftward, feem to partake of the nature of the coaft.
To the Weftward the rocks were high, and the fhores
bold and fteep to; here the land fhelved more, and the
foundings were fhoal, from thirty to ten fathom. It appears extraordinary that none of the old navigators, who
are fo accurate and minute in their defcriptions of the
coaft, have taken any notice of this ifland, fo remarkable
and different from every thing they had feen on the Weftern
coaft; unlefs we fhould fuppofe that it did not then exift,
and that the ftreams from the great ocean up the Weft
fide of Spitfbergen, and through the Waygat's Straits,
meeting here, have raifed this bank, and occafioned the
quantity of ice that generally blocks up the coaft hereabouts.—At four in the afternoon, hoifted out the boat,
and tried the current, which fet N E b E, at the rate of
three quarters of a mile an hour. At midnight, Moffen
Ifland bore from S E b S to S b W, diftant about five
miles.

26th. About two in the morning, we had little
wind, with fog; made the fignals to the Carcafs for

keeping

keeping company. At half an hour after three in the afternoon, we were in longitude 12° 20′ 45″ E; variation, by the mean of five azimuths, 12° 47′ W. At nine we faw land to the Eaſtward; ſteering to the Northward with little wind, and no ice in ſight, except what we had paſſed.

27th. Working ſtill to the N E, we met with ſome looſe ice; however from the opennefs of the ſea hitherto, ſince we had paſſed Deer Field, I had great hopes of getting far to the Northward; but about noon, being in the latitude of eighty and forty-eight, by our reckoning, we were ſtopped by the main body of the icɩ, which we found lying in a line, nearly Eaſt and Weſt, quite ſolid. Having tacked, I brought to, and ſounded cloſe to the edge of the ice, in 79 fathom, muddy bottom.

The wind being ſtill Eaſterly, I worked up cloſe to the edge of the ice, coaſting it all the way. At ſix in the evening we were in longitude 14° 59′ 30″ E, by ob-ſervation.

28th. At midnight the latitude obſerved was 80° 37. The main body of the ice ſtill lying in the ſame direction, we continued working to the Eaſtward, and found ſeveral openings to the Northward, of two or three miles deep; into every one of which we ran, forcing the ſhip, wherever we could, by a prefs of ſail, amongſt the looſe ice

4 which

which we found here in much larger pieces than to the Weſtward. At ſix in the morning the variation, by the mean of ſix azimuths, was 11° 56′ W; the horizon remarkably clear. At noon, being cloſe to the main body of the ice, the latitude by obſervation was 80° 36′: we founded in 1c1 fathom, muddy ground. In the afternoon the wind blew freſh at N E, with a thick fog; the ice hung much about the rigging. The looſe ice being thick and cloſe, we found ourſelves ſo much engaged in it, as to be obliged to run back a conſiderable diſtance to the Weſtward and Southward, before we could extricate ourſelves: we afterwards had both the ſea and the weather clear, and worked up to the North Eaſtward. At half paſt five the longitude of the ſhip was 15° 16′ 45″ E. At ſeven the Eaſternmoſt land bore E ¼ N diſtant about ſeven or eight leagues, appearing like deep bays and iſlands, probably thoſe called in the Dutch charts the *Seven Iſlands*; they ſeemed to be ſurrounded with ice. I ſtood to the Southward, in hopes of getting to the South-eaſtward round the ice, and between it and the land, where the water appeared more open.

29th. At midnight the latitude by obſervation was 80° 21′. At four, tacked cloſe to the ice, hauled up the foreſail and backed the mizen topſail, having too much way amongſt the looſe ice. At noon, latitude obſerved 80° 24′ 56″. An opening, which we ſuppoſed to be

the

the entrance of Waygat's Straits, bore South; the Northernmoft land N E b E; the neareft fhore diftant about four miles. In the afternoon the officer from the deck came down to tell me, we were very near a fmall rock even with the water's edge; on going up, I faw it within little more than a fhip's length on the lee bow, and put the helm down: before the fhip got round, we were clofe to it, and perceived it to be a very fmall piece of ice, covered with gravel. In the evening, feeing the Northern part of the iflands only over the ice, I was anxious to get round it, in hopes of finding an opening under the land. Being near a low flat ifland oppofite the Waygat's Straits, not higher, but much larger than Moffen Ifland, we had an heavy fwell from the Southward, with little wind, and from ten to twenty fathom: having got paft this ifland, approaching to the high land to the Eaftward, we deepened our water very fuddenly to 117 fathom. Having little wind, and the weather very clear, two of the officers went with a boat in purfuit of fome fea-horfes, and afterwards to the low ifland. At midnight we found by obfervation the latitude 80° 27′ 3″, and the dip 82° 2′ ½. At four in the morning I found, by Bouguer's log, that the current fet two fathom to the Eaftward. At fix in the morning the officers returned from the ifland; in their way back they had fired at, and wounded a fea-horfe, which dived immediately, and brought up with it a number of others. They all joined in an attack upon the boat, wrefted an oar from one of the

I   men,

men, and were with difficulty prevented from ftaving or overfetting her; but a boat from the Carcafs joining ours, they difperfed. One of that fhip's boats had before been attacked in the fame manner off Moffen Ifland. From Dr. Irving, who went on this party, I had the following account of the low ifland.

" We found feveral large fir trees lying on the fhore,
" fixteen or eighteen feet above the level of the fea: fome
" of thefe trees were feventy feet long, and had been torn
" up by the roots; others cut down by the axe, and
" notched for twelve-feet lengths: this timber was no
" ways decayed, or the ftrokes of the hatchet in the leaft
" effaced. There were likewife fome pipe-ftaves, and wood
" fafhioned for ufe. The beach was formed of old timber,
" fand, and whale-bones.

" The ifland is about feven miles long, flat, and
" formed chiefly of ftones from eighteen to thirty inches
" over, many of them hexagons, and commodioufly
" placed for walking on: the middle of the ifland is
" covered with mofs, fcurvy grafs, forrel, and a few
" ranunculufes then in flower. Two rein-deer were
" feeding on the mofs; one we killed, and found it fat,
" and of high flavour. We faw a light grey-coloured
" fox; and a creature fomewhat larger than a weafel,
" with fhort ears, long tail, and fkin fpotted white and
" black. The ifland abounds with fmall fnipes, fimilar
" to the jack-fnipe in England. The Ducks were now
" hatching

3

" hatching their eggs, and many wild geefe feeding by
" the water fide."

When I left the deck at fix in the morning, the weather
was remarkably clear, and quite calm. To the N E,
amongft the iflands, I faw much ice, but alfo much water
between the pieces; which gave me hopes that when a
breeze fprung up, I fhould be able to get to the Northward by that way.

30th. Little winds, and calm all day; we got fomething to the Northward and Eaftward. At noon we were
by obfervation in latitude 80° 31'. At three in the afternoon we were in longitude 18° 48' E, being amongft the
iflands, and in the ice, with no appearance of an opening
for the fhip. Between eleven and twelve at night I fent
the mafter, Mr. Crane, in the four-oared boat, amongft
the ice, to try whether he could get the boat through,
and find any opening for the fhip which might give us a
profpect of getting farther; with directions if he could reach
the fhore to go up one of the mountains, in order to difcover
the ftate of the ice to the Eaftward and Northward. At
five in the morning, the ice being all round us, we got
out our ice-anchors, and moored along-fide a field. The
mafter returned between feven and eight, and with him
Captain Lutwidge, who had joined him on fhore. They
had afcended an high mountain, from whence they com-
manded a profpect extending to the Eaft and North Eaft

I 2

ten

ten or twelve leagues, over one continued plain of smooth unbroken ice, bounded only by the horizon: they also saw land stretching to the S E, laid down in the Dutch Charts as islands. The main body of ice, which we had traced from West to East, they now perceived to join to these islands, and from them to what is called the North East land. In returning, the ice having closed much since they went, they were frequently forced to haul the boat over it to other openings. The weather exceedingly fine and mild, and unusually clear. The scene was beautiful and picturesque; the two ships becalmed in a large bay, with three apparent openings between the islands which formed it, but every-where surrounded with ice as far as we could see, with some streams of water; not a breath of air; the water perfectly smooth; the ice covered with snow, low, and even, except a few broken pieces near the edges: the pools of water in the middle of the pieces were frozen over with young ice.

31ft. At nine in the morning, having a light breeze to the Eastward, we cast off, and endeavoured to force through the ice. At noon the ice was so close, that being unable to proceed, we moored again to a field. In the afternoon we filled our cask with fresh water from the ice, which we found very pure and soft. The Carcass moved, and made fast to the same field with us. The ice measured eight yards ten inches in thickness at one end, and seven

yards

Jn.ᵗ Cleveley Junᵣ delinᵗ May 4ᵗʰ 1774.

View of the RACEHORSE *and*

_Pouncy Sculp.ᵗ

ᵇ CARCASS July 31.ˢᵗ 1773.

yards eleven inches at the other. At four in the afternoon the variation was 12° 24′ W : at the fame time the
longitude 19° 0′ 15″ E; by which we found that we had
hardly moved to the Eaftward fince the day before.
Calm moft part of the day; the weather very fine; the ice
clofed faft, and was all round the fhips; no opening to
be feen any where, except an hole of about a mile and a
half, where the fhips lay faft to the ice with ice-anchors.
We completed the water. The fhip's company were
playing on the ice all day. The pilots being much farther
than they had ever been, and the feafon advancing, feemed
alarmed at being befet.

Auguft 1ft. The ice preffed in faft; there was not
now the fmalleft opening; the two fhips were within lefs
than two lengths of each other, feparated by ice, and
neither having room to turn. The ice, which had been
all flat the day before, and almoft level with the water's
edge, was now in many places forced higher than the
main yard, by the pieces fqueezing together. Our latitude this day at noon, by the double altitude, was
80° 37′.

2d. Thick foggy wet weather, blowing frefh to the
Weftward; the ice immediately about the fhips rather
loofer than the day before, but yet hourly fetting in fo
faft upon us, that there feemed to be no probability of
getting the fhips out again, without a ftrong Eaft, or
North

North Eaſt wind. There was not the ſmalleſt appearance of open water, except a little towards the Weſt point of the North Eaſt land. The ſeven iſlands and North Eaſt land, with the frozen ſea, formed almoſt a baſon, leaving but about four points opening for the ice to drift out, in caſe of a change of wind.

3d. The weather very fine, clear, and calm; we perceived that the ſhips had been driven far to the Eaſtward; the ice was much cloſer than before, and the paſſage by which we had come in from the Weſtward cloſed up, no open water being in ſight, either in that or any other quarter. The pilots having expreſſed a wiſh to get if poſſible farther out, the ſhips companies were ſet to work at five in the morning, to cut a paſſage through the ice, and warp through the ſmall openings to the Weſtward. We found the ice very deep, having ſawed ſometimes through pieces twelve feet thick. This labour was continued the whole day, but without any ſucceſs; our utmoſt efforts not having moved the ſhips above three hundred yards to the Weſtward through the ice, at the ſame time that they had been driven (together with the ice itſelf, to which they were faſt) far to the N E and Eaſtward, by the current; which had alſo forced the looſe ice from the Weſtward, between the iſlands, where it became packed, and as firm as the main body.

4th.

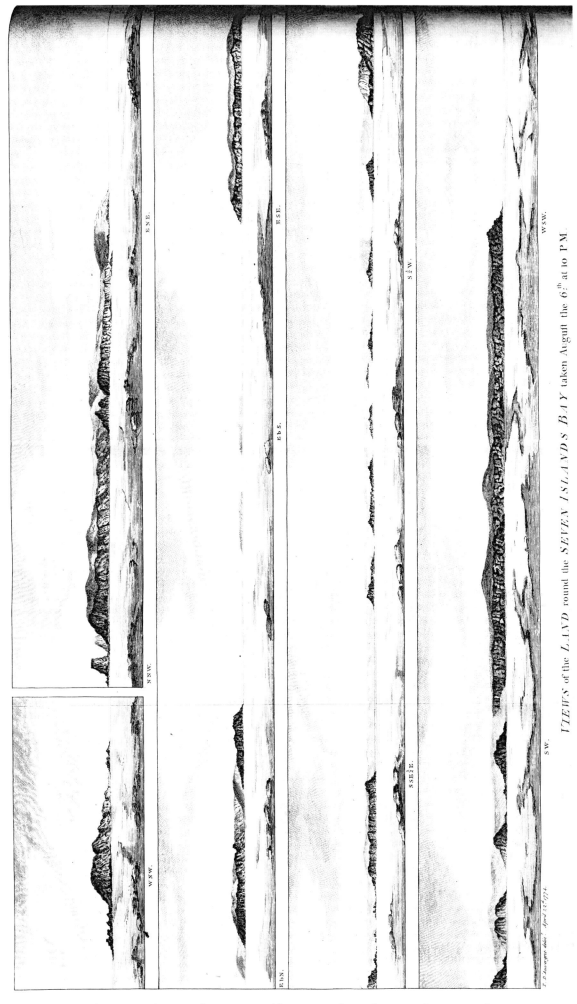

VIEWS of the LAND round the SEVEN ISLANDS BAY taken August the 6.th at 10 P.M.

4th. Quite calm till evening, when we were flattered with a light air to the Eaſtward, which did not laſt long, and had no favourable effect. The wind was now at N W, with a very thick fog, the ſhip driving to the Eaſtward. The pilots ſeemed to apprehend that the ice extended very far to the Southward and Weſtward.

5th. The probability of getting the ſhips out appearing every hour leſs, and the ſeaſon being already far advanced, ſome ſpeedy reſolution became neceſſary as to the ſteps to be taken for the preſervation of the people. As the ſituation of the ſhips prevented us from ſeeing the ſtate of the ice to the Weſtward, by which our future proceedings muſt in a great meaſure be determined, I ſent Mr. Walden, one of the midſhipmen, with two pilots, to an iſland about twelve miles off, which I have diſtinguiſhed in the charts by the name of Walden's Iſland, to ſee where the open water lay.

6th. Mr. Walden and the pilots, who were ſent the day before to examine the ſtate of the ice from the iſland, returned this morning with an account, that the ice, though cloſe all about us, was open to the Weſtward, round the point by which we came in. They alſo told me, that when upon the iſland they had the wind very freſh to the Eaſtward, though where the ſhips lay it had been almoſt calm all day. This circumſtance conſiderably leſſened

the

the hopes we had hitherto entertained of the immediate effeᵭ of an Eaſterly wind in clearing the bay. We had but one alternative; either patiently to wait the event of the weather upon the ſhips, in hopes of getting them out, or to betake ourſelves to the boats. The ſhips had driven into ſhoal water, having but fourteen fathom. Should they, or the ice to which they were faſt, take the ground, they muſt be inevitably loſt, and probably overſet. The hopes of getting the ſhips out was not haſtily to be relinquiſhed, nor obſtinately adhered to, till all other means of retreat were cut off. Having no harbour to lodge them in, it would be impoſſible to winter them here, with any probability of their being again ſerviceable; our proviſions would be very ſhort for ſuch an undertaking, were it otherwiſe feaſible; and ſuppoſing, what appeared impoſſible, that we could get to the neareſt rocks, and make ſome conveniences for wintering, being now in an unfrequented part, where ſhips never even attempt to come, we ſhould have the ſame difficulties to encounter the next year, without the ſame reſources; the remains of the ſhip's company, in all probability, not in health; no proviſions; and the ſea not ſo open, this year having certainly been uncommonly clear. Indeed it could not have been expeᵭed that more than a very ſmall part ſhould ſurvive the hardſhips of ſuch a winter with every advantage; much leſs in our preſent ſituation. On the other hand, the undertaking to move ſo large a body for

ſo

ſo conſiderable a diſtance by boats, was not without very ſerious difficulties. Should we remain much longer here, the bad weather muſt be expected to ſet in. The ſtay of the Dutchmen to the Northward is very doubtful: if the Northern harbours keep clear, they ſtay till the beginning of September; but when the looſe ice ſets in, they quit them immediately. I thought it proper to ſend for the officers of both ſhips, and informed them of my intention of preparing the boats for going away. I immediately hoiſted out the boats, and took every precaution in my power to make them ſecure and comfortable: the fitting would neceſſarily take up ſome days. The water ſhoaling, and the ſhips driving faſt towards the rocks to the N E, I ordered canvaſs bread-bags to be made, in caſe it ſhould be neceſſary very ſuddenly to betake ourſelves to the boats: I alſo ſent a man with a lead and line to the Northward, and another from the Carcaſs to the Eaſtward, to ſound wherever they found cracks in the ice, that we might have notice before either the ſhips, or the ice to which they were faſt, took the ground; as in that caſe, they muſt inſtantly have been cruſhed or overſet. The weather bad; moſt part of the day foggy, and rather cold.

7th. In the morning I ſet out with the Launch over the ice; ſhe hauled much eaſier than I could have expected; we got her about two miles. I then returned with the people for their dinner. Finding the ice rather

K   more

more open near the ſhips, I was encouraged to attempt moving them. The wind being Eaſterly, though but little of it, we ſet the ſails, and got the ſhips about a mile to the Weſtward. They moved indeed, but very ſlowly, and were not now by a great deal ſo far to the Weſtward as where they were beſet. However, I kept all the ſail upon them, to force through whenever the ice ſlacked the leaſt. The people behaved very well in hauling the boat; they ſeemed reconciled to the idea of quitting the ſhips, and to have the fulleſt confidence in their officers. The boats could not with the greateſt diligence be got to the water ſide before the fourteenth; if the ſituation of the ſhips did not alter by that time, I ſhould not be juſtified in ſtaying longer by them. In the mean time I reſolved to carry on both attempts together, moving the boats conſtantly, but without omitting any opportunity of getting the ſhips through.

8th. At half paſt four, ſent two pilots with three men to ſee the ſtate of the ice to the Weſtward, that I might judge of the probability of getting the ſhips out. At nine they returned, and reported the ice to be very heavy and cloſe, conſiſting chiefly of large fields. Between nine and ten this morning, I ſet out with the people, and got the Launch above three miles. The weather being foggy, and the people having worked hard, I thought it beſt to return on board between ſix and ſeven. The ſhips had in the mean time moved ſomething through the ice, and

the

Jn.ᵒ Cleveley, Jun.ʳ delin. May 4.ᵗʰ 1774.

View of the RACEHORSE *and*

CARCASS, August, 7th 1773.

the ice itſelf had drifted ſtill more to the Weſtward. At night there was little wind, and a thick fog, ſo that I could not judge preciſely of the advantage we had gained; but I ſtill feared that, however flattering, it was not ſuch as to juſtify my giving up the idea of moving the boats, the ſeaſon advancing ſo faſt, the preſervation of the ſhips being ſo uncertain, and the ſituation of the people ſo critical.

9th. A thick fog in the morning: we moved the ſhip a little through ſome very ſmall openings. In the afternoon, upon its clearing up, we were agreeably ſurprized to find the ſhips had driven much more than we could have expected to the Weſtward. We worked hard all day, and got them ſomething more to the Weſtward through the ice; but nothing in compariſon to what the ice itſelf had drifted. We got paſt the Launches; I ſent a number of men for them, and got them on board. Between three and four in the morning the wind was Weſterly, and it ſnowed faſt. The people having been much fatigued, we were obliged to deſiſt from working for a few hours. The progreſs which the ſhips had made through the ice was, however, a very favourable event: the drift of the ice was an advantage that might be as ſuddenly loſt, as it had been unexpectedly gained, by a change in the current: we had experienced the inefficacy of an Eaſterly wind when far in the bay, and under the high land; but having now got through ſo much of the

K 2   ice,

ice; we began again to conceive hopes that a briſk gale from that quarter would ſoon effectually clear us.

10th. The wind ſpringing up to the N N E in the morning, we ſet all the ſail we could upon the ſhip, and forced her through a great deal of very heavy ice: ſhe ſtruck often very hard, and with one ſtroke broke the ſhank of the beſt bower anchor. About noon we had got her through all the ice, and out to ſea. I ſtood to the N W to make the ice, and found the main body juſt where we left it. At three in the morning, with a good breeze Eaſterly, we were ſtanding to the Weſtward, between the land and the ice, both in ſight; the weather hazey.

11th. Came to an anchor in the harbour of Smeerenberg, to refreſh the people after their fatigues. We found here four of the Dutch ſhips, which we had left in the Norways when we ſailed from Vogel Sang, and upon which I had depended for carrying the people home in caſe we had been obliged to quit the ſhips. In this Sound there is good anchorage in thirteen fathom, ſandy bottom, not far from the ſhore: it is well ſheltered from all winds. The iſland cloſe to which we lay is called Amſterdam Iſland, the Weſternmoſt point of which is Hacluyt's Head Land: here the Dutch uſed formerly to boil their whale-oil, and the remains of ſome conveniencies erected by them for that purpoſe are ſtill viſible. Once they attempted to make an eſtabliſhment, and left ſome people

to

The RACEHORSE and CARCASS forcing through the ICE, August 10, 1773.

to winter here, who all periſhed. The Dutch ſhips ſtill reſort to this place for the latter ſeaſon of the whale fiſhery.

12th. Got the inſtruments on ſhore, and the tent pitched; but could not make any obſervations this day or the next, from the badneſs of the weather.

13th. Rain, and blowing hard: two of the Dutch ſhips ſailed for Holland.

14th. The weather being fine and little wind, we began our obſervations.

18th. Completed the obſervations. Calm all day. During our ſtay, I again ſet up the pendulum, but was not ſo fortunate as before, never having been able to get an obſervation of a revolution of the ſun, or even equal altitudes for the time. We had an opportunity of determining the refraction at midnight, which anſwered within a few ſeconds to the calculation in Dr. Bradley's table, allowing for the barometer and thermometer. Being within ſight of Cloven Cliff, I took a ſurvey of this part of Fair Haven, to connect it with the plan of the other part. Dr. Irving climbed up a mountain, to take its height with the barometer, which I determined at the ſame time geometrically with great care. By repeated obſervations here we found the latitude to be 79° 44′, which by the ſurvey

correſponded

correfponded exactly with the latitude of Cloven Cliff,
determined before; the longitude 9° 50′ 45″ E; dip 82°
8′ ¼ ; variation 18° 57′ W; which agrees alfo with the
obfervation made on fhore in July. The tide flowed here
half paft one, the fame as in Vogel Sang harbour.

Oppofite to the place where the inftruments ftood, was
one of the moft remarkable Icebergs in this country.
Icebergs are large bodies of ice filling the vallies between
the high mountains; the face towards the fea is nearly perpendicular, and of a very lively light green colour. That
reprefented in the engraving, from a fketch taken by Mr.
D'Auvergne upon the fpot, was about three hundred feet
high, with a cafcade of water iffuing out of it. The
black mountains, white fnow, and beautiful colour of the
ice, make a very romantick and uncommon picture. Large
pieces frequently break off from the Icebergs, and fall
with great noife into the water: we obferved one piece
which had floated out into the bay, and grounded in twenty-
four fathom; it was fifty feet high above the furface of
the water, and of the fame beautiful colour as the Iceberg.

A particular defcription of all the plants and animals
will have a place in the Appendix. I fhall here mention fuch general obfervations as my fhort ftay enabled
me to make. The ftone we found was chiefly a kind of
marble, which diffolved eafily in the marine acid. We
perceived no marks of minerals of any kind, nor the leaft
appearance of prefent, or remains of former Volcanoes.
Neither did we meet with infects, or any fpecies of

W. Pars del.

View of a

W. Byrne Sculp. 1774

n Iceberg.

reptiles; not even the common earthworm. We saw no springs or rivers, the water, which we found in great plenty, being all produced by the melting of the snow from the mountains. During the whole time we were in these latitudes, there was no thunder or lightning. I must also add, that I never found what is mentioned by Marten (who is generally accurate in his observations, and faithful in his accounts) of the sun at midnight resembling in appearance the moon; I saw no difference in clear weather between the sun at midnight and any other time, but what arose from a different degree of altitude; the brightness of the light appearing there, as well as elsewhere, to depend upon the obliquity of his rays. The sky was in general loaded with hard white clouds; so that I do not remember to have ever seen the sun and the horizon both free from them even in the clearest weather. We could always perceive when we were approaching the ice, long before we saw it, by a bright appearance near the horizon, which the pilots called the *blink of the ice*. Hudson remarked, that the sea where he met with ice was blue; but the green sea was free from it. I was particularly attentive to observe this difference, but could never discern it.

The Driftwood in these seas has given rise to various opinions and conjectures, both as to its nature and the place of its growth. All that which we saw (except the pipe-staves taken notice of by Doctor Irving on the Low Island) was fir, and not worm-eaten. The place of its growth I had no opportunity of ascertaining.

The

The nature of the ice was a principal object of attention in this climate. We found always a great ſwell near the edge of it; but whenever we got within the looſe ice, the water was conſtantly ſmooth. The looſe fields and flaws, as well as the interior part of the fixed ice, were flat, and low: with the wind blowing on the ice, the looſe parts were always, to uſe the phraſe of the Greenlandmen, *packed*; the ice at the edges appearing rough, and piled up; this roughneſs and height I imagine to proceed from the ſmaller pieces being thrown up by the force of the ſea on the ſolid part. During the time that we were faſt amongſt the Seven Iſlands, we had frequent opportunities of obſerving the irreſiſtible force of the large bodies of floating ice. We have often ſeen a piece of ſeveral acres ſquare lifted up between two much larger pieces, and as it were becoming one with them; and afterwards this piece ſo formed acting in the ſame manner upon a ſecond and third; which would probably have continued to be the effect, till the whole bay had been ſo filled with ice that the different pieces could have had no motion, had not the ſtream taken an unexpected turn, and ſet the ice out of the bay.

19th. Weighed in the morning with the wind at N N E. Before we got out of the bay it fell calm. I obſerved for theſe three or four days, about eleven in the evening, an appearance of duſk.

20th.

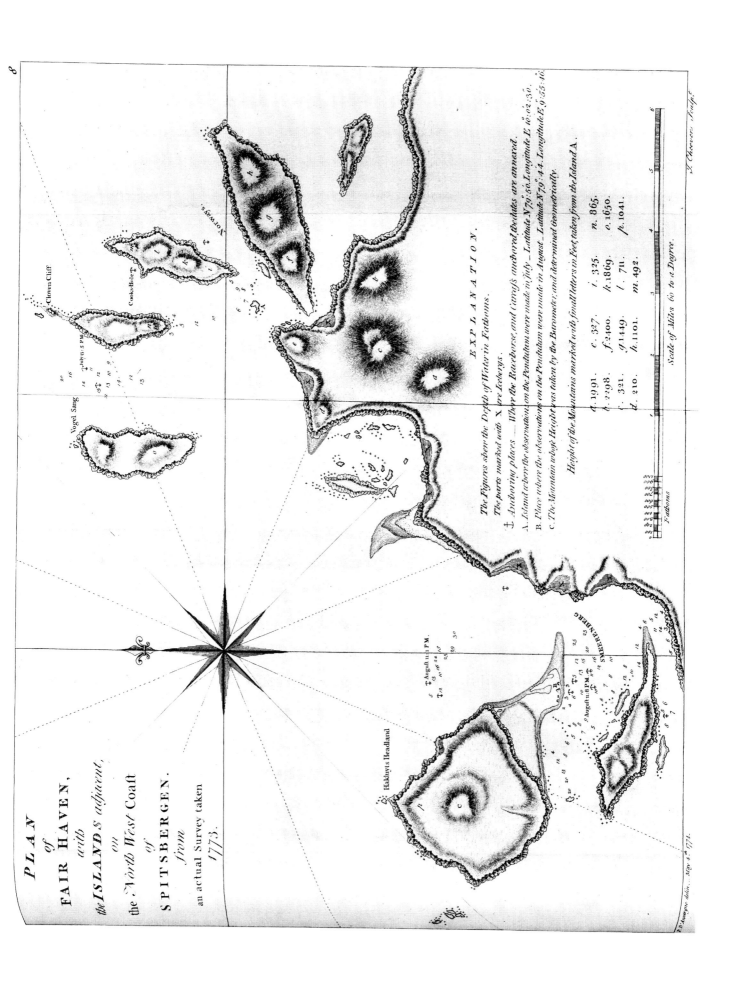

20th. At midnight, being exactly in the latitude of Cloven Cliff, Mr. Harvey took an obſervation for the re-fraction; which we found to agree with the tables. The wind Southerly all day, blowing freſh in the afternoon. About noon fell in with a ſtream of looſe ice, and about four made the main ice near us. We ſtood to the W N W along it at night, and found it in the ſame ſituation as when we ſaw it before; the wind freſhened and the weather grew thick, ſo that we loſt ſight of it, and could not venture to ſtand nearer, the wind being S S W.

21ſt. At two in the morning we were cloſe in with the body of the Weſt ice, and obliged to tack for it; blowing freſh, with a very heavy ſea from the Southward. The wind abated in the afternoon, but the ſwell continued, with a thick fog.

22d. The wind ſprung up Northerly, with a thick fog; about noon moderate and clearer; but coming on to blow freſh again in the evening, with a great ſea, and thick fog, I was forced to haul more to the Eaſtward, left we ſhould be embayed, or run upon lee ice.

The ſeaſon was ſo very far advanced, and fogs as well as gales of wind ſo much to be expected, that nothing more could now have been done, had any thing been left untried. The ſummer appears to have been uncommonly

L   favourable

favourable for our purpofe, and afforded us the fulleft op-portunity of afcertaining repeatedly the fituation of that wall of ice, extending for more than twenty degrees between the latitudes of eighty and eighty-one, without the fmalleft appearance of any opening.

I fhould here conclude the account of the voyage, had not fome obfervations and experiments occurred on the paffage home.

In fteering to the Southward we foon found the weather grow more mild, or rather to our feelings warm. Auguft 24th, we faw Jupiter: the fight of a ftar was now become almoft as extraordinary a phenomenon, as the fun at midnight when we firft got within the Arctic circle. The weather was very fine for fome part of the voyage;

on the 4th of September, the water being perfectly fmooth with a dead calm, I repeated with fuccefs the attempt I had made to get foundings in the main ocean at great depths, and ftruck ground in fix hundred and eighty-three fathoms, with circumftances (which will be men-tioned in the Appendix) that convince me I was not mif-taken in the depth; the bottom was a fine foft blue clay. From the 7th of September, when we were off Shetland, till the 24th, when we made Orfordnefs, we had very hard gales of wind with little intermiffion, which were conftantly indicated feveral hours before they came on by the fall of the barometer, and rife of the manometer: this

5

proved

proved to me the utility of those instruments at sea. In one of these gales, the hardest, I think, I ever was in, and with the greatest sea, we lost three of our boats, and were obliged to heave two of our guns overboard, and bear away for some time, though near a lee shore, to clear the ship of water. I cannot omit this opportunity of repeating, that I had the greatest reason on this, as well as every other critical occasion, to be satisfied with the behaviour both of the officers and seamen. In one of these gales on the 12th of September, Dr. Irving tried the temperature of the sea in that state of agitation, and found it considerably warmer than that of the atmosphere. This observation is the more interesting, as it agrees with a passage in Plutarch's Natural Questions, not (I believe) before taken notice of, or confirmed by experiment, in which he remarks, " that the sea becomes warmer " by being agitated in waves."

The frequent and very heavy gales at the latter end of the year, confirmed me in the opinion, that the time of our sailing from England was the properest that could have been chosen. These gales are as common in the Spring as in the Autumn : there is every reason to suppose therefore, that at an early season we should have met with the same bad weather in going out as we did on our return. The unavoidable necessity of carrying a quantity of additional stores and provisions, rendered the ships so deep in the water, that in heavy gales the boats, with many of the stores, must probably have been thrown

L 2   overboard;

overboard; as we experienced on our way home, though the fhips were then much lightened by the confumption of provifions, and expenditure of ftores. Such accidents in the outfet muft have defeated the voyage. At the time we failed, added to the fine weather, we had the further advantage of nearly reaching the latitude of eighty without feeing ice, which the Greenlandmen generally fall in with in the latitude of feventy-three or feventy-four. There was alfo moft probability, if ever navigation fhould be practicable to the Pole, of finding the fea open to the Northward after the folftice; the fun having then exerted the full influence of his rays, though there was enough of the fummer ftill remaining for the purpofe of exploring the feas to the Northward and Weftward of Spitfbergen.

A P P E N D I X.

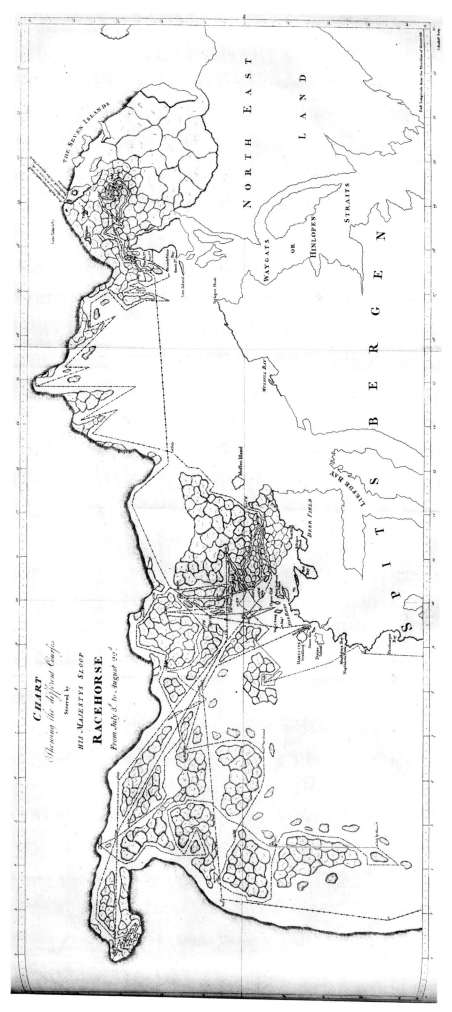

The material originally positioned here is too large for reproduction in this reissue. A PDF can be downloaded from the web address given on page iv of this book, by clicking on 'Resources Available'.

A P P E N D I X.

Eſtabliſhment of OFFICERS and MEN for the RACEHORSE

ONE Commander.
Three Lieutenants.
One Maſter.
One Boatſwain.
One Gunner.
One Carpenter.
One Purſer.
One Surgeon.
One Surgeon's Mate.
One Cook.
Three Maſter's Mates.
Six Midſhipmen.
One Captain's Clerk.
Two Quarter Maſters.
One Quarter Maſter's Mate.
Two Boatſwain's Mates.
One Coxſwain.
One Maſter Sail-maker.
One Sail maker's Crew.
One Gunner's Mate.
One Yeoman of the Powder Room.
One Quarter Gunner.
One Armourer.

Two

Two Carpenter's Mates.
Two Carpenter's Crew.
One Steward.
One Corporal.
Fifty Seamen.
Two Pilots.

    In all Ninety-two.

Comparative Table of the Latitudes and Longitudes of some remarkable Places.								
Places.	By Sir Jonas Moore.		By the Atlas Maritimus.		By Robertson's Navigation.		By Observations made this Voyage.	
	Latitude.	Longitude.	Latitude.	Longitude.	Latitude.	Longitude.	Latitude.	Longitude.
	° ′	° ′	° ′	° ′	° ′	° ′	° ′	° ′
Queenborough,	51 30	0 37E	. .	. . .	. .	. . .	. .	. . .
Sheernefs,	. .	0 37E	. .	. . .	. .	. . .	51 31	0 30E
Orfordnefs,	52 20	1 11E	52 14	1 36E	52 17	1 11E	. .	. . .
Southwold,	. .	. . .	. .	. . .	. .	. . .	. .	1 18E
Flamborough Head,	54 8	0 49W	54 9	0 10E	54 8	0 11E	54 9	0 19E
Whitby,	54 35	1 14W	54 28	0 22W	54 30	0 50W	. .	1 55W
Hangcliff,	. .	. . .	. .	. . .	. .	. . .	60 9	0 56W
Black Point,	78 32	13 10E	77 58	. . .	78 0	10 50E	78 13	10 33E
Hakluyt's Head Land,	. .	. . .	. .	. . .	79 55	12 0E	79 47	9 11E

T A B L E

APPENDIX.

Table of Days Works.

Day of the Month	Course	Distance	Latitude in	Longitude — By the Watch	By Kendal	By Arnold	By Lunar Observations	By the Reckoning	Magnetic Observations — Dip	Variation West	Bearings and Distances
June 6									73 22		Southwold, WNW ¼ N, distance 3 leagues.
7	N 27 E	107	52 17 obf.	1 30 15 E	1 59 0 E	1 45 15 E		2 39 E			Southwold, S 27° W, distance 36 leagues.
8	S 54 W	70	54 0 obf.	0 37 0 E	1 19 45	1 5 15		0 56			Southwold, S 10° 30' E, distance 22 leagues.
9	NW	45	53 39 obf.					0 12			Southwold, S 22° 10' E, distance 35 leagues.
10	NW	36	54 5 obf.	1 55 30 W	1 22 30	1 33 15		0 31 W			Southwold, S 27° 50' E, distance 47 leagues.
11			54 27					1 0 E			In Whitby Road.
12	N 15 E	123	56 28					0 10 E			Whitby, S 15° W, distance 41 leagues.
13	N by E	190	59 32 obf.	0 3 0 W	0 36 15 E	0 27 15 E	1 39 15 E	0 10 W		21 53	Whitby, S 12° 40' W, distance 103 leagues.
14	N 29 W	48	60 17 obf.	0 56 45 W	0 25 0 W	0 17 0 W	2 42 30 E	0 40 W	73 30	23 46	Whitby, S 6° 10' W, distance 122 Leagues. Hangcliff, S 59° W, 10 or 11 miles.
15			60 19 obf.	0 39 0 W	0 10 15 W	0 15 45 W	0 26 0 W		75 0		Hangcliff, S 55° W, distance 10 or 11 miles.
16	N 27 E	27	60 29 obf.					0 31	76 45		Hangcliff, S 27° W, distance 9 leagues.
17	N 6 E	147	62 59 obf.	0 19 45 W	0 26 45 E	0 22 15 E		0 2 W		19 22	Hangcliff, S 9° 34' W, distance 56 leagues.
18	N 4 W	141	65 18 obf.	1 0 30 W	0 11 45 W	0 15 15 W		0 17			Hangcliff, S 3° 30' W, distance 102 leagues.
19	N 4 W	54	66 14	1 7 0 W	0 19 45 W	0 31 30 W		0 27		19 11	Hangcliff, S 2° 52' W, distance 121 leagues.
20	N 30 E	59	67 5					0 46 E			Hangcliff, S 6° 14' W, distance 138 leagues.
21	N 5 W	60	68 5 obf.	0 37 0 W	0 20 0 E	0 22 0 E		0 32			Hangcliff, S 3° 44' W, distance 157 leagues.
22	North	161	70 45					0 32	77 52	23 18	Hangcliff, S 3° 44' W, distance 211 leagues.
23	N 2 E	97	72 22					0 46			Hangcliff, S 28' W, distance 243 leagues.
24	N 41 E	81	73 22					3 53	81 30		Hangcliff, S 7° 59' W, distance 265 leagues.
25	N 63 E	116	74 5 obf.	8 14 0 E	9 29 30	9 43 0	11 11 30 E	9 44	79 30	17 9	Hangcliff, S 16° 9' W, distance 289 leagues.
26	N 58 E	33	74 25 obf.	9 18 15	10 44 45	11 1 0	10 10 0	11 46	79 22	7 47	Hangcliff, S 18° 38' W, distance 296 leagues.
27	N 21 W	51	75 21					9 43			Hangcliff, S 15° 17' W, distance 314 leagues.
28	N 10 W	137	77 36 obf.	8 0 15	9 29 45	9 53 45		8 52	81 7		Hangcliff, S 11° 6' W, distance 350 leagues.
29	N 26 E	28	77 59 obf.	9 1 0	10 35 30	11 4 30		9 48	80 26		Hangcliff, S 11° 24' W, distance 360 leagues.
30	N 37 W	20	78 8 obf.	9 18 0	10 57 30	11 28 0		10 58	79 30		Black Point, ENE ¼ E, distance 9 miles.
July 1	N 7 W	11	78 13 obf.					10 53		11 38	Black Point, East, distance 18 miles.
2	N 31 W	15	78 23 obf.	9 35 30	11 57 15	10 17 30		10 15			Black Point, S 61° E, distance 27 miles.
3	North	12	78 36					10 15			Black Point, S 42° E, distance 11 leagues.
4	N 2 E	57	79 31 obf.					9 57	80 45	14 55	Magdalena Hook, N 25° E, distance 4 miles.
5	N 33 W	17	79 55	9 5 0	10 30 30	11 49 45		9 7			Magdalena Hook, S 33° E, distance 17 miles.
6			79 57 obf.								Vogel Sang Point, S 83° E, distance 5 leagues.
7											Cloven Cliff S 65° W, distance 5 leagues.
8											Cloven Cliff S 26° W, Vogel Sang Point, S 48° W, distance 7 or 8 miles.
9	N 47 W	55	80 29 obf.	10 54 30	13 13 15	14 18 15	9 32	5 56	81 52		Vogel Sang Point, S 47° E, distance 55 miles.
10	West	35	80 29				E	2 21			Vogel Sang Point, S 63° 15' E, distance 8¼ miles.
11			80 4 obf.								Vogel Sang Point, S 48° W, distance 9 miles.
12											Vogel Sang Point, S 25° W, distance 6 miles.

M

APPENDIX.

Table of Days Works.

Day of the Month.	Course.	Distance.	Latitude in	Longitude, By the Watch.	By Kendal.	By Arnold.	By Lunar Observations.	By the Reckoning.	Magnetic Observations. Dip.	Variation West.	Bearings and Distances.
July 13											⎫
14											⎮ In Vogel Sang.
15			79 53	10 2 30 E	12 6 30 E	13 55 0 E			81 52½	20 38	⎮
16									82 7		⎭
17											
18											
19	N 58 W	65	80 27								The North End of Vogel Sang, S 15° W, distance 8 leagues.
20	S 10 E	64	79 27 obf.					4 52 E			Cloven Cliff, S 58° E, distance 22 leagues.
21	N 32 E	40	80 1					4 29			Cloven Cliff, N 63° 18' E, distance 21 leagues.
22	N 57 E	43	80 24					6 32			Cloven Cliff, S 82° 15' E, distance 10 leagues.
23			80 16								Vogel Sang, S 4° W, distance 9 leagues.
24											Cloven Cliff, S 15° W, 7 leagues.
25											The Westernmost Land of Cloven Cliff, S 88° W.
26			80 17								Cloven Cliff, S 61° W, distance 40 miles.
27	N 23 E	34	80 48	14 50 30	15 45 0			14 42		12 47	Cloven Cliff, S 42° W, distance 23 leagues.
28	N 70 E	17	80 36 obf.	15 13 45	17 6 0			15 30		11 56	Cloven Cliff, S 58° 46' W, distance 26 leagues.
29	S 58 E	21	80 25 obf.					18 18	80 2¼		Northernmost Land, N 44° E, distance 10 miles. The middle of the Opening, S 12° E. supposed the Waygat, S 12° E.
30			80 31 obf.	18 33 0	20 18 0						The Westernmost of the Seven Islands, N 3° E. Table Island, N 14° E.
31			80 37 obf.	19 0 15	20 45 0						The Westernmost of the Seven Islands, N 60° W, distance 7 miles.
August 1										12 24	Black Point, S 75° W, Table Island, N 45° E, distance 7 miles.
2											Black Point, N 80° W, distance 4 leagues.
3											Black Point, S 50° W, Great Table Island, N 23° W.
4											Black Point, S 78° W, Great Table Island, N 19° W.
5											Great Table Island, N 27° W.
6											Black Point, S 61° W, Table Island, N 39° W.
7											Black Point, S 61° W, Table Island, N 46° W.
8											Table Island, N 35° W, Black Point, N 62° W.
9											A thick Fog.
10											⎧ The Westernmost of the Seven Islands, N 16° W. Black Point, S 32° E, distance 3 leagues.
11											⎩ Hakluyt's Head Land, S 31° W, distance 3 miles. The North End of Vogel Sang, N 67° E.
12											⎫
13											⎮
14											⎮ At Smeerenberg.
15											⎮
16			79 44	9 50 45	12 46 15				82 8¼	18 57	⎮
17											⎮
18											⎮
19											⎭

N

Table

A P P E N D I X.

Table of Days Works.

Day of the Month	Course	Distance	Latitude in	Longitude					Magnetic Observations		Bearings and Distances.
				By the Watch	By Kendal	By Arnold	By Lunar Observations	By the Reckoning	Dip	Variation West	
Auguſt 20	N 34° W	30	80 11					7 40 E			Hakluyt's Head Land, S 34° E, diſtance 10 leagues,
21	S 83 W	50	80 5					2 54			Hakluyt's Head Land, S 74° E, diſtance 70 miles.
22	S 14 W	42	79 24					1 56			Hakluyt's Head Land, N 74° 27' E, diſtance 82 miles.
23	S 15 E	139	77 10					4 58			Hakluyt's Head Land, N 16° 20' E, diſtance 188 miles.
24	S 12 E	77	75 58 obſ.					6 13			Hakluyt's Head Land, N 9° 34' E, diſtance 232 miles.
25	S 25 W	48	75 15 obſ.					4 51			Hakluyt's Head Land, N 11° 30' E, diſtance 278 miles.
26	S 23 W	127	73 19					1 46			Hakluyt's Head Land, N 14° 30' E, diſtance 133 leagues.
27	S 28 W	57	72 29 obſ.					0 14			Hakluyt's Head Land, N 15° 18' E, diſtance 151 leagues.
28	S 61 W	44	72 9					1 49 W			Hakluyt's Head Land, N 19° 21' E, diſtance 162 leagues.
29	S 5 E	70	70 59					1 28			Hakluyt's Head Land, N 16° 24' E, diſtance 183 leagues.
30	S 41 E	54	70 17 obſ.					0 18 E			Hakluyt's Head Land, N 14° 15' E, diſtance 195 leagues.
31	South	96	68 47 obſ.	3 24 0 E	6 28 30 E			0 18	79 4		Hakluyt's Head Land, N 11° 44' E, diſtance 225 leagues.
Sept. 1	S 64 W	7	68 44					0 2		24 17	Hakluyt's Head Land, N 12° 16' E, diſtance 227 leagues.
2	S 12 E	33	68 11 obſ.					0 38			Hakluyt's Head Land, N 10° 57' E, diſtance 237 leagues.
3	S 5 W	133	65 59 obſ.	2 41 30 E	6 8 45 E			0 8			Hakluyt's Head Land, N 10° 14' E, diſtance 280 leagues.
4	S 8 W	60	64 59 obſ.					0 12 W		22 14	Hakluyt's Head Land, N 12° 51' E, diſtance 303 leagues.
5	S 17 W	63	64 0					0 54			Hakluyt's Head Land, N 10° 38' E, diſtance 321 leagues.
6	S 5 W	92	62 29	0 58 30 E	4 7 15 E			1 12		25 46	Hakluyt's Head Land, N 10° 12' E, diſtance 351 leagues.
7	S 17 W	142	60 14 obſ.					2 35			Hakluyt's Head Land, N 10° 39' E, diſtance 394 leagues.
8	S 59 E	51	59 48 obſ.					1 9			Hakluyt's Head Land, N 9° 16' E, diſtance 403 leagues.
9	S 32 E	31	59 22 obſ.					0 37			Hakluyt's Head Land, N 8° 43' E, diſtance 413 leagues.
10	S 43 W	96	58 9 obſ.					1 40 E			Hakluyt's Head Land, N 6° 25' E, diſtance 435 leagues.
11	S 7 E	33	57 37 obſ.					1 32			Hakluyt's Head Land, N 5° 15' E, diſtance 446 leagues.
12	S 17 E	42	56 57 obſ.					1 55			Hakluyt's Head Land, N 6° 3' E, diſtance 459 leagues.
13	S 14 W	55	56 4 obſ.					1 31			Hakluyt's Head Land, N 6° 15' E, diſtance 477 leagues.
14	S 66 W	61	55 40 obſ.					0 0			Hakluyt's Head Land, N 7° 27' E, diſtance 486 leagues.
15	S 14 E	69	54 33					0 29			Hakluyt's Head Land, N 6° 56' E, diſtance 507 leagues.
16	S 21 W	83	53 15					0 1			Hakluyt's Head Land, N 7° 2' E, diſtance 535 leagues.
17	S 59 W	6	53 12					0 7 W			Hakluyt's Head Land, N 7° 4' E, diſtance 537 leagues.
18	S 8 W	19	52 53 obſ.					0 11			Hakluyt's Head Land, N 7° 6' E, diſtance 543 leagues.
19	S 37 E	14	52 42					0 29			Hakluyt's Head Land, N 7° 5' E, diſtance 546 leagues.
20	S 36 E.	15	52 31 obſ.					0 16		20 47	Hakluyt's Head Land, N 7° 2' E, diſtance 550 leagues.
21	S 24 E.	16	52 17 obſ.					0 5			Hakluyt's Head Land, N 7° 2' E, diſtance 555 leagues.
22	W by N	55	52 28 obſ.					1 35			Hakluyt's Head Land, N 8° 2' E, diſtance 552 leagues.
23	S 50 E	39	52 4 obſ.					0 49			Catwick, N 62° E, diſtance 12 leagues.
24	N 80 W	63	52 16					2 33			Orfordneſs, SW by S, diſtance 5 miles.
25				0 43 45 E	3 24 25						[In Hoſely Bay, Orfordneſs Lighthouſe N 36° 30' E. Hoſely Church, S 82° W, diſtance from the ſhore, 1 mile.

O

OBSERVATIONS on different METHODS of meafuring a
SHIP'S WAY

THE degree of accuracy with which the diftance run
by a fhip can be meafured, is a thing of great importance, but unfortunately not eafily to be afcertained,
from the great variety of circumftances which may occafion errors in the reckoning, and which, though not
depending upon the meafure of the fhip's way, may in
voyages not nearly upon a meridian be confounded with
thofe that do. The circumftances of the prefent voyage
gave me the faireft opportunity of trying this experiment,
the weather being fine, and the courfe very nearly upon
a meridian; fo that an error of one point could not make
more than the difference of one mile in fifty in the
diftance. When the difference of latitude is the fame as
the diftance, it gives frequent opportunities of comparing
the reckoning with the obfervation, and whatever error is
found muft be attributed to the imperfections in the
manner of meafuring the diftance. Moft of the writers on
this fubject have attributed the errors to a faulty divifion
of the log-line.

Before Norwood meafured a degree, the length of a
minute had been erroneoufly fuppofed 5000 feet; in

confequence

confequence of which, the log line, from the firft ufe of that inftrument about the year 1570, was invariably marked forty-two feet to thirty feconds. Norwood, when he publifhed his Seaman's Practice, ftated the true meafure to be fifty-one feet to thirty feconds; but, as the fhip would really run more than is given by the log, and it is right to have the reckoning ahead of the fhip, he recommended marking the log line fifty feet to thirty feconds. It does not appear at what time an alteration either in the marking the log, or the length of the glafs, took place in confequence of thefe obfervations: Sir Jonas Moore in his Navigation which was publifhed in the reign of Charles II. mentions, that the feamen, having found the old log not to anfwer, had fhortened the glafs to twenty-five feconds, which was equal to a line marked fifty feet with a glafs of thirty feconds; but he rather recommends reftoring the half minute glafs, and making the correction on the line. Since that time the feamen, whether from finding the allowance of one foot in fifty not a fufficient compenfa- tion for the accidental errors to which the log is fubject, or from a preference of a meafure nearly equal to the ftatute mile, have ufed a line of forty-five feet to thirty feconds, or a glafs of twenty-eight feconds to forty-two feet.

All the writers I have met with, who have treated of the log, except Wilfon, have complained of the feamen not having adhered to Norwood's meafure. Norwood himfelf, himself, however, seems to have been aware of the neceffity of fubmitting to the teft of experiment the advantages of a new meafurement derived from theory. In the preface to his *Seaman's Practice* he fays, "Becaufe I "am perfuaded we have at this day as many excellent navi-"gators in this kingdom, and as great voyages performed, "as from any other place in the world, I fhould be glad "to hear of the experimental refolution of this problem by "fome of them, though it were but running eight or ten "degrees near the meridian; for fo I doubt not but what "I have here written thereof, would receive further con-"firmation and better entertainment than happily it will "now, being fo much different from the common "opinion."

Had the errors in the diftance arifen only from a fault in marking the line, nothing would have been more eafy than to have removed that difficulty, by comparing carefully the different meafures with the obfervations, and adhering to that which had been found to correfpond beft with them. But the diftance meafured by the log being rendered uncertain by many accidental circumftances, it becomes difficult, or rather impoffible, to find any length of line which will fhew invariably the diftance run by the fhip, or even to afcertain with precifion that meafure which will at all times come neareft the truth. Some of thefe circumftances are:

1. The

1. The effects of currents.

2. The yawing of the ship going with the wind aft, or upon the quarter, when she is seldom steered within a point each way : this I mention as an error in the distance, and not in the course; since, though the ship by being yawed equally each way may make the intended course good upon the whole, yet the distance will be shortened as the versed sine of the angle between the line intended and that steered upon.

3. By the ship being driven on by the swell, or the log during the time of heaving being thrown up nearer the ship.

4. By the log *coming home*, or being drawn after the ship, by the friction of the reel and the lightness of the log. Norwood mentions these two last, and says, " For " these causes, it is like, there may sometimes be allowed " three or four fathoms more than is veered out; but this, " (as a thing mutable and uncertain) being sometimes " more, sometimes less, cannot be brought to any certain " rule, but such allowance may be made as a man in his " experience and discretion finds fit."

5. By the log being only a mean taken every hour, and consequently liable to error from the variations in the force of the wind during the intervals, for which an arbitrary correction is made by the officer of the watch; and though men of skill and experience come near the truth, yet this allowance must, from its nature, be inaccurate.

These

Thefe circumftances did not efcape M. Bouguer's attention, and his ingenuity fuggefted to him an improvement of the common log, which would correct the errors
likely to arife from the moft material of thefe circumftances: a defcription of this improvement he publifhed at
large in the Memoirs of the Academy of Sciences for the
year 1747 ; it has fince been abridged in the edition of his
Navigation by De la Caille   It appears extraordinary that
this log fhould never have been made, ufe of by others;--
the great reputation of the author, as well as the very good
reafons he offers in favour of his improvement, were fufficient inducements to me to try the experiment.

In the log which I made ufe of,

The length of the cone was	—	12 inches.
The diameter of the bafe	—	5$\frac{1}{10}$.
The weight of the cone	—	25 ounces.
The diagonal length of the diver	—	14 inches.
The length of each fide	—	9$\frac{1}{4}$.
The weight of the diver	——	26$\frac{1}{2}$ ounces.

The length of line from the diver to the cone, 50 feet;
the log line 51 feet to a knot.

Whether M. Bouguer's log will (as he expected) correct
the errors arifing from currents in the common log, I had
no opportunity of difcovering in this voyage.

The fecond error, which no log will correct, cannot
be attended with any bad effect, as it muft make the
reckoning,

reckoning, in whatever degree it takes place, ahead of the ſhip.

By obſerving M. Bouguer's rules in comparing it with the common log, which for that purpoſe muſt be reckoned at fifty-one feet, it will, I think, very fully correct the third and fourth, which are the moſt material errors; as the agitation of the ſea from winds does not exceed the depth to which the diver is let down, and the weight of the whole machine prevents the friction of the reel from having an effect in any degree equal to that which it has on the common log.

The fifth ariſes from the imperfection it has in common with the log generally uſed.

At firſt, on the paſſage out, I contented myſelf with heaving Bouguer's log occaſionally, to obſerve what precautions were neceſſary to be taken to prevent errors, as well as to find whether its variations from the common log were on the ſame ſide as the meridian obſervation required. I found that it was neceſſary to take care that the diver ſhould be of ſuch a weight as to let only the top of the cone ſwim; but not heavy enough to ſink it, as in that caſe it would be liable to an error in exceſs, by meaſuring the depth that the diver would ſink in addition to the ſhip's way. It was neceſſary to put a weight of lead to the bottom of the diver, to ſink it down to its

palce

place before the ftray line was out   The line between the diver and the cone fhould not be more than fifty feet, that being as great a depth as it will fink to whilft the ftray line is running off the reel when the fhip has much way through the water.

On the paffage out, the longeft period of my trying this log between two obfervations, was from the twenty-fifth to the thirtieth; in which time the fhip had run four degrees, and the reckoning by Bouguer's log was eighteen miles aftern of the fhip: but as it appears that the fhip on the twenty-fixth, with the wind Northerly, and making barely an Eaft courfe, was found by the obfervation to be twenty miles to the Northward of her reckoning, that diftance muft be attributed to a current; therefore if that current had not taken place, Bouguer's log would have been, inftead of eighteen miles aftern, two miles ahead of the fhip.

On the paffage home it was tried from the latitude of eighty degrees eleven minutes to fixty-eight degrees eleven minutes; in which diftance, though the fhip was much yawed from the fea being frequently upon the quarter, this log was only thirty-one miles ahead of the fhip, which might be owing entirely to that circumftance without any other caufe.

The ftate of the common log on the paffage out, when the weather was remarkably fine and water in general fmooth, was, from the latitude of fixty degrees thirty-feven minutes to feventy-eight degrees eight minutes, with

the

the line marked fifty-one feet to thirty feconds, one degree fifty-eight minutes aftern of the fhip, with the line marked forty-five feet to thirty feconds, four miles ahead of the fhip. On the paffage home, the log at fifty-one feet to thirty feconds, thirty-five miles aftern of the fhip; at forty-five to thirty feconds, one degree feven minutes ahead of the fhip. As far therefore as the experience of this voyage extends, it appears that the errors of the log marked forty-five feet are always on the fafe fide, and that thofe of the longer marked line are always fhort of the run; but that Bouguer's is much more accurate than either.

It is not to be expected that the obfervations of a fingle voyage can be fufficient to determine the merit of any inftrument, particularly one of fo much confequence as the log. I thought it right, however, to give an account of the trial I made of the different methods, and of fuch remarks as occurred to me.

In the following table the courfe is put down, in the firft column, for all the diftances and latitudes; after the diftance and latitude, according to each marking of the log, there is a column for the difference between that latitude, and the latitude obferved. I thought it beft to continue the reckonings without corrections, as if there had been no obfervation, in order to fhew the difference upon the whole run, as well as from one obfervation to another.

T A B L E

TABLE.

Day of the Month.	Course.	By the Common Log, marked 49 Feet.			By the Common Log, marked 45 Feet.			By the Common Log, marked 51 Feet.			By Bouguer's Log, marked 51 Feet.		Difference of the Distance by the Common and Bouguer's Log, each marked 51 Feet.	Bouguer's Log, increased by ¼ of the Difference of the Distance by the Common and Bouguer's Log.			Latitude by Observation.
		Distance.	Latitude by Account.	Difference between the Latitude by Account and Observation.	Distance.	Latitude by Account.	Difference between the Latitude by Account and Observation.	Distance.	Latitude by Account.	Difference between the Latitude by Account and Observation.	Distance.	Latitude by Account.		Distance.	Latitude by Account.	Difference between the Latitude by Account and Observation.	
	°		° '	° '		° '	° '		° '	° '							° '
On the Voyage Out.																	
June 16	N 27 E	27	60 37	0 8	29	60 39	0 10	26	60 36	0 7	...	...	...	...	...	...	60 29
17	N 7 E	136	62 52	0 7	147	63 5	0 6	131	62 46	0 13	...	...	...	...	...	...	62 59
18	N 7 W	131	65 2	0 16	141	65 25	0 7	126	64 51	0 27	...	...	...	...	...	...	65 18
19	N 4 W	54	65 56	...	58	66 23	...	52	65 43	...	...	...	...	...	...	...	...
20	N 30 E	59	66 47	...	63	67 17	...	57	66 32	...	...	...	...	...	...	...	...
21	N 5 W	60	67 47	0 18	65	68 22	0 17	58	67 30	0 35	...	...	...	...	...	...	68 5
22	North	149	70 16	...	161	71 2	...	143	69 53	...	...	...	...	...	...	...	...
23	N 2 E	89	71 45	...	97	72 40	...	86	71 19	...	...	...	...	...	...	...	...
24	N 41 E	81	72 46	...	88	73 46	...	78	72 18	...	...	...	...	...	...	...	...
25	N 73 E	99	73 15	0 50	107	74 18	0 13	95	72 42	1 23	...	...	...	...	...	...	74 5
26	East	33	73 15	1 10	36	74 18	0 7	32	72 42	1 43	33½	74 5	1½	34	74 5	0 20	74 25
27	N 21 W	59	74 10	...	64	75 18	...	57	73 35	...	64½	75 5	7½	66½	75 7	...	...
28	N 10 W	126	76 14	...	137	77 33	...	121	75 34	...	126	77 9	5	127¼	77 12	...	...
29	N 26 E	28	76 39	1 20	30	77 59	0 0	27	75 58	2 1	27	77 34	0	27	77 36	0 23	77 59
30	N 52 E	20	76 51	1 17	22	78 12	0 4	19	76 10	1 58	21	77 47	2	21¼	77 50	0 18	78 8
On the Voyage Home.																	
August 20	N 34 W	30	80 12	...	32	80 14	...	29	80 11	...	...	...	...	...	...	...	...
21	S 83 W	50	80 5	...	54	80 8	...	48	80 5	...	50	80 5	2	50½	80 4½	...	...
22	S 14 W	42	79 24	...	45	79 24	...	40	79 26	...	41	79 25	1	41¼	79 24½	...	...
23	S 15 E	139	77 10	...	151	76 59	...	133	77 18	...	142	77 8	9	144¼	77 6	...	...
24	S 12 E	77	75 55	0 3	83	75 38	0 20	74	76 6	0 8	78	75 52	4	79	75 49	0 9	75 58
25	S 25 W	48	75 12	0 3	52	74 51	0 24	46	75 24	0 9	50	75 7	4	51	75 3	0 12	75 15
26	S 23 W	127	73 19	...	137	72 45	...	122	73 32	...	130	73 7	8	132	73 1½	...	...
27	S 37 W	45	72 40	0 11	49	72 6	0 23	43	72 58	0 28	46	72 30	3	46¾	72 24	0 5	72 29
28	S 61 W	44	72 19	...	48	71 43	...	42	72 38	...	45	72 9	3	45¾	72 2	...	...
29	S 5 E	70	71 9	...	76	70 38	...	67	71 31	...	77	70 52	10	79½	70 43	...	...
30	S 41 E	54	70 29	0 12	59	69 43	0 34	52	70 52	0 35	55	70 11	3	55¾	70 1	0 16	70 17
31	South	86	69 3	...	93	68 10	...	83	69 29	...	86	68 45	3	86¾	68 34	...	...
September 1	S 64 W	7	69 0	...	7	68 7	...	7	69 27	...	4	68 43	3	3¼	68 32	...	...
2	S 12 E	45	68 14	0 3	49	67 19	0 52	43	68 44	0 33	51	67 53	8	53½	67 40	0 31	68 11
3	S 5 W	138	65 57	0 2	148	64 52	1 7	131	66 34	0 35	...	...	...	...	...	...	65 59

Q

I also

The material originally positioned here is too large for reproduction in this reissue. A PDF can be downloaded from the web address given on page iv of this book, by clicking on 'Resources Available'.

I alfo tried two perpetual logs; one invented by Mr. Ruffell, the other by Foxon, both conftructed upon this principle, that a Spiral, in proceeding its own length in the direction of its axis through a refifting medium, makes one revolution round the axis; if therefore the revolutions of the fpiral are regiftered, the number of times it has gone its own length through the water will be known. In both thefe the motion of the fpiral in the water is communicated to the clock-work within board, by means of a fmall line, faftened at one end to the fpiral, which tows it after the fhip, and at the other to a fpindle which fets the clock-work in motion. That invented by Mr. Ruffell has a half fpiral of two threads, made of copper, and a fmall dial with clock-work, to regifter the number of turns of the fpiral. Foxon's has a whole fpiral of wood with one thread, and a larger piece of clock-work, with three dials, two of them to mark the diftance, and the other divided into knots and fathoms, to fhew the rate by the half minute glafs, for the convenience of comparing it with the log.

This log, like all others, is liable to the firft error, as well as to the fecond. The third it partakes of in a very fmall degree, only affecting the reckoning by that quantity which the fpiral is thrown towards the fhip; whereas in the log the fame circumftance affects the whole rate for the hour. The fourth it is entirely free from, as well as the fifth. It will have the advantage of every other in

R   fmooth

smooth water and moderate weather, when it is neceffary to ftand on one courfe for any particular diftance, efpe-cially in the night, or a fog, as it meafures exactly the diftance run. It will alfo be very ufeful in finding the trim of a fhip when alone; as well as in furveying a coaft in a fingle fhip, or in meafuring diftances in a boat be-tween headlands or fhoals, when a bafe is not otherwife to be obtained; both which it will do with the greateft ac-curacy in fmooth water, with a large wind, and no tide or current. But notwithftanding thefe advantages, which will make it very ufeful and worth having, I doubt much whether it might ever be fubftituted entirely in the room of the common log. Machines eafily repaired or replaced have advantages at fea, which fhould not lightly be given up for others more fpecious

OBSERVATIONS

OBSERVATIONS on the Ufe of the MEGAMETER in Marine Surveying.

THE greateft difficulty in marine furveying is that of obtaining an accurate bafe, from the extremities of which the angles may be taken with precifion, for afcertaining the bearings and diftance of headlands and fhoals, when either want of time or other circumftances make it impracticable to land and meafure a bafe. The ufual way is, to eftimate the diftance by the log, and to take the angles by the compafs. This method is liable to many errors, and affords no means of correcting or difcovering them. The Megameter, conftructed upon the principles of the object-glafs micrometer, defcribed by M. de Charniere and applied by him to find the longitude at fea, I thought might be ufefully applied to marine furveying. That which I ufed was made by Ramfden, with fome improvements. The advantages I imagined might be derived from this inftrument were, a more correct and expeditious manner of determining the pofition of coafts, and the diftance of fhoals or the fhip from headlands. This inftrument being divided to ten feconds, an angle may be taken by it with great accuracy to five feconds. The height of a fhip's maft-head above the water being known, it is eafy to find with this inftrument, by a fingle obfervation, the diftance between

two

two fhips, and confequently to determine a bafe. The angles being taken with an Hadley's quadrant from each of the fhips, to the objects whofe fituations are defigned to be afcertained, the diftance may be found; and, confequently, their relative fituations. If there is a megameter in each fhip, the altitudes taken from both fhips at one inftant, and the angles of the different parts of the coaft intended to be furveyed obferved with an Hadley's quadrant at the fame time, will give the fituation with more accuracy and expedition than any method of furveying from fhips hitherto practifed; with the farther advantage of the certain means of detecting any error in the obfervation, fo as to judge whether it is of fufficient importance to be attended to. The only precautions neceffary are; to make the obfervations at the fame inftant, to prevent their being affected by any alteration in the relative pofition of the fhips, as a very fmall one there would occafion a confiderable error in the diftance; and to be careful in chufing objects fufficiently defined and remarkable. This method of furveying has the further advantage of giving the fcale of a coaft; Seamen, though they judge very accurately of their diftance from places upon coafts well known to them, are very often miftaken when they fall in with land they have never feen before; of which we had, at firft, fome inftances in this voyage, the height of the mountains, before we knew the fcale of the coaft, making us always think ourfelves nearer the land than we really were. Where the coaft is at all

2   high,

high, the megameter affords a very accurate and expeditious method of determining the height of all the points, when their diftances are found; and thence, the heights being known, of afcertaining immediately by a fingle obfervation the fituation of the fhip, or the latitude of any point by the bearings at the time of a meridian obfervation: the direction and rate of currents or tides may alfo be found in this manner with great accuracy. I made feveral obfervations during this voyage with the megameter, fome of which I fhall give as examples; they were fufficient to prove to me the great accuracy that may be attained with this inftrument after fome practice. The utility of fuch a method of obtaining a furvey on an enemy's or undefcribed coaft, as well as that of being able to prove the truth of charts by a fingle obfervation, is obvious.

June the fifteenth, the fhip being in latitude 60° 19', longitude 0° 39' W, Hangcliff bore S 63° 00' W; variation, 23° W.

The altitude of the Carcafs's maft, by the megameter, was 35' 48"; height of the maft, 102,75 feet; hence the diftance between the Racehorfe and Carcafs was 9861 feet: angle between the Carcafs and Hangcliff, 85° 48'; between the Racehorfe and Hangcliff, 87° 00'; From whence the difference of latitude was found 10' S; difference of longitude 17' W. Therefore, the latitude of Hangcliff is 60° 9'; longitude 0° 56' W.

July

July the fecond, to try how far the megameter could be depended upon, I obferved the altitude of the Carcafs's maft 2° 23′ 48″; the angle between the main-yard and main-topfail yard, 0° 44′ 26″; hence the dif-tance between the main-yard and main-topfail yard came out ————   ————   31,750 feet.
By meafurement it was found   —   34,125 feet.

Difference 2,375 feet.

The diftance between the two fhips, deduced from the altitude of the maft, was   ———   2457 feet.
By the angle of the main and main-topfail yard, the diftance between them being 34,125 feet,   2640 feet.

Difference   183 feet.

Which is not more than the fhips might have changed their pofition in the time of reading off and fetting down the firft obfervation before taking the fecond.

An error of ten feconds in the obfervation of the angle fubtended by the maft at this diftance, would make an error of two feet and three quarters in the diftance. At the diftance of a nautical mile it would produce an error of fixteen feet. At other diftances the error decreafes as the fquares of the diftances decreafe; and at other heights it decreafes as the heights decreafe.

Whenever

Whenever the diftance of the objeƈt, whofe angle is taken by the megameter, does not exceed that of the vifible horizon, the very fmall portion of the earth's furface intercepted between the objeƈt and obferver, may be confidered as a plane, to which the objeƈt is perpendicular, and the diftance may be concluded by refolving the right-angled triangle, formed by the upright objeƈt, and lines drawn from the obferver's ftation to the top and bottom of it.

But in greater diftances, the bottom of the objeƈt being concealed from the fight of the obferver, it becomes neceffary to have recourfe to a different calculation.

The only cafes which can occur in praƈtice are two; the one when the height is given to find the diftance; the other when, the diftance being known, the height of the objeƈt is to be deduced from the obfervation: both which are eafily folved by the following praƈtical rules.

To find the Diftance.

To the apparent altitude of the objeƈt above the fenfible horizon, add the complement of the dip anfwering to the height of the obferver's eye above the fea; the fum is the angle BAE (fig. 1:); and fay: As the femidiameter of the earth increafed by the height of the objeƈt, is to the femidiameter increafed by the height of the

I eye

eye; fo is the fine of B A E, to another fine, which is that of the angle B; the difference between 180°, and the fum of the two angles B A E and B, is the value, in degrees and minutes, of the arc G C of the earth's furface intercepted between the eye and object. Multiply the number of minutes and decimal parts of a minute in this arc by the value of one minute in miles, fathoms, or fuch meafure as may be moft convenient, and you will have the diftance in the like meafure.

E X A M P L E

The height of Snow Peak being 1503 yards, its apparent altitude above the horizon of the fea was obferved to be — — — 1° 47' 6"

The height of the eye being 16 feet,
the complement of the dip is - - - 82° 56' 11"

The fum is E A B 91° 43' 17"

To the femidiameter of the
earth in yards 6966382 - - - - - 6966382

Add the height   Add the height
of the object   1503   of the eye   5⅓

Semidiam. height   Semidiam.+height
of the object   6667885   of the eye   6966387⅓

As

As 6967885   Co Ar   3,1568990

To 6966387 ⅓   6,8430076

So is Sine E A B 90° 43′ 17″   9,9998040

To ſine B   87   54   30   9,9997106

179   37   47

Subtracted from   180   0   0

0   22   13   the diſtance.

Therefore the diſtance is 22,22 minutes, or nautical miles.
This multiplied by ‑ 2040   the number of yards in
one minute,

The product 45328,8 is the diſtance in yards.

To find the Height.

To the apparent altitude of the object above the ſenſible horizon, add the complement of the dip anſwering to the height of the obſerver's eye above the ſea, the ſum is the angle B A E ; to this add the horizontal diſtance of the eye and object in degrees and minutes, and ſubtract the ſum from 180°, the remainder is the angle B : then ſay, as the ſine of B is to the ſine of B A E, ſo is the ſemidiameter of the earth increaſed by the height of the eye to a fourth number ; from which ſubtracting the ſemidiameter of the earth, the remainder is the height of the object.

S   E X A M P L E.

E X A M P L E

July the second, the apparent altitude
of Snow Peak was obſerved to be, at the
distance of 37507 yards or 18′ 30″,   2°   12′ 20″
The height of the eye being 5 ⅓ yards,
the complement of the dip is - -   89   56   11

Hence the angle B A E 92   8   31
Horizontal distance   18   30

92   27   1
Subtracted from 180

Angle B 87   32   59

Semidiameter of the earth   6966382
Height of the eye   5⅓
Semidiameter + height of the eye 6966387⅓

As fine B   87° 32′ 59″ Co. Ar. 0,0003972
To fine B A E 92   8   31   9,9996965
So is femidiameter + height
of the eye =   6966387⅓ yards 6,8430076

To 6967888   6,8431013

Semidiameter 6966382

Height   1506 in yards.

DEMON

DEMONSTRATION.

Let G F C (plate I. fig. 1.) reprefent the furface of the earth, E its center, B C the height of a hill or other object rifing perpendicular from C; A is the place of the obferver's eye, whofe height above the level of the fea is A G. Draw A H perpendicular to A E, and A F touching the circle G F C in F. Then H A F is the dip, E A F its complement, D A B is the apparent altitude of the object above the fenfible horizon; to this add E A D, the fum is E A B. In the triangle E A B, the fide E A is the fum of the femidiameter E G and G A the height of the obferver's eye; E B the fum of the femidiameter E C and C B the height of the object; the angle A E B is meafured by G C the horizontal diftance between the obferver and object. Now in the firft cafe there are given in the triangle E A B, the fides E A, E B, and the angle B A E, to find the angle A E B; and in the fecond there are given the angles B A E, A E B and the fide E A, to find the fide E B and confequently B C. The trigonometrical folutions of thefe cafes are the above practical rules.

OBSERVATIONS on the VARIATION.

T H E Variation of the compaſs, always an intereſting
object to navigators and philoſophers, became peculiarly ſo in this voyage from the near approach to the
Pole. Many of the theories that had been propoſed on
this ſubject, were to be brought to the teſt of obſervations made in high latitudes, by which alone their
fallacy or utility could be diſcovered. They of courſe
engaged much of my attention, and gave me the fulleſt
opportunity of experiencing, with regret, the many imperfections of what is called the Azimuth compaſs. This
inſtrument, though ſufficiently accurate to enable us to
obſerve the variations ſo as to ſteer the ſhip without any
material error, with the precaution of always uſing the
ſame compaſs by which they are taken, is far from being
of ſuch a conſtruction as to give the variation with that
degree of preciſion, which ſhould attend experiments on
which a theory is to be founded, or by which it is to be
tried. The obſervations taken in this voyage will fully
evince this, by their great variations from one another in
very ſhort intervals of time ; nor is this diſagreement of
ſucceſſive obſervations peculiar to the higher latitudes,
and to be imputed to a near approach to the Pole, as I
found it to take place even upon the Engliſh coaſt.

As to the obſervations themſelves, they were taken
with the greateſt care, and the moſt ſcrupulous attention

to

to remove every circumftance which might be fuppofed to create an accidental error; the obfervations being taken fometimes by different people with the fame compafs, in the fame and different places; fometimes with different compaffes, changing the places and the obfervers repeatedly, to try whether there was any error to be imputed to local attraction, or the different mode of obfervation by different perfons. I have fince my return tried the compaffes by a meridian as well as by taking azimuths, and find them to agree with one another, though the fame compafs fometimes differs from itfelf a degree in fucceffive obfervations.

That every perfon may (as far as is poffible without having been prefent at the time) be enabled to judge of the degree of accuracy to be expected in fuch obfervations, as well as the degree of attention paid to thofe made by us, I have fet down every circumftance that I thought material, giving every part of each obfervation, with each feparate refult, and the mean of every fet, with the weather at the time. Whenever I mention its blowing frefh, it was only comparatively with refpect to the reft of the voyage, no obfervation having been made in any weather which might not generally fpeaking be called fine.

Having faid fo much of the inaccuracy of the inftrument, I muft add, that I think fome general and rather curious inferences may fafely be drawn from thefe

S 3 obfervations.

obfervations. One is, that the variation near the latitude of eighty, if it alters at all with time, does not alter in any degree as it does in thefe latitudes : the variation having been found by Poole in 1610 to be 22° 30′ W in latitude 78° 37′; 18° 16′ W in Crofs Road in latitude 79° 15′ N; and 17° 00′ within the foreland in latitude 78° 24′. By Baffin in 1613, in Horne Sound, latitude 76° 55″, the variation from the meridian was 12° 14′ W; but by his compafs 17°: his compafs " was touched 5½ Eafterly," that being the variation in London at that time : in Green Harbour, latitude 77° 40′, he obferved the variation 13° 11′ W. Fotherby in 1614, made the variation in Magdalena Bay, latitude 79° 34′ N, 25° 00′ W; and in latitude 79° 8′, two points. Neither Poole nor Fotherby mention whether their variations are reckoned from the meridian, or whether their compaffes, like Baffin's, were fitted to the variation at that time in London. If Fotherby's were taken with a compafs in which a correction was made for the variation at London, his obfervation agrees exactly with thofe made by me in Vogel Sang and Smeerenberg; and thofe of Poole and Baffin differ fo little from mine, that the difference need not be regarded. But the variation in London now differs from what it was at that time above twenty-fix degrees.

The other inference is, that in going to the Eaftward in the latitude of eighty, the Wefterly variation decreafes very confiderably from a difference in the longitude.

5   Table

A P P E N D I X.

Table of the Observations of the Variation.

Day of the Month.	Latitude in	Longitude in	Altitude of the Sun's Lower Limb.	Sun's Magnetic Azimuth.	Sun's true Azimuth from the North.	West Variation from each Observation.	Mean of the Observations.	Remarks.
June 6th at 7 AM.	52 20		36 50	S 62 15 E	100 42	17 3	} 16 55	The Weather very fine, and the Water smooth.
			37 4	62 20	101 2	16 37		
			37 39	61 0	101 54	17 5	} 16 22	
			37 56	61 30	102 19	16 10		
			38 20	60 30	102 55	16 34		
14th at 7 AM.	60 20	1 7 W	31 44	S 59 30 E	98 44	21 46	21 53	The Weather very fine, and the Water smooth.
			32 2	58 45	99 17	21 58		
			32 16	57 30	99 44	22 46		
			32 36	57 30	100 22	22 8		
			33 15	56 50	101 36	21 34		
			33 35	56 35	102 16	21 9		
14th at 6 PM.	60 20	0 39 W	13 51	N 44 5 W	67 16	23 11	22 58	
			13 25	43 15	66 30	23 15		
			13 3	43 0	65 30	22 30		
15th at 7 AM.	60 20	0 39 W	29 48	N 117 50 E	95 6	22 44	} 23 31	
			30 29	120 30	96 20	24 10		
			31 50	122 30	98 50	23 40		
			31 56	122 52	99 2	23 50	} 24 2	
			32 19	123 10	99 45	23 25		
			32 34	124 15	100 14	24 1		
			32 52	125 40	100 48	24 52		
15th at 1 PM.	60 20	0 39 W				26 16		Some Sea.
17th at 8 AM.	62 30	0 4 W	32 8	N 120 30 E	101 20	19 10	19 22	
			32 50	122 15	102 48	19 27		
			33 16	123 10	103 44	19 26		
			33 45	124 10	104 46	19 24		
19th at 6 PM.							19 11	Fresh Breezes, and some swell.

Table

APPENDIX.

Table of the Observations of the Variation.

Day of the Month.	Latitude in.	Longitude in.	Altitude of the Sun's Lower Limb.	Sun's Magnetic Azimuth.	Sun's true Azimuth from the North.	West Variation from each Observation.	Mean of the Observations.	Remarks.
June 21st at 6 AM.	68 12	0 37 W	17 20	N 95 30 E	70 20	25 10		
			17 43	95 30	71 18	24 12		
			18 47	97 50	74 0	23 50		Fresh Breezes, not much Sea.
			19 0	96 30	74 32	21 58	23 18	
			19 11	98 30	75 0	23 30		
			19 30	98 0	75 48	22 12		
			19 55	100 0	76 50	23 10		
			20 0	99 30	77 2	22 28		
25th at 7 AM.	73 55	7 15 E	28 12	E 34 30 S	103 36	20 54		
			29 1	34 0	107 22	16 38		Blowing fresh, a good deal of Sea.
			29 34	36 30	110 26	16 4	17 9	
			29 57	38 30	110 56	17 34		
			30 6	37 30	111 30	16 0		
			30 16	37 30	114 46	15 44		
25th at 3 PM.	74 10	8 36	19 36	N 65 30 W	73 46	8 16		
			19 30	65 30	73 21	7 51	7 47	Blowing fresh, with some Sea; but not enough, in my opinion, to have occasioned so great a difference.
			19 17	65 50	73 6	7 16		
			17 12	57 40	64 57	7 17		
			17 0	56 30	64 16	7 46	7 47	
			16 58	55 40	63 49	8 9		
			16 45	55 28	63 24	7 56		
27th at 7 AM.	74 20	9 43	25 40	E 24 30 S	95 25	19 5	17 15	
			25 26	22 30	96 24	16 6		
			26 2	23 20	96 45	16 35		
			26 16	25 30	97 36	17 54	16 50	
			26 35	25 30	98 52	16 38		
			26 55	26 0	100 2	15 58		
			27 8	29 30	100 50	18 40	17 22	
			27 36	28 40	102 36	16 4		
			28 35	35 35	106 20	19 15	19 0	
			28 50	36 5	107 20	18 45		

APPENDIX.

Table of the Obſervations of the Variation.

Day of the Month.	Latitude in.	Longitude in.	Altitude of the Sun's Lower Limb.	Sun's Magnetic Azimuth.	Sun's true Azimuth from the North.	Weſt Variation from the Obſervation.	Mean of the Obſervations.	Remarks.
June 27th at 7 AM.	74 20	9 43 E	27 52 / 28 2 / 28 14 / 28 22	E 35 40 S / 36 33 / 35 30 / 35 20	103 36 / 104 14 / 105 0 / 105 30	22 9 / 22 16 / 20 30 / 19 50	21 11	
27th at 7 AM.	74 20	9 43	30 1 / 30 17 / 30 41	E 46 0 S / 47 20 / 46 1	112 2 / 113 7 / 114 47	23 58 / 24 19 / 21 13	23 8	
29th at 8 PM.	78 2	7 50	21 26 / 21 9 / 21 0 / 20 50 / 20 42 / 17 13 / 17 10 / 17 5 / 16 58 / 16 55 / 16 51	N 70 30 W / 67 30 / 68 30 / 67 40 / 66 20 / 47 5 / 45 45 / 45 30 / 44 15 / 44 35 / 44 30	79 50 / 78 31 / 77 48 / 77 0 / 76 24 / 59 2 / 58 46 / 58 20 / 57 42 / 57 26 / 57 4	9 20 / 11 1 / 9 11 / 9 20 / 10 4 / 11 57 / 13 1 / 12 50 / 13 27 / 12 51 / 12 54	10 10 / 9 34 / 12 36 / 12 57	Light winds, the water fmooth.
29th at 8 PM.	78 2	7 50	16 41 / 16 38 / 16 30 / 16 29 / 16 24 / 16 20 / 16 14 / 16 4	N 43 40 W / 43 30 / 43 0 / 43 0 / 41 42 / 41 0 / 41 15 / 40 30	56 10 / 56 52 / 55 8 / 55 4 / 54 35 / 54 12 / 53 38 / 52 42	12 30 / 12 22 / 12 8 / 12 4 / 13 13 / 13 12 / 12 23 / 12 12	12 16 / 12 16	Light winds, the water fmooth.
July 2d at 5 PM.	78 22	9 8	By the Mean of Three Obſervations.				14 55	Light winds, the water fmooth.
	79 50	10 2					20 38	
26th at 4 PM.	80 18	12 12	At the Iſland. 22 37 / 22 33 / 22 25 / 22 23 / 22 22	S 84 0 W / 84 10 / 84 25 / 84 40 / 85 10	109 14 / 108 48 / 107 57 / 107 46 / 107 45	13 14 / 12 58 / 12 22 / 12 26 / 12 25	12 47	Light airs, the water fmooth.

Table

Table of the Observations of the Variation.

Day of the Month.	Latitude in.	Longitude in.	Altitude of the Sun's Lower Limb.	Sun's Magnetic Azimuth.	Sun's true Azimuth from the North.	West Variation from each Observation.	Mean of the Observations.	Remarks.
	° ′	° ′	° ′	° ′	° ′	° ′	° ′	
June 28th at 6 AM.	80 30	15 14 E				11 28 12 54 11 24 11 24 11 56 12 30	11 56	Light Breezes, and the Water smooth.
July 31st at 4 PM.	80 35	19 0				12 24		The Weather very fine, and the Water quite still.
	79 44	9 51		At Smeerenberg.		18 57		
Aug. 31st at 4 PM.	68 46	3 24	15 3	N 87 59 W	107 32	19 33		
31st at 6 PM.	68 47	3 24	4 35 4 31 4 10 4 2 3 51 3 44	N 53 45 W 53 30 53 35 53 15 53 30 52 30	79 49 78 37 77 41 77 19 76 51 76 30	25 4 25 7 24 6 24 4 23 21 24 0	24 17	Calm, and the Water very smooth.
Sept. 3d at 6 PM.	65 47	2 27	17 13 16 42 15 59 15 10 13 42 13 0	N 86 25 W 84 30 82 35 78 40 75 30 73 45	111 48 110 34 109 24 106 24 103 34 100 34	25 23 26 4 26 49 28 24 28 4 26 49	26 55	Light Breezes, not much swell.
4th at 8 AM.	65 4	2 21	18 33 19 2 19 27 19 56 20 45 21 45	S 43 30 E 41 0 40 30 39 15 37 45 33 30	114 56 116 12 117 14 118 32 120 40 123 38	21 31 22 48 22 16 22 13 21 35 23 2	22 14	Light Breezes, and the Water very smooth.
5th	63 45	2 16	Moon's true Amplitude	. .	25 16	25 46		Fresh Breezes, and some Sea.
20th	52 57	1 30	. . .	. .	.	20 38 20 56	20 47	

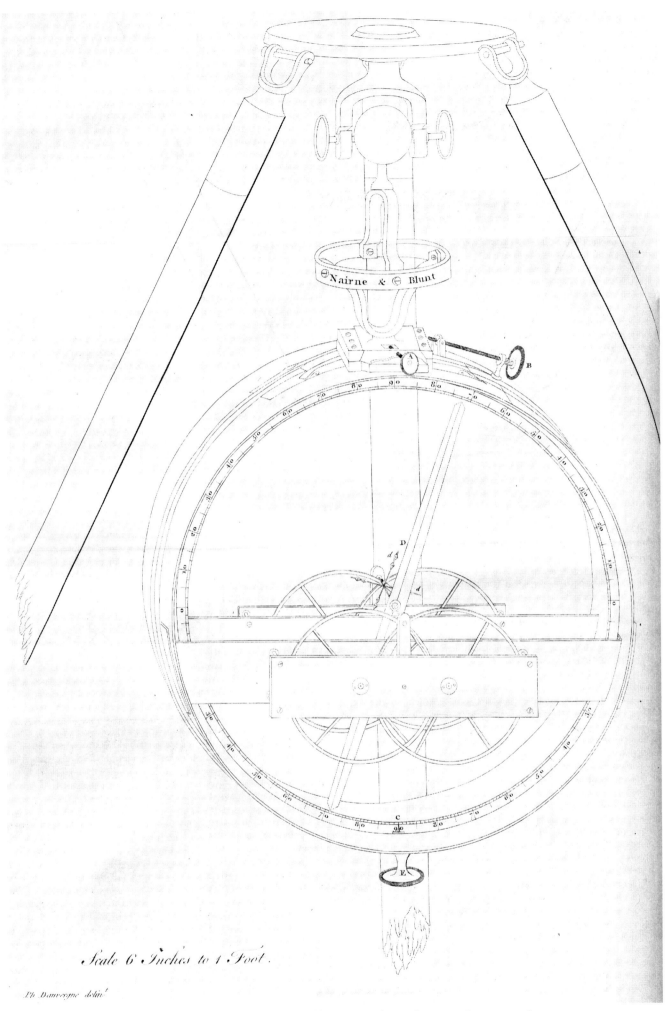

Nairne & Blunt

Scale 6 Inches to 1 Foot.

Ph. Danvergne delin.ᵗ

Account of the Observations made with the Marine Dipping Needle, conftructed for the Board of Longitude by Mr. Nairne, from whom I received the following defcription of the inftrument.

" THE figure (plate 9.) is a reprefentation of the
" inftrument, hanging by an univerfal joint on a
" triangular ftand. It is adjufted fo as to hang in a plane
" perpendicular to the horizon, by means of a plumb line,
" which is to be fufpended on a pin above the divided
" circle, and the dovetail work, which alters the pofition
" of the inftrument, by turning the button A. The two
" 90° on the divided circle, are adjufted fo as to be per-
" pendicular to the horizon, by the fame plumb line and
" the adjufting fcrew B: and at the loweft 90°, when
" it is adjufted, the pointer C is fixed. The length of the
" magnetic needle is twelve inches, and its axis (the ends
" of which were of gold alloyed with copper) refted on
" friction wheels of four inches diameter, each end on two
" friction wheels; which wheels were balanced with great
" care. The ends of the *axes* of the friction wheels were
" likewife of gold alloyed with copper, and moved in fmall
" holes made in bell metal; and oppofite the ends of the
" *axes* of the needle and the friction wheels, were flat
" agates finely polifhed   The magnetic needle vibrated
S 8   " within

" within a circle of bell metal, divided from the lower 90°

" each way, as far as fixty-five degrees, into degrees and

" half-degrees: the other divifions were two degrees and a

" half; the needle being very nearly balanced before it was

" made magnetical: but by means of the crofs D, fixed

" on the axis of the needle (on the arms of which were cut

" very fine fcrews, to receive the fmall buttons dd, that

" might be fcrewed nearer or farther from the axis) the

" needle could be adjufted both ways to a great nicety,

" after it was made magnetical, by changing the fides of

" the needle, and reverfing the Poles. As this needle at

" fea could feldom remain at reft; to remedy in a great

" meafure this inconvenience, the divided circle is made

" moveable by turning the button E; fo that when it is

" ufed at fea, the divided circle is moved till fome prin-

" cipal divifion is the mean of the vibrations: then that

" number of degrees and half-degrees diftant from the

" pointer, fubtracted from ninety, gives the dip, if the

" needle is properly balanced: but left it fhould be fome-

" what out of balance, the moft certain way is, firft, to

" take the dip with the face of the divided circle to the Eaft,

" and afterwards to the Weft, and then changing the ends

" of the needle by reverfing the Poles, and taking the dip

" as before, with the divided circle fronting the Eaft and

" Weft: and the mean of thofe four dips will be the moft

" accurate. In each cafe, when the dip is taken, the in-

" ftrument muft be fo placed that the needle vibrates in

" the magnetic meridian."

2   The

The obfervations on the dip of the needle, during this voyage, were made with great care : firft the dip was obferved with the divided arch to the Eaft, the inftrument being placed as near as poffible in the magnetic meridian ; it was then turned, and the obfervation made with the divided arch to the Weft : the poles being changed, the obfervation was repeated in the fame manner. The actual obfervations are expreffed in the fecond, third, fourth, and fifth columns; and the mean refult in the fixth. It appears by thefe obfervations that the dip increafes in going North.

There is no reafon at prefent to fuppofe that the dip is liable to any variation in the fame place at different periods of time, it having been obferved in London by Norman, who firft difcovered it in 1592, to be 71° 50'; and by Mr. Nairne, in 1772, about 72°. The difference between thefe obfervations, taken at fuch diftant periods, is fmaller than that found between feveral of Mr. Nairne's obfervations compared with each other; and therefore we have no reafon to conclude that the dip has altered fince Norman's time : the care with which his inftrument was conftructed, and his obfervations made, leaves no room to doubt of their accuracy.

T   TABLE

TABLE of the OBSERVATIONS made with the Marine DIPPING-NEEDLE.

Day of the Month.	West.		East.		West.		East.		Mean Dip.		Place of Observation.
	°	′	°	′	°	′	°	′	°	′	° ′
June 2 P. M.	73	0	73	15	73	20	74	30	73	31	} Latitude 51 35 near the
2 P. M.	74	30	73	0	73	20	73	30	73	35	} Buoy of the Upper Middle.
5 P. M.	70	20	73	0	73	15	72	15	72	12	Off Harwich.
6 P. M.	72	0	75	0	72	0	74	30	73	22	In Southwold Bay.
14 P. M.	72	30	73	30	74	0	74	0	73	30	} Off Shetland.
8 P. M.	75	15	75	30	74	0	76	30	75	18	° ′
15, 8 A. M.	74	30	74	30	75	0	75	30	74	52	} Latitude 60 18
P. M.	74	30	75	30	75	0	75	0	75	0	
16 P. M.	77	0	76	30	76	30	77	0	76	45	
22 Noon	78	0	77	30	78	0	78	0	77	52	Latitude 70 45
23, 9 P. M.	81	30	80	0	83	0	81	30	81	30	Latitude 72 40
24 Noon	82	30	79	30	81	30	79	0	80	35	Latitude 73 22
P. M.	77	30	77	30	81	0	82	0	79	30	Latitude 73 36
26, 2 P. M.	77	30	80	0	82	0	78	0	79	22	Latitude 74 30
28 Mid.	83	30	80	0	82	0	79	0	81	7	Latitude 77 48
29, 2 P. M.	79	15	81	0	78	30	83	0	80	26	Latitude 78 2
30 Noon	76	45	79	30	82	30	79	45	79	30	Latitude 78 8
July 2, Mid.	80	30	82	30	80	30	79	30	80	45	Latitude 78 24
9, 6 P. M.	82	45	81	45	83	0	80	0	81	52	Latitude 80 12
	81	45	81	15	82	0	82	30	81	52½	} On Shore.
15	82	45	81	15	82	50	81	10	82	7½	} Latitude 79 50
29 M d.	83	15	83	0	80	40	81	15	82	2½	Latitude 80 27
Auguſt 14	83	0	83	0	81	15	81	20	82	8¾	At Smeerenberg. Latitude 79° 44′ on ſhore.
31 P. M.	79	30	77	45	80	0	79	0	79	4	Latitude 69° 2′

ACCOUNT

ACCOUNT of the INSTRUMENTS made ufe of for keeping the
METEOROLOGICAL JOURNAL.

THE Marine Barometer was made by Mr. Nairne,
from whom I received the following defcription:

" The bore of the upper part of the glafs tube of this ba-
" rometer, is about three-tenths of an inch in diameter, and
" four inches long. To this is joined a glafs tube, with a
" bore about one-twentieth of an inch in diameter. The
" two glafs tubes being joined together, form the tube of
" this barometer ; and being filled with mercury, and in-
" verted into a ciftern of the fame, the mercury falls down
" in the tube till it is counterbalanced by the atmofphere.

" In a common barometer, the motion of the mercury up
" and down in the tube is fo great at fea, that it is not
" poffible to meafure its perpendicular height; confequently,
" cannot fhew any alteration in the weight of the atmo-
" fphere : but in this marine barometer, that defect is reme-
" died. The inftrument is fixed in gimmals, and kept in a
" perpendicular pofition by a weight faftened to the bottom
" of it.

T 2   " The

" The perpendicular rifing or falling of the mercury is
" meafured by divifions, on a plate divided into inches and
" tenths, and by a Vernier divifion into hundredths of an
" inch, which is fixed to the fide of the tube."

The HYGROMETER I was favoured with by M. De Luc;
and the following account is a literal tranflation of that
which he gave me in French.

THE part of M. De Luc's Hygrometer which is affected
by the impreffions of the moifture of the air, is a hollow
cylinder of ivory, two inches eight lines long, and inter-
nally two lines and a half in diameter. It is open only
at one end; and the thicknefs of its fides, for the length
of two inches fix lines from the bottom, is but three-
fixteenths of a line. It is this thin part which does the
office of an hygrometer; the remaining part of the
cylinder, towards its orifice, muft be kept a little thicker,
being deftined for joining it to a tube of glafs, thirteen or
fourteen inches long. This junction is effected by means
of a piece of brafs, and the whole is cemented together
with gum lac.

M. De Luc's reafon for chufing ivory as the hygrometer, is, that this matter appeared to him more proper
than any other for receiving the impreffions of the moifture
of the air, without fuffering thereby any effential change.

3   The

The cylinder made of it becomes more capacious, in proportion as it grows moifter. This is the fundamental principle of the inftrument. M. De Luc has fince found,
that upon letting this cylinder lie fome time in water of
an uniform temperature, it fwells to a certain point, after
which it dilates no further. This circumftance furnifhed
him with a *maximum* of humidity; and, confequently, with
one point of comparifon in the fcale of the hygrometer;
and this point he has fixed at the temperature of melting
ice. For meafuring the differences in the capacity of
this ivory cylinder, and thereby difcovering its different
degrees of moifture, M. De Luc makes ufe of quickfilver,
with which he fills the cylinder, and a part of the communicating glafs tube. The more capacious this cylinder
is, or, which is the fame, the moifter it is, the lower does
the mercury ftand in the glafs tube; and *vice verfâ*. Now
M. De Luc has found, that the loweft point to which it
can fink, is that where it ftands when the ivory cylinder is
foaked in melting ice: he therefore names this point *zero*,
in the fcale of his hygrometer; and confequently, the degrees of this fcale are *degrees of drynefs*, counted from
below upwards, as the quickfilver rifes in the glafs tube.

To give thefe degrees a determinate length, and thus
render the hygrometers capable of being compared with
each other, M. De Luc employs in conftructing them
fuch glafs tubes as have been previoufly prepared, by being
made into thermometers, and filled with mercury, fo as

to

to afcertain upon them the points of melting ice and boiling water, and to take exactly the diftance between thofe points by any fcale at pleafure. That done, the bulb of this preparatory thermometer muft be broken, and the quickfilver it contains exactly weighed. It is by knowing the weight of this, together with the diftance between the fixed points of the thermometer, that the fcale of the hygrometer is determined. For inftance, let the weight of the quickfilver be one ounce, and the diftance between the two abovementioned points, one thoufand parts of a certain fcale: then fuppofe that the quickfilver in the hygrometer, to which this tube is to be applied, weighs only half an ounce; this will give a fundamental line, confifting of five hundred parts of the fame fcale. The fundamental line, thus found, is applied to the fcale of the hygrometer, beginning at *zero*, and meafuring it off about four times over, that the whole variation of the inftrument may be comprehended. Each of thofe fpaces being afterwards divided into forty equal parts, gives fuch degrees as M. De Luc has found moft convenient. In general terms, the length of the fundamental line of the hygrometer, muft be to the interval between the two fixed points of the preparatory thermometer, as the weight of the quickfilver in the hygrometer, is to the weight of the quickfilver in that thermometer.

This proportion between the fcale of the hygrometer and that of the preparatory thermometer, furnifhes an

eafy

eafy method of correcting in this inftrument the effects of heat upon the mercury it contains.

It will eafily be conceived, from the conftruction of the fcale of this hygrometer, that if its cylinder of ivory was fuddenly changed into glafs, the inftrument would become a true thermometer, in which the interval between the points, anfwering to melting ice and boiling water, would be divided into forty parts. If, therefore, a thermometer, with a fcale fimilarly divided into forty parts between the fixed points, be placed near the hygrometer, it will fhew immediately the correction to be made on that inftrument for its variation as a thermometer; with fome reftrictions, however; of which M. De Luc has given an account in the paper he fent to the Royal Society on the fubject of this hygrometer.

That part of the frame of the inftrument on which the fcale is marked, is moveable; fo that, before obferving the points at which the mercury ftands, it may be pufhed upwards or downwards, according as the thermometer has rifen or fallen with refpect to the point of melting ice : and thus the indications of the hygrometer can at once be freed from the errors which would arife from the difference in the volume of the quickfilver, on account of the different degrees of heat.

Defcription

Defcription of the Manometer, conftructed by Mr.
Ramfden.

THE Manometer ufed in this voyage was compofed of
a tube of a fmall bore, with a ball at the end; the barometer being at 29,7, a fmall quantity of quickfilver was
put into the tube to take off the communication between
the external air, and that confined in the ball and the part
of the tube below this quickfilver. A fcale is placed on
the fide of the tube, which marks the degrees of dilata-
tion arifing from the increafe of heat in this ftate of the
weight of the air, and has the fame graduation as that of
Fahrenheit's thermometer, the point of freezing being
marked 32. In this ftate therefore it will fhew the
degrees of heat in the fame manner as a thermometer.
But if the air becomes lighter, the bubble inclofed in the
ball, being lefs compreffed, will dilate itfelf, and take up a
fpace as much larger, as the compreffing force is lefs;
therefore the changes arifing from the increafe of heat will
be proportionably larger; and the inftrument will fhew
the differences in the denfity of the air, arifing from the
changes in its weight and heat. Mr. Ramfden found, that
a heat, equal to that of boiling water, increafed the magnitude of the air from what it was at the freezing
point $\frac{404}{1000}$ of the whole. From this it follows, that the
ball and the part of the tube below the beginning of the

fcale

fcale is of a magnitude equal to almoſt 414 degrees of the ſcale.

If we have the height of both the manometer and thermometer, the height of the barometer may be thence deduced by this rule; as the height of the manometer increaſed by 414, is to the height of the thermometer increaſed by 414; ſo is 29,7, to the height of the barometer.

This inſtrument, though far from complete, having been conſtructed in a hurry for the purpoſe of a firſt experiment, and liable to ſome inaccuracies in the obſervations from not having the thermometer with which it was compared attached to it, ſeldom differed from the marine barometer $\frac{1}{10}$ of an inch. Should it be improved to that degree of accuracy of which it ſeems capable, it will be of great uſe in determining refractions for aſtronomical obſervations, as well as indicating an approaching gale of wind at ſea.

U   Meteorological

Meteorological Journal.

Day of the Month.	Time.	Fahrenheit's Thermometer.	Barometer.	Hygrometer.	Manometer.	Latitude.	Longitude.	Winds and Weather.	Remarks, &c.
		°	In. dec.	°	°	° ′	° ′		
June 4th	6 A. M.	58½	…	…	…	…	…	NNW, hazy weather.	
	Noon.	58½	29,99	77	…	…	…	NW,	
	4 P. M.	58½	…	…	…	…	…	NW, } cloudy.	
	6 P. M.	58	29,95	81	…	…	…	NNW,	
	Midnight.	58	…	…	…	…	…	E by N,	
5th	6 A. M.	58½	…	…	…	…	…	N by W, cloudy.	
	Noon.	59½	29,93	75	…	…	…	NE, } hazy.	
	6 P. M.	54	29,96	79½	…	…	…	NE by E,	
6th	6 A. M.	54	…	…	…	…	…	SSW, fair.	
	Noon.	61	29,90	73½	…	57 17	1 30 E	SW, } hazy.	
	6 P. M.	56	29,93	73	…	…	…	SW by S,	
7th	Noon.	54	29,88	74	…	53 59	2 39	N by E, hazy.	
8th	Noon.	58	30,04	75	…	53 36	0 56	NNE, } hazy.	
	6 P. M.	53	30,08	75½	…	…	…	SSE,	
9th	Noon.	58	30,05	70	…	54 2	0 12	SSE, } hazy.	
	6 P. M.	56	29,99	70	…	…	…	S by E,	
10th	Noon.	54½	30,05	68	…	54 27	0 31 W	NNE, cloudy.	
11th	Noon.	58	29,90	70	…	…	0 31	SE, cloudy.	
12th	Noon.	54	29.73	62	…	56 28	1 0	SE. hazy.	
13th	6 A. M.	51½	…	…	…	…	…		
	Noon.	57	30.07	65¼	…	59 34	0 10 E	} E, clear weather.	
	6 P. M.	51½	…	…	…	…	…		
14th	Noon.	60	30,16	62	…	60 21	0 40 W	N, clear weather.	
15th	Noon.	58½	29,96	64	…	60 19	0 48	NE, foggy.	
16th	6 A. M.	49	…	…	…	…	…	SSW, hazy.	
	Noon.	55	29,54	64	…	60 37	0 31	SW, foggy.	
17th	Noon.	52	29,64	63	…	63 0	0 2	SSW, } cloudy.	
	Midnight.	49	…	…	…	…	…	SSE,	
18th	6 A. M.	48½	…	…	…	…	…	SSE, cloudy.	
	Noon.	52	29,72	62	54½	65 20	0 17		
	6 P. M.	50	…	…	…	…	…	} SE, foggy.	
	Midnight.	48	…	…	…	…	…		
19th	Noon.	49	29,73	62½	54½	66 14	0 27	SE, cloudy.	

Meteorological

Meteorological Journal.

Day of the Month.	Time.	Fahrenheit's Thermometer.	Barometer.	Hygrometer.	Manometer.	Latitude.	Longitude.	Winds and Weather.	Remarks, &c.
		°	In. dec.	°	°	° '	° '		
June 20th	4 A. M.	43						N, fair weather.	
	Noon.	48½	29,90	62	47	67 5	0 46 E	Calm, cloudy,	
	Midnight.	44¼						SSW, fair.	
21st	Noon.	50	29,85	65	47	68 4	0 32	SSE, fresh, cloudy.	
	Midnight.	41½						S, cloudy.	
22d	6 A. M.	41						W,	Thermometer in the air being 43°, in the surface water of the sea it was 31°. At 6 A. M. Thermometer exposed to the Sun 5' rose 12°.
	Noon.	42½	29,80	66	44	70 45	0 32	WSW, } cloudy.	
	Midnight.	37½						E,	
23d	6 A. M.	38						SE,	
	Noon.	40	29,77	61	44	72 22	0 45	SSW, } foggy.	
	6 P. M.	38						SE,	
	Midnight.	37						SE by E,	
24th	6 A. M.	37½						SE by E, } foggy.	
	Noon.	40	30,03	63	38	73 22	3 53	WSW,	
	6 P. M.	37	30,15					N, clear weather.	
	Midnight.	34						NNE, cloudy.	
25th	2 A. M.	41						NNE,	
	3 A. M.	35						NE by N, } hazy.	
	4 A. M.	36						N,	
	6 A. M.	36						N by E, } cloudy.	
	Noon.	36	30,13	67	34	74 5	9 44	{ N, squally, hail and sleet.	
	8 P. M.	37½						NNE, cloudy.	
26th	Noon.	40¼	30,33	82½	39½	74 25	11 46	NE by N, fair weather.	
	8 P. M.	41						almost calm, cloudy.	
27th	Noon.	40	30,00	87	41½	75 21	9 43	WSW. cloudy and snow	
	6 P. M.	39						WSW, cloudy.	
	Midnight.	39						SSW, rain.	
28th	6 A. M.	38						SSW, rain.	
	Noon.	39	29,65			77 36	8 52	S, hazy and rain.	
	Midnight.	38½						ENE, cloudy.	
29th	Noon.	39				78 1	9 48	N by E. hazy.	At Midnight Thermometer exposed to the Sun 30' rose 20°.
	Midnight.	37½						NNE, fair.	

Meteorological

Meteorological Journal.

Day of the Month.	Time.	Fahrenheit's Thermometer.	Barometer.	Hygrometer.	Manometer.	Latitude.	Longitude.	Winds and Weather.	Remarks, &c.
		°	In. dec.	°	°	° ′	° ′		
June 30th	Noon.	42	29,57	106	. .	78 8	10 58 E	Calm and cloudy.	The rife of the Hygrometer was occafioned by a fire being lighted in the cabin.
	Midnight.	42	. . .	. .	. .	. . .	. . .	{ Variable winds and fair.	
July 1st	Noon.	44	29,63	84	50	78 18	10 53	WSW, hazy weather.	At Noon, Thermometer expofed to the fun rofe 10° in 10′.
	8 P. M.	50	. . .	. .	. .	. . .	. . .	Calm and fair.	
	Midnight.	49	. . .	. .	. .	. . .	. . .	N, fine weather.	
2d	Noon.	43½	29,71	79	50	78 22	10 15	SSW, fair weather.	At 6 P. M. Thermometer expofed 10′ to the Sun rofe to 76°.
	Midnight.	45	. . .	. .	. .	. . .	. . .	Calm and cloudy.	
3d	Noon.	43½	. . .	. .	. .	78 36	10 15	S, hazy.	
	Midnight.	40½	. . .	. .	. .	. . .	. . .	SE, cloudy.	
4th	Noon.	44½	29,94	. .	. .	79 31	9 57	Calm and fair.	
	6 P. M.	40	. . .	. .	. .	. . .	. . .	Calm and clear.	
	Midnight.	40	. . .	. .	. .	. . .	. . .	Variable and foggy.	
5th	Noon.	41	29,94	. .	. .	79 55	9 17	SW, foggy.	
	Midnight.	37½	. . .	. .	. .	. . .	. . .	S, cloudy.	
6th	Noon.	39½	29,80	. .	. .	79 57	8 37	SE, fair.	
	6 P. M.	41	. . .	. .	. .	. . .	. . .	} SE, cloudy.	
	8 P. M.	38½	. . .	. .	. .	. . .	. . .		
7th	Noon.	39½	29,78	. .	. .	. . .	. . .	} N, rainy.	Thermometer placed clofe to a piece of ice, fell from 39°½ to 37°.
	6 P. M.	. . .	29,81	. .	. .	. . .	. . .		
	Midnight.	39½	. . .	. .	. .	. . .	. . .	N by E, cloudy.	
8th	6 A. M.	40	. . .	. .	. .	. . .	. . .	N by E, } cloudy.	Near the ice.
	Noon.	39½	29,83	. .	. .	. . .	. . .	W by S, }	
	6 P. M.	37	. . .	. .	. .	. . .	. . .	SE, foggy.	
	Midnight.	39	. . .	. .	. .	. . .	. . .	SW, cloudy.	
9th	1 A. M.	. . .	29,78	. .	. .	. . .	. . .	SW, cloudy.	At 3 P. M. Thermometer expofed to the wind blowing from the ice, fell in 5′ from 42° to 39°. Near the ice.
	Noon.	40	29,83	. .	. .	80 7	5 5	} SW by S, cloudy.	
	6 P. M.	39	. . .	. .	. .	. . .	. . .	S by W, thick fog.	
	Midnight.	38	. . .	. .	. .	. . .	. . .		
10th	Noon.	39½	29,86	. .	. .	80 22	2 12	SSW, thick fog.	Among the ice.
	Midnight.	38½	. . .	. .	. .	. . .	. . .	SSW, cloudy.	

Meteorological

Meteorological Journal.

Day of the Month.	Time.	Fahrenheit's Thermometer.	Barometer.	Hygrometer.	Manometer.	Latitude.	Longitude.	Winds and Weather.	Remarks, &c.
		°	In. dec.	°	°	° ′	° ′		
July 11th	3 A. M. 4 A. M. Noon. Midnight.	41 37 42 44	29,66			80 4		} SSW, with rain. Calm and fair. Light airs and fair.	At 10 A. M. Thermometer exposed to the Sun 30′ rose 26°. At 7 P.M. Thermometer fell suddenly to 37°, then rose again about 8°.
12th	Noon. 8 P. M. Midnight.	45 45 44	29,58					ENE, cloudy. Calm, cloudy. Calm and fair.	Light winds.
13th	Noon. 8 P. M.	46 42	29,63					Calm and cloudy. { SW by S, squally and cloudy.	
14th	Noon. Midnight.	36 38						ENE, foggy. ENE, cloudy.	Thermometer exposed to the Sun rose to 86°½.
15th	Noon. Midnight.	45 46						NNE, W, } fair.	
16th	Noon. Midnight.	49 48						} Light airs and clear.	Thermometer exposed to the Sun rose to 89°½.
17th	Noon. Midnight.	49 45						} Light airs and clear.	
18th	Noon. Midnight.	45½ 42						} NW by W, cloudy.	Among the loose ice.
19th	Noon. Midnight.	42 39	29,60					SE, foggy. E, cloudy.	Thermometer exposed to the Sun 30′ rose to 89°.
20th	Noon. Midnight.	37 33½	29,70	110	37½	80 30	3 26 E	NE, } E, } snow and sleet.	Near the ice. The rising of the Hygrometer was occasioned by a fire lighted in the cabin.
21st	4 A. M. 9 A. M. Noon. 6 P. M. 10 P. M. Midnight.	33 33½ 34 35 32½ 32½	29,74 29,77	73 73	34½ 34	79 27	4 29	E, hazy and snow. SW, } NW, } hazy. WNW, cloudy. SW, hazy. SW by S, cloudy.	Close to the ice.

Meteorological Journal.

Day of the Month.	Time.	Fahrenheit's Thermometer.	Barometer.	Hygrometer.	Manometer.	Latitude.	Longitude.	Winds and Weather.	Remarks, &c.
		°	In. dec.	°	°	° ′	° ′		
July 22d	6 A. M.	34	. . .	. .	30½	. . .	. . .	SW by S, cloudy.	Thermometer placed near the frozen ropes fell to 32°½.
	Noon.	35	29,76	. .	33	80 1	6 32	SW, } foggy.	
	6 P. M.	39½	. . .	. .	. .	. . .	. . .	S	
	Midnight.	35½	. . .	. .	. .	. . .	. . .	E by N, hazy.	
23d	4 A. M.	37	. . .	. .	36	. . .	. . .	E by N, hazy.	Hygrometer placed in Bittacle.
	Noon.	36	29,74	48	40	80 24	9 59 E	} E, rain.	
	6 P. M.	36½	. . .	. .	39½	. . .	. . .		
	Midnight.	37½	. . .	44	. .	. . .	. . .	E, cloudy.	
24th	Noon.	39	29,41	43	41	. . .	. . .	E, } cloudy.	Near the floating ice.
	Midnight.	37	. . .	. .	44	. . .	. . .	ENE,	
25th	Noon.	39½	29,64	39	41	. . .	. . .	NW by N, hazy.	
	4 P. M.	38	. . .	. .	41	. . .	. . .	N, cloudy.	
	Midnight.	39½	. . .	39½	. .	. . .	. . .	Light airs and foggy.	
26th	Noon.	39	29,90	39	32½	80 17	13 22	NNW, foggy.	
	Midnight.	39	. . .	. .	41	. .	. . .	SSE, cloudy.	
27th	4 A. M.	39	. . .	. .	40¾	. . .	. . .	E, cloudy.	
	Noon.	38	30,17	. .	. .	80 48	14 42	ENE, } hazy.	
	8 P. M.	39	. . .	. .	32	. . .	. . .	E,	
	Midnight.	. . .	30,30	. .	. .	. . .	. . .	E by N, cloudy.	
28th	4 A. M.	36	. . .	. .	26¼	. . .	. . .	Hazy.	6 A. M. Thermometer exposed to the Sun 15′ rose 9°½. Among the ice.
	8 A. M.	37	. . .	. .	27½	. . .	. . .	Foggy.	
	Noon.	37	30,35.	62	33	80 36	15 30	E by N, foggy.	
	4 P. M.	35½	. . .	. .	26$\frac{3}{8}$	. . .	. . .	} SE, hazy.	
	6 P. M.	36	. . .	. .	27	. . .	. . .		
	Midnight.	40	. . .	. .	. .	. . .	. . .		
29th	Noon.	42	30,43	. .	33	80 25	18 18	ESE, clear.	
	Midnight.	42	. . .	. .	. .	. . .	. . .	SSE, fair.	
30th	Noon.	48	30,43	86½	27	80 31	. . .	NE by N, clear.	
	Midnight.	44	. . .	. .	. .	. . .	. . .	Calm and fair.	
31st	Noon.	48	30,43	92	40	. . .	. . .	Light airs at E, fair.	
	Midnight.	48	30,45	. .	. .	. . .	. . .	Calm and fair.	
August 1st	Noon.	48	30,45	73	36½	80 37	. . .	Light airs at E, hazy.	
	Midnight.	. . .	30.43	. .	. .	. . .	. . .	NNW, foggy.	
2d	Noon.	44	30,34	. .	. .	. . .	. . .	NW, } foggy.	
	Midnight.	45	30,33	. .	. .	. . .	. . .	NNW,	
3d	Noon.	47	30,17	96	38	. . .	. . .	} Light airs and fair weather.	
	6 P. M.		0.13						

Meteorological Journal.

Day of the Month.	Time.	Fahrenheit's Thermometer.	Barometer.	Hygrometer.	Manometer.	Latitude.	Longitude.	Winds and Weather.	Remarks, &c.
		°	In. dec.	°	°	°	°		
Auguſt 4ᵗʰ	Noon.	46	. . .	88	30	. . .	. . .	ENE, foggy.	
7ᵗʰ	Midnight.	38	. . .	. .	. .	. . .	. . .	W, foggy.	
8ᵗʰ	8 A. M. 8 P. M.	32 36½	. . . . . .	. . . .	. . . .	. . . . . .	. . . . . .	} Calm and foggy.	
9ᵗʰ	4 A. M. Noon. Midnight.	35 34 32	. . . 30,02 . . .	. . 47 . .	. . . . . .	. . . .	. . . .	SE, foggy. Variable and foggy. NE, cloudy.	
10ᵗʰ	Noon. 8 P. M. Midnight.	33 33 33	29,87	53	27	. . . .	. . . .	NNE, cloudy and ſnow. ENE, } NE, } cloudy.	
11ᵗʰ	Noon. 8 P. M.	33 33	29,70 . . .	46 . .	32 . .	. . . . . .	. . . . . .	} ENE, hazy weather.	
12ᵗʰ	Noon.	36	29,60	46	31			NE, ſnow.	
13ᵗʰ	Noon. 8 P. M.	37 35	29,68 . . .	46 . .	32 . .			{ NE, cloudy, ſnow and ſleet.	
14ᵗʰ	Noon. 8 P. M.	40 45	29,68 . . .	47 . .	35 . .			Calm, and fair. N, hazy.	
15ᵗʰ	Noon. 8 P. M.	39 35	29,85 . . .	43 . .	34 . .	At Smeeren-berg, Latitude 79° 44′. Longitude 9° 50′ 45″ E.		NE, hazy. Variable and cloudy.	
16ᵗʰ	Noon. 8 A. M.	38 37	29,97 . . .	41 . .	34 . .			ENE, hazy. E, cloudy.	
17ᵗʰ	Noon.	40	29,80	54	35			NE, hazy.	
18ᵗʰ	Noon.	46	29,78	45	37			NE, clear.	
19ᵗʰ	Noon. Midnight.	37 39	29,70 . . .	35 . .	35 . .			NNW, rain. ESE, cloudy.	
20ᵗʰ	Noon. 8 P. M.	40 38	29,50 . . .	35 . .	35 . .	80 12 . . .	7 40 E . . .	SW, cloudy. SSW, rain.	
21ˢᵗ	4 A. M. 8 A. M. Noon. 4 P. M. Midnight.	38 40 40 36 36	. . . . . . 29,06	. . . . 29	34 35 34 35 35	. . . . . . 80 5	. . . . . . 2 54	} SE, hazy and rain. SE by S, SE, } foggy. SE.	

Meteorological Journal.

Day of the Month.	Time.	Fahrenheit's Thermometer.	Barometer.	Hygrometer.	Manometer.	Latitude.	Longitude.	Winds and Weather.	Remarks, &c.
		°	In. dec.	°	°	° ′	° ′		
Aug. 22d	Noon.	37	. . .	. .	. .	79 24	1 56 E	NE, hazy.	
	Midnight.	36½	. . .	. .	. .	. . .	. . .	NNE, rain.	
23d	2 A. M.	32½	. . .	. .	. .	. . .	. . .	NNE, rain and sleet.	
	Noon.	37	29,98	30	31	77 10	4 58	W by N, cloudy.	
	4 P. M.	35½	. . .	. .	34	. . .	. . .		
	Midnight.	35	. . .	. .	. .	. . .	. . .		
24th	4 A. M.	35	. . .	. .	31½	. . .	. . .	SW, cloudy.	
	Noon.	42	29,79	31	33	75 59	6 13	Calm and cloudy.	
25th	4 A. M.	36½	. . .	. .	. .	. . .	. . .	E, cloudy.	
	Noon.	42	29,79	31	40½	75 12	4 51	S by E, cloudy.	
	Midnight.	37	. . .	. .	35½	. . .	. . .	SE, rain and sleet.	
26th	Noon.	42	29,71	26	42	73 19	1 46	SE by S, rainy.	
	6 P. M.	45	29,71	25	41	. . .	. . .	S, hazy.	
	Midnight.	42	29,78	25½	. .	. . .	. . .	S, cloudy.	
27th	4 A. M.	43	. . .	. .	47½	. . .	. . .	SW by S, hazy.	
	Noon.	45	29,79	23	42	72 40	0 14	SSW, hazy.	
	Midnight.	46	. . .	. .	. .	. . .	. . .	SSW, hazy.	
28th	4 A. M.	45¼	. . .	. .	42¼	. . .	. . .	SSW, foggy.	
	Noon.	46	29,93	25	42	72 19	1 49 W	W by S, fog and rain.	
	4 P. M.	45	. . .	. .	42½	. . .	. . .	NW, hazy.	
	8 P. M.	41½	. . .	. .	. .	. . .	. . .		
	Midnight.	42	. . .	. .	. .	. . .	. . .		
29th	Noon.	40½	30,00	28	35	71 9	1 28	SW, fair.	
30th	4 A. M.	44	. . .	. .	35½	. . .	. . .	W by S, cloudy.	
	8 A. M.	44	. . .	. .	35¼	. . .	. . .	W by S, cloudy.	
	Noon.	53	30,28	33	39	70 29	0 18 E	W by S, cloudy.	
	8 P. M.	48	. . .	. .	. .	. . .	. . .	WNW, cloudy.	
31st	4 A. M.	44	. . .	. .	. .	. . .	. . .	WNW, cloudy.	
	8 A. M.	48	. . .	. .	42½	. . .	. . .		
	Noon.	55	30,23	39	38	69 3	0 18	Variable and fair.	
Sept. 1st	Noon.	50	30,23	54	38	69 0	0 2	S, cloudy.	
	9 P. M.	46½	. . .	. .	38	. . .	. . .	WNW, cloudy.	
2d	Noon.	57	30,09	32½	49	68 14	0 38	E, cloudy.	
	6 P. M.	52	. . .	44½	39	. . .	. . .	ESE, hazy,	
	8 P. M.	52½	. . .	40¾	39¾	. . .	. . .	ESE, foggy.	

Day of the Month.	Time.	Fahrenheit's Thermometer.	Barometer.	Hygrometer.	Manometer.	Latitude.		Longitude.		Winds and Weather.	Remarks, &c.
		°	In. dec.	°	°	°	'	°	'		
Sept. 3ᵈ	1 A. M.	52½	· · ·	25	39½	· ·		· · ·		ESE, foggy.	
	4 A. M.	52¼	· · ·	23½	40					ESE, } hazy.	
	Noon.	65	30,06	34½	59	65	57	0	8 E	SE, }	
	8 P. M.	56	· · ·	32½	48½	· ·		· · ·		SSE, cloudy.	
	Midnight.	53	· · ·	30	48¾	· ·		· · ·		ESE, clear.	
4ᵗʰ	8 A. M.	62	· ·	29	51	· ·		· · ·		ESE, clear.	
	Noon.	58	30,00	37	51	64	58	0	12 W	Calm and cloudy.	
5ᵗʰ	4 A. M.	56	· · ·	· ·	51½	· ·		· · ·		SE, cloudy.	
	8 A. M.	58	· · ·	· ·	51	· ·		· · ·		SE, clear.	
	Noon.	57	29,81	30	52	63	58	0	54	{ SE by E, cloudy and rain.	
	Midnight.	56	· · ·	44	51	· ·		· · ·		SE by E, cloudy.	
6ᵗʰ	2 A. M.	55½	· · ·	44	51	· ·		· · ·		} SE by E, cloudy.	
	4 A. M.	56½	· · ·	45	52	· ·		· · ·			
	Noon.	59	29,13	39	60	62	27	1	12	} E by S, hazy.	
	8 P. M.	56	· · ·	· ·	54	· ·		· · ·			
	Midnight.	56½	· · ·	· ·	58	· ·		· · ·			
7ᵗʰ	8 A. M.	58	· · ·	· ·	61	· ·		· · ·		} SE, hazy.	
	Noon.	61	29,02	36	64	60	1	2	35		
8ᵗʰ	4 A. M.	54	· ˙ ·	·33½	65	· ·		· · ·		SW, small rain.	
	8 A. M.	54½	· · ·	33	64½	· ·		· · ·		Squally and rain.	
	Noon.	56	28,71	36	66	59	35	1	9	SW by S, hazy.	Fresh gales.
9ᵗʰ	Noon.	56	28,70	41	66½	59	9	0	37	WSW, hazy.	Fresh gales.
10ᵗʰ	· · ·	· · ·	· · ·	· · ·	· · ·	· ·		· · ·		· · · · · ·	The weather was so bad, and the ship had so much motion, that the barometer could not be observed this day.
11ᵗʰ	Noon.	58	29,20	41	59	57	25	1	32 E	SW, hazy.	Fresh gales.
12ᵗʰ	Noon.	57	29,30	39	61	56	57	1	55	NW, squally.	
13ᵗʰ	Noon.	56	29,70	30	53	56	4	1	31	SSW, rain.	At 1 A. M. a very hard gale of wind. Squally weather.
14ᵗʰ	9 A. M.	· · ·	29,79	· ·	· ·	· ·		· · ·		} NW, ditto.	} Hard gales.
	Noon.	52	29,89	30	55	55	40	· · ·			

Meteorological

Meteorological Journal.

Day of the Month.	Time.	Fahrenheit's Thermometer.	Barometer.	Hygrometer.	Manometer.	Lati tude.	Longitude.	Winds and Weather.	Remarks, &c.
			In. dec.	°	°	° ′	° ′		
15th	Noon.	57	29,59	32	53	54 33	0 29 E	WSW, rain.	Very hard gales.
16th	Noon. 9 P. M. 10 P. M.	57	29,90 29,70 29,60	40 . . . -	53	53 13	0 1	W, cloudy. } Rain.	Moderate. } Squally.
17th	Noon.	55	29,50	37	54	53 12	0 7	WNW, hazy and rain.	
18th	Noon.	57	29,77	44	. .	52 53	0 11 W	W by S, cloudy.	
19th	Noon.	61	30,08	50	. .	52 42	0 29	W by S, cloudy.	
20th	Noon. Midnight.	61 . . .	30,00 29,90	48 . .	. . . .	52 31 . . .	0 16 . . .	SW by W, hazy. W by S, cloudy.	Fresh gales. Moderate.
21st	10 A. M. Noon. 10 P. M.	61 63 . . .	. . . 29,88 29,23	44 44 . .	. . . . . .	. . . 52 17 . . .	. . . 0 5 . . .	SW by W, cloudy. SW by S, moderate. S, hazy.	Fresh gales. Fresh gales.
22d	Noon. 6 P. M.	60 . . .	29,23 29,43	45 . .	. . . .	52 28 . . .	1 35 . . .	{ SW by S, hard gales { and squally. WNW, rain.	Squally. Strong gales.
23d	Noon. 6 P. M.	51 . . .	29,91 29,70	50 . .	. . . .	52 2 . . .	0 49 . . .	W, cloudy. SW by W, ditto.	} Moderate.
24th	Noon.	57	29,50	45	. .	52 16	2 33	SSW, cloudy.	
25th	8 A. M. Noon. 11 P. M.	. . . 61 . . .	29,66 29,66 29,80	. . 44 . .	. . . . . .	. . . .	. . . .	SW, SW by W, } cloudy. WSW, }	

MISCELLANEOUS OBSERVATIONS.

OBSERVATIONS for determining the refraction in high latitudes.

JUNE the thirtieth, at midnight, the diftance of the two oppofite horizons, taken by me with Ramfden's fextant, was 179° 54′; the height of the eye being fixteen feet above the level of the fea.

August the fifteenth, at midnight, by the aftronomical Quadrant, the altitude of the fun's upper limb 4° 16′ 55″ lower limb 3° 46′ 0″

Error of the Quadrant	— 32		-	-		— 32	
	4	16	23	-	-	3	45	28
Semidiameter	— 15	51	-	-	+ 15	51	

App. Alt. Sun's center	-	-	4	0	32	-	-	4	1	19
Co. Declin.	-	75	56	13	-	-	75	56	13
App. Lat.	-	79	56	45	-	-	79	57	32
True Lat.	-	79	44	3	-	-	79	44	3
Refraction	-	-	12	42	-	-	13	29
By Dr. Bradley's tables	11	18	-	-	12	27
Allowing for the therm.	11	53	-	-	13	2

Barometer, 29,6   Thermometer, 37°

5   Auguft

Auguſt the twentieth, at midnight, the ſun's meridian
altitude by Mr. Harvey,   2° 25' 00"
                    Dip — 3 49
                    ─────────────
                          2 21 11
        Semidiameter + 15 52
                    ─────────────
Altitude of the Sun's center 2 37   3
        Co. Declin. 77 31 26
                    ─────────────
            App. Latitude 80   8 29
    Refr. by the tables   16 44
                    ─────────────
        True Latitude 79 51 45
                    ─────────────

Hakluyt's Head-land S B E
Cloven Cliff - - - E B S ½ S
Variation - - - - 19° 30' S.

It may not be improper to mention here that Baffin, in
1613, made an obſervation of the refraction when the ſun
was in the horizon, in latitude 78° 46', which alſo agrees
exactly with Dr. Bradley's tables. It may therefore be
preſumed that the refractions in the higher latitudes follow
the ſame law as in theſe.

Specific

Specific Gravity of Ice, tried by Dr. Irving.

A piece of the moſt denſe ice he could find, being im-
merſed in ſnow water, thermometer thirty-four degrees,—
fourteen fifteenth parts ſunk under the ſurface of the
water.

In brandy juſt proof, it barely floated: in rectified
ſpirits of wine it fell to the bottom at once, and diſſolved
immediately.

September the fourth, at two in the afternoon, we ſounded
with all the lines, above eight hundred fathom. Some
time before the laſt line was out, we perceived a ſlack,
and that it did not run off near ſo quick as before. When
we got the lines in again, the firſt coil came in very eaſily,
and twenty fathom of the next, after which it took a
great ſtrain to move the lead; a mark was put on at the
place where the weight was perceived, and the line
meaſured, by which the depth was found to be ſix hundred and eighty-three fathoms. The lead weighed above
one hundred and fifty pounds, and had ſunk, as appeared
by the line, near ten feet into the ground, which was
a very fine blue ſoft clay. A bottle fitted properly by

Y   Dr.

Dr. Irving (none of thofe fent out having given fatisfaction) was let down, faftened to the line, about two fathom from the lead. A thermometer plunged into the water from the bottom ftood at forty degrees:—in water from the furface at fifty-five degrees;—in the fhade, the heat of the air was fixty-fix degrees.

Experiments to find the Temperature of the Water at different Depths, made with Lord Charles Cavendifh's Thermometer.					
Day of the Month.	Depth in Fathoms to which it was funk.	Temperature of the Water as fhewn by the Inftrument.	Correction for Compreffion and unequal Expanfion of Spirits.	Temperature of the Sea at the greateft Depth to which it was funk, corrected for Compreffion and Expanfion.	Heat of the Air.
		°	°	°	°
June 20	780	15	11	26	48½
30 A.M.	118	30	1	31	40½
P. M.	115	33	0	33	44¾
Auguft 31	673	22	10	32	59½

It appears from the Experiment of July 1ft, in which the Inftrument was compared with Fahrenheit's Thermometer at different Heats, that the Experiment cannot be depended on to lefs than two or three Degrees, as the Refults drawn from the different Comparifons would differ by about five Degrees.

Experiments

Experiments to determine the Temperature of the Water at different Depths of the Sea, and Quantity of Salt it contains; made with the Bottle fitted by Dr. Irving. A Meafure, containing 29 Ounces 59 Grains of pure Snow-water, was ufed as a Standard; Thermometer 59°, Barometer 30,06.

Day of the Month.	Weight of the Water.	Depth in Fathoms.	Thermometer at the Surface.	Thermometer in Water from the Bottom.	Thermometer in the Air.	Weight of the Salt.	Latitude, &c.
1773	Oz. Grs.		•	°	°	Grs.	° ′
June 1	29 404				59	393	{51 31 Nore
9	30 2					500	{54 8 Off Flamborough Head.
11		32	51	49	55		
12 {	29 440	Surface	50		50	490	}60 Off Shetland.
	29 442	65		44		490	
26	29 462				36	496	74 At Sea.
July 3	29 454		40		44	500	78
19	29 369				44	476	80 Near the Ice.
Aug. 4	30 15	60	36	39	32	510	80 30 Under the Ice.
31	12 360	80	51		48	220	
Sept. 4 {	12 365	683	55	40	66¼	192	75 At Sea.
	12 365					216	
7		56	57	50	60		60 14

Sea water taken up at the back of Yarmouth Sands, was in the following ratio to diftilled water:

$$\left.\begin{array}{l} \text{Sea-water} - - - \quad 21 \quad 16 \quad 13{,}7 \\ \text{Diftilled water} \quad 21 \quad 4 \quad 16 \end{array}\right\} \text{Thermometer, } 53°;$$

oz. dwts. grs.

which is, as 10192 : 10477,7; or, as 1 : 1,02803. The quantity of dry falt produced from the above water, was 13 dwts. 15 grs.; it appears, therefore, that fea-water contains more air than diftilled water.

Y 2   The

The refults of the experiments made with Lord Charles
Cavendifh's thermometer, and thofe with the bottle fitted
by Dr. Irving, differ materially as to the temperature of
the fea at great depths; I fhall give an account, therefore, of the precautions ufed by Dr. Irving to prevent the
temperature from being altered, as well as of the allowance
made by Mr. Cavendifh for compreffion, as they communicated them to me.

The following is the account of the precautions taken
by Dr. Irving to prevent the temperature of the water
being changed in bringing up from the bottom:

" The bottle had a coating of wool, three inches thick,
" which was wrapped up in an oiled fkin, and let into a
" leather purfe, and the whoie inclofed in a well-pitched
" canvafs-bag, firmly tied to the mouth of the bottle, fo
" that not a drop of water could penetrate to its furface.
" A bit of lead fhaped like a cone, with its bafe downwards
" and a cord fixed to its fmall end, was put into the bottle;
" and a piece of valve leather, with half a dozen flips of
" thin bladder, were ftrung on the cord, which, when
" pulled, effectually corked the bottle in the infide."

The

The following is Mr. Cavendish's account of the corrections to be made for Lord Charles Cavendish's thermometer.

" The Thermometer ufed in thefe experiments is fully
" defcribed in the Philofophical Tranfactions, Vol. L. Page
" 308; fo that I imagine it is unneceffary to mention it
" here. But fince the publication of that volume, the late
" Mr. Canton difcovered, that fpirits of wine and other
" fluids are compreffible; which muft make the thermometer
" appear to have been colder than it really was, and renders
" a correction neceffary on that account. There is another
" fmaller correction neceffary, owing to the expanfion of
" fpirits of wine by any given number of degrees of
" Fahrenheit's thermometer being greater in the higher
" degrees than the lower. As the method of computing
" thefe two corrections is not explained in that paper, it
" may be proper juft to mention the rule which was made
" ufe of in doing it.

" In adjufting the degrees on the fcale of this thermo-
" meter, the tube was intirely full of Mercury, or the
" Mercury ftood at no degrees on the fcale, when its real heat
" was 65° of Fahrenheit. Let the bulk of the Mercury con-
" tained at that time in the cylinder be called M, and that
" of the fpirits, S; let the expanfion of fpirits of wine by
" 1° of Fahrenheit, about the heat of 65°, be to its whole
" bulk

" bulk at that heat, as s to 1; and let its expansion by one

" degree at any other heat, as $65° — x$, be to its bulk at $65°$,

" as $s \times \overline{1 — d\,x}$ to 1; let the expansion of Mercury by one

" degree of heat be to its bulk at $65°$, as m to 1; and let

" $\frac{Ss + Mm}{Ss}$ be called G; let the compression of spirits of

" wine by the pressure of 100 fathom of sea-water,

" when the heat of the spirits is nearly the same as

" that of the sea at the depth to which the thermo-

" meter was let down, be to its bulk at $65°$, as C to 1;

" the compression of the Mercury is so small that it may

" be neglected; let the thermometer be let down N

" hundred fathom, and when brought up and put into water

" of $65° — F$ degrees of heat let the Mercury in the tube

" stand at E degrees; consequently the heat, as shewn by

" the thermometer, is $65° — F — E$: and let the real heat of

" the sea at the depth to which it was sunk be $65 — x$ degrees;

" then $65° — x = 65° — F — E + \dfrac{CN}{sG} - \dfrac{E\,d \times \overline{E + F + x}}{2\,G} + \dfrac{CN\,d \times \overline{F + x}}{2\,s\,G^2}$.

" In this thermometer $S = 1160$; $M = 97$; the expansion of

" the spirits used in making it by $1°$ at the heat of $65°$, was

" found to be $\frac{1}{1786}$ of their bulk at that heat; that is $s =$

" $\frac{1}{1786}$; $m = \frac{1}{11500}$; therefore $G = 1{,}013$. From M. DeLuc's

" experiments * it appears, that the expansion of spirits of

" wine by $1°$ at any degree of heat, as $65° — x$, is to its

" expansion by $1°$ at $65°$, nearly as $1 — \frac{x}{315}$ to 1: there-

" fore, $d = \frac{1}{315}$. The compressibility of the spirits used for

" this thermometer at the heat of $58°$, was found to be

* Modifications de l'Atmosphere, vol. I. page 252.

" exactly

" exactly the fame as Mr. Canton determines it to be at that
" heat; and therefore its compreffibility at all other degrees
" of heat is fuppofed to be the fame as he makes it. Ac-
" cording to his experiments *, the compreffion of fpirits of
" wine by the preffure of 29½ inches of Mercury at the
" heat of 32°, *id eft*, nearly the heat of the fea in thefe ex-
" periments, is 59½ millionth parts of its bulk at that heat;
" therefore $\frac{C}{G} = 1,9$ and $65 - x = 65 - F - E + N \times$

" $1,9 - \dfrac{E \times \overline{E+F+x}}{638} + \dfrac{N \times 1,9 \times \overline{F+x}}{638}.$ "

OBSERVATIONS made by Dr. Irving of the heat of the fea
agitated by a gale of wind, and that of the atmofphere.

September the twelfth, the thermometer plunged
into a wave of the fea, rofe to 62°; the heat of the
atmofphere 50°.

This experiment was frequently repeated during the
gale, and it gave nearly the fame difference. At night,
when the weather became moderate, the heat of water
30 fathoms below the furface was 55°; the furface and
the atmofphere were 54°.

September the twenty-fecond. The fea-water was 60°;
the atmofphere, 59°: the wind at S W, a frefh gale.

* Philofophical Tranfactions, Vol. LIV. page 261.

OBSERVATIONS

Observations for determining the height of a Mountain in Latitude 79° 44′; by the Barometer, and Geometrical Measurement.

Observations taken by the Barometer, by Dr. Irving.

AUGUST the eighteenth, the day remarkably clear:

At 6ʰ in the morning, the barometer by the sea   Inches.
side stood at -   -   -   -   -   30,040
The thermometer 50°
On the summit of the mountain, about an hour
and three quarters later than the first obser-
vation below, -   -   -   -   -   28,266
Thermometer 42°
About an hour later at the same place - - 28,258
Thermometer 42°
By the sea side, where the first observation was
made, and about three hours later - - 30,032
Thermometer 44°

Height of the mountain calculated by M. De Luc from
the first observation -   -   -   1585 feet
From the second observation - - 1592
─────
Mean -   -   -   -   -   1588¼ feet
─────
Means

Means ufed to afcertain the Height of the Mountain Geometrically.

A point was fixed upon, in the moft convenient place the ground would admit of between the fummit of the mountain (a well-defined object) and the fea fide; from hence, in a right line from the mountain, a ftaff was placed at the fea fide, by a Theodolite made by Ramfden, with two telefcopes and double Vernier divifions. The inftrument was carefully adjufted; firft, by levelling the ftand with a circular level, and afterwards the whole inftrument by the crofs levels. From hence (A) at right angles to the ftation at the fea fide (C) and the top of the mountain (E), a bafe was meafured each way to (B) and (D) of eight lines of feventeen fathom each; in all, five hundred and forty-four yards. The divifions of both the Verniers were carefully examined, both at fetting off the ftation by the fea fide, and thofe at the extremities of each bafe, the fixed telefcope being kept directed to the fummit of the mountain, and the moveable one directed at right angles each way, both divifions of the Vernier coinciding exactly. Station ftaves were fixed perpendicular by the vertical hair of the telefcope. The altitude of the mountain was then taken with the vertical arch, as a means of detecting any error in the obfervation, and was found to be

Z   8° 50.

8° 50′. The diſtance not enabling me to take the depreſſion of any particular part of the ſtaff by the ſea ſide
under the land on the other ſide accurately, I ſent a man
to ſtand cloſe before it, and took the depreſſion nearly to
his eye, which was found to be 1° 54′. The inſtrument
was then removed to the ſtation on the right (B). The
inſtrument being adjuſted with the ſame precautions as
before, and the fixed teleſcope pointing to the center
ſtation (A); the angle to the mountain was 84° 58′, the
angle to the ſtation by the water ſide (C) 294° 44′. The
inſtrument was then removed to the ſtation by the ſea ſide
(C), the ſame precautions uſed in adjuſting, and the fixed
teleſcope pointing to the center (A) in one with the
mountain, the angle to the ſtaff on the right (B) was
24° 44′. Intending to make the triangle B C D iſoſceles,
and imagining there might be ſome little error from the
unevenneſs of the ground, I ſet off on the theodolite an
angle equal to the laſt, having a perſon ready with a
ſtaff on the baſe line to fix it where that angle ſhould
interſect on looking through the teleſcope; I found it cut
exactly at the ſtaff D 335° 16′, and from thence concluded
the meaſure of the baſe to be exact. I then took the altitude of the mountain by the vertical arch 7° 44′. I then
removed the inſtrument to the ſtation (D) to take the third
angle; but from the badneſs of the ground, I could not
place the inſtrument exactly over the ſpot where the ſtaff
ſtood; from hence I took the third angle of the triangle;
the fixed teleſcope pointing to (A) and the ſame precau-

7   tions

tions of adjuſtment being obſerved, the angle to **C** came out 65° 15′; leſs by one minute than it ſhould have been. I then took from the ſame place the angle to the mountain (E) 275° 1′; more by one minute than the correſponding angle at the oppoſite ſtation (B): but the errors correcting each other, the whole angle C D E=150° 14′= the whole angle C B E.

By the triangle A B C, A C comes out 1771,4 feet:

By the triangle A B E, A E comes out 9265,0 feet:

Therefore the diſtance C E is   -   11036,4 feet.

Angle of the mountain's elevation ſeen from C   7° 44′:

Height of the mountain above C   -   1498,8 feet:

+ height of C above the water's edge   5:

Height of the mountain above the water's edge 1503,8 feet.

I prefer this obſervation to the others, becauſe the three angles of the triangle A B C came out exactly 180 degrees by the obſervation. The diſtance A C found by the computation, differed only four feet from that by the meaſure; but, the ground being uneven, I did not depend upon the meaſure, but took it merely as a check upon the operation, to detect an error, in caſe of any great difference.

The diſtance found by the ſimilar triangles

B C E and C D E comes out   -   11037 feet;

The angle of the mountain's elevation ſeen

from A was   -   -   8° 50′;

Hence the height of the mountain above

A was found   -   -   -   1439,8 feet:

Depreſſion of C ſeen from A was   1° 54′;

Hence

Hence the height of A above C is   -   58,7 feet ;
Height of the mountain above C   1498,5 feet :
+ height of C above water's edge   -   5 ;
Height of mountain above the level of the fea 1503,5 feet;
which differs from that found by the fingle angle three
tenths of a foot.

I cannot account for the great difference between the
geometrical meafure and the barometrical one according
to M. De Luc's calculation, which amounts to 84,7 feet.
I have no reafon to doubt the accuracy of Dr. Irving's obfervations, which were taken with great care.   As to the
geometrical meafure, the agreement of fo many triangles,
each of which muft have detected even the fmalleft error,
is the moft fatisfactory proof of its correctnefs.   Since my
return, I have tried both the theodolite and barometer,
to difcover whether there was any fault in either, and find
them upon trial, as I had always done before, very
accurate.

OBSERVATIONS

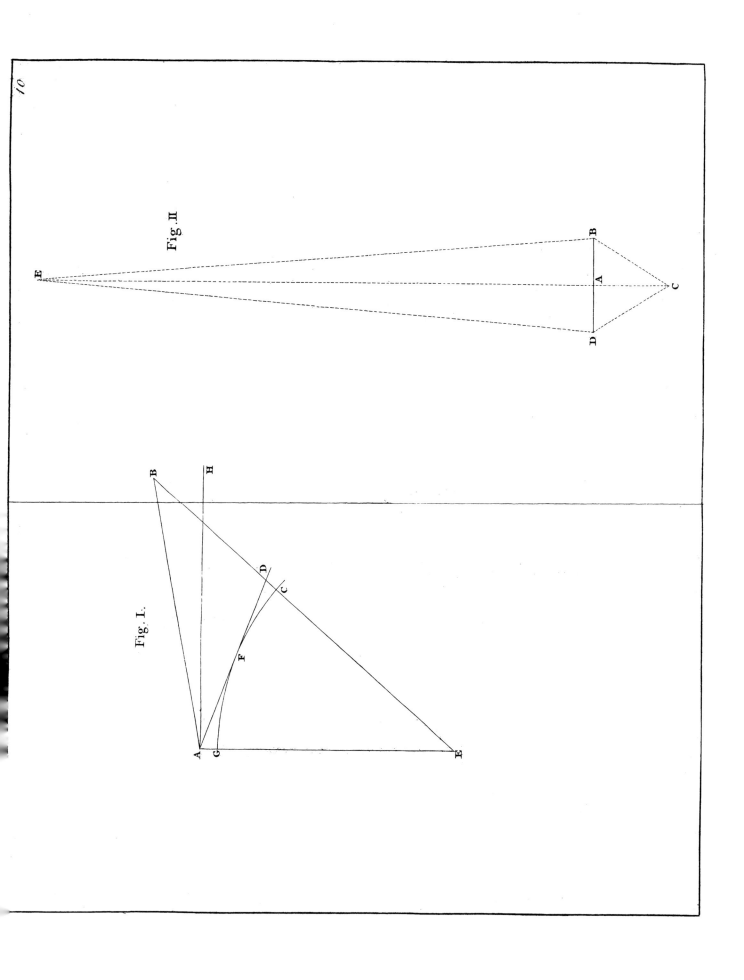

Fig. I.

Fig. II

OBSERVATIONS for determining the Acceleration of the
PENDULUM.

Defcription of the Pendulum with which the Obfervations
were made, by Mr. Cumming.

" THE apparatus with which the following experi-
" ments were made, was prepared for the voyage
" with all the care which the fhortnefs of the time
" would admit, and particular attention was paid to its
" fimplicity. The pendulum was that which the late Mr.
" George Graham had conftructed, to afcertain the exact
" diftance between the center of motion and center of
" ofcillation of a pendulum to vibrate feconds at London.

" The ball is a fphere of folid brafs, whofe diameter is
" three inches and ninety two hundredth parts of an inch;
" and whofe weight is nine pounds and one quarter.

" The rod is a round fteel wire, one tenth of an inch
" thick, and is fo firmly fcrewed into the ball, that it
" cannot be unfcrewed by hand, nor the length of the
" pendulum altered without the application of proper
" inftruments for that purpofe, there being no adjufting
" fcrew as in clock-pendulums.

" The

" The axis of the pendulum is of hard-tempered fteel,
" nearly two inches long, and moves on angular or knife-
" pivots, whofe edges are formed with great care, fo as to
" lie exactly in the fame right line ; the pivots are formed
" nearly to an angle of thirty-eight degrees from the edge
" to the back ; the fharpnefs of the edges is taken off,
" and they are carefully rounded, fo that the lower parts
" of both (on which the pendulum moves) form parts of
" one continued cylinder, whofe diameter is rather lefs
" than the two hundredth part of an inch.

" Thofe pivots move in angular notches made in two
" pieces of hardened fteel, each a quarter of an inch thick ;
" the notches are formed to an angle of one hundred
" and twenty degrees, with their bottoms fomewhat
" rounding, and formed fo that the whole length of the
" pivot has an equal bearing in them ; the ends or extremi-
" ties of the pivots are floped from the edges on which
" they move, towards the backs, or upper fide ; and
" two plates of hardened fteel are fcrewed againft the
" angular notches in which the pivots move, fo as to
" confine them always to the fame place in the notches,
" and prevent fuch irregularities as might otherwife happen
" if the fhoulders of the pivots fhould chance to touch.

" Towards one end of the axis is pierced an oblong
" fquare hole, from the upper to the under fide, into
" which the upper end of the pendulum rod (having its
" fides

" fides fomewhat flattened) is fitted, without fhake, but
" in fuch manner that it moves freely therein from back
" to front, round a fteel pin which paffes horizontally
" through it and the axis, that both the pivots may
" have an equal bearing, and the pendulum may hang
" truely perpendicular, without any tendency to bend its
" rod, and by that means alter its time of vibration, even
" though the axis be not accurately adjufted to a level
" pofition : The error which might arife from accidental
" friction on the above fuppofition, of an inaccurate
" levelling of the axis, is obviated by means of the fteel
" plates againft which the *very central point* of the loweft
" pivot muft in fuch cafe act.

" To the other end of the axis, is fcrewed a pair of
" pallets, conftructed nearly on Mr. Graham's principle
" of the *dead-beat*, but differing from it in having a
" degree of recoil which tends to render the longer vibra-
" tions of the pendulum as quick as the fhorter : but
" this precaution is the lefs neceffary, becaufe the weight
" which keeps the machine in motion is fo adjufted, as
" to make the angle of conftant vibrations as nearly as
" poffible the fame with the angle of fcapement ; that is,
" to make the vibrations the fhorteft, that will admit
" of the wheel to efcape the pallets : by this means,
" if the oil applied fhould become glutinous, fo as to
" diminifh the action of the wheel on the pendulum, or
" if any other circumftance fhould happen to fhorten the
" arc

" arc of vibration of the pendulum, the weight which
" keeps it in motion muſt be increaſed, till it is found juſt
" ſufficient to keep the machine going; by which means
" there is a certainty that the pendulum vibrates ſimilar
" arcs in each experiment, even if the obſerver ſhould not
" attend to that circumſtance.

" The ſwing-wheel is made of tempered ſteel, and the
" points of its teeth are left much thicker than they
" uſually are in clocks, in order to avoid accidents; it
" has thirty teeth, and carries with it a divided circle
" which ſhews ſeconds.

" On the axis of the ſwing-wheel there is a pinion, on
" which another wheel acts : and in the axis of this laſt,
" there is a ſmall pulley, in the groove of which is applied
" the line which keeps the machine going, by means of
" a weight and counter-weight, in the manner deſcribed
" by Huygens in the eighth and eighteenth pages of his
" *Horologium oſcillatorium :* this method is the ſimpleſt
" of any for keeping the wheels in motion while the
" weight is winding up, and is peculiarly advantageous
" in ſuch machines as this, which require frequent
" winding : the weight applied to this machine was ſix
" ounces Troy, which with a deſcent of thirty-two inches
" kept it going for three hours, with a vibration of three
" degrees.

" The

5

" The whole is contained in a ſtrong braſs frame,
" ſcrewed on the top of a three-legged wooden ſtand,
" three feet four inches high : the front legs extend three
" feet eight inches in the direction of the vibration, and
" the back leg extends three feet four inches from each of
" the front legs, at which diſtance the three legs are
" ſo connected at bottom, by horizontal rods, that
" they cannot poſſibly alter their relative poſition ; by
" theſe means the point of ſuſpenſion of the pendulum
" is rendered much more immovable than could be
" done in any portable clock having a caſe of the uſual
" dimenſions, without great trouble, and an apparatus ill
" ſuited for experiments of this nature.

" In the middle of the horizontal bar that connects the
" front legs is fixed a piece of ſilvered-glaſs, by means of
" which the whole machine is readily adjuſted to its
" proper poſition : the lower part of the pendulum-
" ball hangs directly over this mirror, on which is drawn
" a line from back to front ; and when the image of a
" ſmall pin, which is ſcrewed into the lower part of the
" pendulum, is ſeen biſected by this line viewed directly in
" front, the poſition of the machine is properly adjuſted.

" On the back leg of the ſtand, immediately behind the
" pendulum, is a hook to hang a thermometer on, for
" making frequent obſervations of the temperature of the
" air. In order to prepare for an experiment, the pendulum
A a   " is

" is made to vibrate till 60 on the fecond-circle comes to
" the index, and is then to be held at the extremity of
" its vibration by a trigger; on preffing which with the
" finger, the pendulum is difengaged in an inftant: hence
" the vibrations muft be of equal extent in every experi-
" ment.

" The wooden ftand which fupports the pendulum is
" fo conftructed, that it forms an oblong fquare box, in
" which the pendulum, with every part of its apparatus,
" is with great facility and expedition packed ; fo fecurely
" that no part can receive damage; and the whole is fo
" portable, that it may with eafe be carried on a man's
" fhoulder to any acceffible place.

" This pendulum immediately before the voyage was
" compared with a well-regulated eight-day clock, and in
" twelve hours its beat did not differ fenfibly from that of
" the clock; Fahrenheit's thermometer being then at 60°."

July the fixteenth the Pendulum and the Equatorial Inftrument were landed on a fmall rocky ifland in latitude
79° 50′ N; and the pendulum being carefully fet up in
a fmall tent erected for that purpofe, and its pofition truly
adjufted, a thermometer was fufpended on the hook
behind the pendulum-rod; and the pendulum being re-

2   peatedly

peatedly put in motion, it was found to ftop, till a mufket bullet and a half was added to the weight, which was found fufficient to keep it in motion; when it was thus found to continue its vibration, it was locked by the trigger at 60″. The equatorial inftrument was fet up on a bafis of folid rock, and being in this cafe to be ufed only as a tranfit inftrument, no attempt was made to adjuft it either to the latitude or meridian of the place; but the azimuth and equatorial circles being truely levelled, the telefcope was directed towards the fun, and fo elevated that it fhould pafs as near as poffible through the middle of the field. The inftrument being thus prepared, the Weft limb of the fun was obferved to touch the Eaft fide of the vertical wire in the telefcope at 5ʰ 19′ 28′ in the afternoon, by the watch; and at the fame inftant the pendulum was unlocked, and kept vibrating till after the fun had completed its revolution, and its Weft limb was again feen to touch the fame fide of the vertical wire.

From the vertical pofition of the wire and the time of the day, the fun's motion had a degree of obliquity with refpect to the wire, which muft occafion its diameter to take a longer time in paffing than if it croffed the wire at right angles: this pofition of the wire, together with the change of the fun's declination, prolong the time of the fun's coming again to the wire; fo that there was an interval of twenty-four hours, forty-nine feconds and a half, from the time that the fun's limb touched the wire on the fixteenth day of July, to

A a 2 the

the time of its return to the fame wire on the feventeenth day *.

During the time of this revolution of the fun, an account was kept of the thermometer, and feveral comparifons made of the rate of the going of the pendulum with my fecond-watch: in making which, I always took the time by the watch, when the pendulum fhewed 60″: thefe comparifons were chiefly intended to prevent a miftake of a whole minute in eftimating the acceleration of the pendulum, which only fhewed feconds, having no index for minutes:

* July the fixteenth P. M. at 5^h 19′ 28″ by the watch : the angle S between the vertical and circle of declination was 10° 49: the fun's altitude 20°; its declination 21° 8′: the change in the fun's declination in 24^h, was 10′ 11″ : hence the time of the fun's coming to the fame vertical hair of a telefcope, will be retarded 44″,1 : for (by Cotes, *Æftimatio Errorum*, Theor. 35.)

As fine Z P or cofine latitude, — — Comp. Ar. 0,75322
Is to tang. S. 10° 49′; — — — 9,28117
So is the change in declin. 10′ 11″ fine, — — 7,47161

To 11′ 1″ the change in the hor. angle fine, —— 7,50600

Which turned into time, gives —— — 44″,1
The change in the equation of time is —— — 5,4

Therefore the interval between the two tranfits is — 24^h 0′ 49,5
It was obferved —— —— — 24 (2) 4,5

The difference is the gain of the pendulum — — (1) 15

To

minutes: and as a candid inveſtigation of a matter that had ſo much engaged the attention of the beſt philoſophers and mathematicians was the only objeḋ of my wiſh, I judged it beſt, in the firſt place, to give the obſervations juſt as they were made, regularly numbered, that they may be readily referred to from the following tables, in which the order of the original obſervations is varied, according to the periods of time between each pair of obſervations. By thus giving the foundations on which the concluſions depend, all perſons, who chuſe it, may trace and examine every ſtep towards the concluſion, and by that means be enabled to deteḋ any error that may have crept into the operation; or draw ſuch further concluſions as their ingenuity may ſuggeſt, and the materials here given may warrant.

To find the time of the ſun's diameter paſſing a vertical hair. (Cotes, *Æſtim. Error.* Theor. 21.)

As the produḋ of { Coſine declination — — Comp. Ar. 0,03024
{ Coſine S. — — Comp. Ar. 0,00778

Is to the produḋ of Radius and Coſ. Altitude; — — 19,97298

So is the ſun's diameter in time 135″,6, — — 2,13226

To the time ſought — 139″,1 = 2′ 19″,1 — 2,·4326

It was obſerved — 2′ 21″,0

Difference 1″,9

Although the obſervation of the ſun's diameter paſſing the wire has no immediate conneḋion with our concluſion; yet the agreement between the calculated and the obſerved time of its paſſing, ſerves to ſhow that the proper allowance was made for the obliquity of the direḋion in which it paſſed the wire.

Day

Day of the Month.	N°	Time by the Watch.	Time by the Pendulum.	Thermo-meter.	Remarks.
		h ''	''		
July 16th P. M. }	1	5 19 28	60	50 {	Equatorial fixed.
	2	6 30 00	. .	49½	
	3	7 00 00	. .	50	
	4	8 00 00	. .	49	
	5	8 30 00	. .	49	
	6	9 00 00	. .	45	
	7	9 30 00	. .	45	
	8	10 00 00	. .	45	
	9	11 00 00	. .	45	
	10	11 30 00	. .	48½	
	11	12 00 00	. .	48½	
	12	12 30 00	. .	46	
	13	12 39 14	60	51	
17th A. M.	14	1 00 00	. .	50½	
	15	2 55 9	60	49	
	16	5 00 00	. .	45	
	17	6 00 00	. .	44	
	18	7 00 00	. .	49½	
	19	8 00 00	. .	47	
	20	9 00 00	. .	49½	
	21	11 2 23	60	58½	
	22	12 00 20	60	56	
P. M.	23	1 00 00	. .	54	
	24	2 30 00	. .	52½	
	25	3 30 00	. .	56	
	26	4 00 00	. .	55½	
	27	4 46 10½	60	52½	
	28	[5 19 24]	4½	{	Tranfit of the Sun's Weft limb.
	29	. . .	25	{	Tranfit of the Sun's Eaft limb.
	30	5 24 9	60	51	

It

It has already been faid that the watch was ufed only to prevent an error of *whole minutes*, in eftimating the time gained by the pendulum in twenty-four hours; the exact period of twenty-four hours being determined by the revolution of the fun.

In order to obtain the acceleration of the pendulum, the original obfervations are transferred from the foregoing table, to that which follows, for the convenience of arranging them according to the length of the intervals, beginning with thofe of the fhorteft duration: fo that the conclufion from each period becomes a check upon thofe that follow.

In this table *the firft column* refers to the original obfervations, from which a conclufion is here to be drawn; thus, in the firft line, we find 27 — 30, by which is meant that a conclufion is to be drawn in this line from obfervations 27 and 30, that is, from the acceleration of the pendulum from four hours, forry-fix minutes, ten feconds and a half, to five hours, twenty-four minutes nine feconds in the afternoon, July 17.

The fecond column exprcffes the interval of time by the watch, between each pair of obfervations referred to in the firft.

The third column fhews how much the pendulum gained on the watch, in each period expreffed in the fecond.

The fourth column fhews the mean height of the Thermometer for each period.

The

The fifth column expreffes the difference between this mean height, and 60°, the height of the thermometer at London when the pendulum was adjufted.

The fixth column fhews the contraction of the pendulum rod by the degree of cold expreffed in the fifth column, according to Mr. Smeaton's experiments, publifhed in N° 79 of the Philofophical Tranfactions for the year 1754.

The feventh column fhews how much this contraction would make the pendulum gain during each period of the fecond column.

The eighth column fhews how much the pendulum would have gained on the watch in each period, if the thermometer had remained at 60°, and therefore no contraction of the pendulum-rod had taken place.

The ninth column fhews how much the watch ought to have loft in each period, allowing it to have loft uniformly at the rate of four feconds in twenty-four hours, as was obferved by the tranfit.

The tenth column fhews how much the pendulum would have gained on the watch, in each period; allowing for its lofing at the rate of four feconds in twenty-four hours, and fuppofing the thermometer to have remained conftantly at 60°.

The eleventh column fhews how much the pendulum would gain *per* hour according to the rate of acceleration given in the tenth column for each period.

T A B L E

T A B L E [*A.*]

Obſervations with the *Pendulum* from the 16th to the 18th of July, 1773, in Latitude 79° 50′ N.

1 Obſervations referred to.	2 Duration in Time by the Watch.	3 Seconds gained by the *Pendulum*, on the Watch.	4 Mean Height of the Thermometer.	5 Difference between the Height of the Thermometer at the Time of adjuſtment at London, and at the Time of Obſervation.	6 Contraction of the *Pendulum* rod by the cold, in parts of an Inch.	7 Time gained on the Watch by the contraction of the *Pendulum* rod.	8 Time gained by the *Pendulum* on the Watch, corrected for the Thermometer.	9 Time loſt by the Watch, according to its Rate of going, as determined by the tranſit.	10 Time gained by the *Pendulum* on the Mean Time, allowing for the Thermometer, and Rate of the Watch's loſing.	11 *Ratio* of Acceleration *per* Hour.
	H ′ ″	″	°	°		″	″	″	″	″
27——30	0 37 58½	1½	52	8	,0020	0,06	1,44	0,10	1,34	2,12
21——22	0 57 57	3	57	3	,0007	0,03	2,97	0,15	2,82	2,93
13——15	2 15 55	5	49¼	10¼	,0027	0,28	4,72	0,37	4,35	1,92
22——27	4 45 50½	9½	53¾	6¼	,0015	0,35	9,15	0,78	8,37	1,75
22——30	5 23 49	11	53	7	,0017	0,44	10,56	0,90	9,66	1,79
21——27	5 43 47½	12½	54½	5½	,0014	0,37	12,13	0,95	11,18	1,95
21——30	6 21 46	14	54½	5½	,0014	0,41	13,59	1,05	12,54	1,97
1——13	7 19 46	14	47½	12½	,0031	1,06	12,94	1,21	11,73	1,60
15——21	8 7 14	46	48¾	11¼	,0028	1,05	44,95	1,34	43,61	5,37
15——22	9 5 11	49	50¾	9¼	,0023	0,98	48,02	1,51	46,51	5,12
1——15	9 35 41	19	48	12	,0030	1,33	17,67	1,60	16,07	1,67
13——21	10 23 9	51	49½	10½	,0026	1,26	49,74	1,72	48,02	4,62
13——22	11 21 6	54	50	10	,0025	1,31	52,69	1,88	50,81	4,47
15——27	13 51 1½	58½	52	8	,0020	1,28	57,22	2,30	54,92	3,96
15——30	14 29 0	60	51¾	8¼	,0021	1,38	58,62	2,41	56,21	3,88
13——27	16 6 56½	63½	54	6	,0015	1,11	62,39	2,68	59,71	3,70
13——30	16 44 55	65	53¾	6¼	,0016	1,22	63,78	2,78	61,00	3,64
1——21	17 42 55	65	48¾	11¼	,0028	2,30	62,70	2,94	59,76	3,37
1——22	18 40 52	68	49¼	10¾	,0027	2,33	65,67	3,11	62,56	3,34
1——27	23 26 42½	77½	50½	9½	,0024	2,58	74,92	3,90	71,02	3,02
1——30	24 4 41	79	50¼	9¾	,0024	2,72	76,28	4,01	72,27	3,00

It appears by the original obfervations that the pendulum began its vibrations at 60″, the inftant in which the
firft limb of the fun was obferved to touch the fide of the
vertical wire in the telefcope of the Equatorial, that
is, at five hours, nineteen minutes, twenty-eight feconds
in the afternoon by the watch, on the 16th of July; and
by every comparifon of the pendulum with the watch,
that the pendulum was conftantly gaining on the watch,
and in a period of twenty-four hours, four minutes,
forty-one feconds, had gained on the watch feventy-
nine feconds; and when the revolution of the fun was
completed, it appeared, that the watch had loft four
feconds in the exact period of twenty-four hours; therefore, if four feconds loft by the watch, be fubtracted from
feventy-nine, the time gained by the pendulum on the
watch, it will leave feventy-five feconds for the time
gained by the pendulum on the *mean*, or true time, no
deduction being here made for the contraction of the pendulum-rod by the cold.

The odd fifteen feconds are determined by obferving,
that the pendulum fhewed four feconds and a half exactly
when the fun had again returned to the vertical wire; fo
that this period is determined wholly by the fun, and
totally independent of the watch; but as the watch is
found by the fame obfervation to have loft only four
feconds, recourfe is had to the intermediate comparifons
of it with the pendulum, which clearly fhow that the

C c   pendulum

pendulum had gained *one whole minute*, together with the fifteen feconds determined by the pendulum and the revolution of the fun: and although it appears by the eleventh column of the foregoing table that the watch did not lofe uniformly at the rate of four feconds in twenty-four hours, yet its mean rate leaves as little doubt with regard to the *whole minute* gained by the pendulum, as if its going had been perfectly uniform during the whole time. For, if from the fum of all the periods in the fecond column, and of all the accelerations in the tenth, a mean rate be taken, it makes the acceleration of the pendulum on the watch to be $80''{,}79$ in twenty-four hours, which differs from the acceleration obferved by the revolution of the fun only $5''{,}75$; and from the rate of going of the watch, determined by the revolution of the fun, only $1''{,}79$: hence there can be no poffible room to fuppofe an error of a whole minute.

Although the period of twenty-four hours, and the rate of going of the watch for that time, are very accurately determined by the revolution of the fun; it may not be improper here to take notice, that from a mean of fix altitudes of the fun, taken by a very good aftronomical quadrant of eighteen inches radius, the watch was computed to have loft $5''\frac{1}{4}$, in twenty-four hours, which differs from the rate given by the revolution of the fun only $1''\frac{1}{4}$; this may ferve to fhew how far the mean of a great number of obfervations by the fame obferver and

inftrument

inſtrument may be relied on, when there is no other
obſervation to check or corroborate.

It may alſo be proper here to mention, that the time
by the watch was not obſerved at the inſtant that the ſun
had returned to the vertical wire, and at which the pendulum was obſerved to ſhow 4¼ ſeconds, my attention
being wholly engaged in obſerving the pendulum. The
watch was found to have loſt 77″¼ by the pendulum, in
twenty-three hours, twenty-ſix minutes, forty-two ſeconds
and a half. An allowance according to this rate for
34′ 4″ (the ſupplement of the laſt obſervation by the
watch to the time of the ſun's paſſage when the pendulum
ſhewed 4″¼) amounts to 1″¼.

From whence it follows, that the Weſt limb of the ſun
touched the Eaſt ſide of the vertical hair at five hours,
twenty minutes, thirteen ſeconds and a half, by the
watch; which had therefore loſt four ſeconds in twenty-
four hours.

As the compariſon of the watch and the pendulum in
this one inſtance is not from actual obſervation, *at the inſtant*, but ſuppoſes that the watch had kept for thirty-
four minutes to the ſame rate of loſing at which it had
been obſerved to loſe for nearly twenty-four hours
immediately preceding; the time by the watch *thus
found* is inſerted in the table of obſervations within

hooks

hooks to diftinguifh it, that every perfon may have an opportunity of judging how far it ought to be admitted. Upon the whole it appears, that by the revolution of the fun, corrected for the oblique direction in which it paffed the vertical wire in the telefcope, the change of declination and the equation from the time of its Weft limb touching the wire on the 16th, to the time of its touching the fame wire on the 17th of July, that the pendulum gained feventy-five feconds in twenty-four hours. But as the mean height of the thermometer for the time of this experiment was $9°\frac{3}{4}$ lower than 60°, the height at which it was at London when the pendulum was compared with the clock; the pendulum ought on this account, according to Mr. Smeaton's experiments, to have been contracted $\frac{24}{10000}$ of an inch, and to have gained on that account 2,″72; fo that the acceleration of the pendulum arifing only from the difference between the latitude of London and 79° 50′ N, is 72″,28.

The pendulum was continued in motion, and the comparifons between it and the watch made as before, with intention to take a fecond revolution of the fun: but at eleven o'clock next morning, the wind being fair, and the weather cloudy fo as to afford no profpect of feeing the fun in the afternoon, the inftruments were taken on board, and the fhips failed immediately.

Auguft

Auguſt the fourteenth, we landed the Pendulum, Equatorial Inſtrument, and aſtronomical Quadrant on Smeerenberg Point, latitude 79° 44′ N; and ſet up the pendulum in every reſpect as formerly deſcribed. The equatorial and quadrant were alſo ſet up, and prepared for obſervation.

The pendulum was ſet a going when it was exactly 6^h 0′ 0″ P. M. by my watch, from which time it was frequently compared with the watch, till 5^h 50′ A. M. the 15th; when the pendulum ſtopped. It was again ſet a going with the additional weight which had formerly been uſed, when the watch was exactly 6^h 00′ 00″, and continued going from that time till after five in the morning of the 18th, in which time the thermometer was obſerved, and the watch and pendulum compared, as in the following table: many altitudes of the ſun were taken with the quadrant, on the 15th A. M. but without any further opportunity till the 18th A. M. when they were repeated to aſcertain the rate of the watch's loſing.

Day

Day of the Month.	N°	Time by the Watch.			Time by the Pendulum.	Thermometer.	Remarks.
		h	′	″	″	°	
Aug. 14th, } P. M. }	1	6	00	00	60	44	
	2	7	29	53½	60	43	
	3	12	13	30½	60	40	
15th, A. M.	4	5	00	09	60	36	The *Pendulum* set agoing with the additional Weight.
	5	6	00	00	60	35	
P. M.	6	2	09	22½	60	{ 36 36	
	7	8	59	49	60	37	
16th, A. M.	8	2	00	00	.	{ 36 36½	
	9	3	00	00	.	37	
	10	4	00	00	.	36	
	11	5	00	00	.	37	
	12	6	00	00	.	36½	
	13	7	00	00	.	37	
	14	8	00	00	.	37	
	15	9	00	00	.	37	
	16	10	00	00	.	37	
	17	11	00	00	.	37	
Noon	18	12	00	00	.	37	
P. M.	19	1	00	00	.	37	
	20	2	01	39½	60	37	
	21	3	01	34½	60	37	

Day

Day of the Month.	N°	Time by the Watch.			Time by the Pendulum.	Thermometer.	Remarks.
		h	′	″	′ ″	°	
	22	7	13	16	60	38	
	23	9	00	00	.	38	
	24	10	00	00	.	37½	
	25	11	00	57	60	37	
Midnight,	26	12	00	00	.	38	
Aug. 17th, A. M.	27	1	00	00	.	38	
	28	2	00	00	.	38	
	29	3	00	00	.	38	
	30	4	00	00	.	37½	
	31	5	00	00	.	37½	
	32	6	00	00	.	38	
	33	7	00	00	.	37½	
	34	8	00	00	.	37¼	
Noon	35	9	00	00	.	37½	
P. M.	36	10	00	00	.	38½	
	37	11	00	00	.	37	
	38	12	00	00	.	39½	
	39	1	00	00	.	40	
	40	2	02	58	60	41	
	41	4	23	45½	60	40	
	42	10	00	19½	60	39	

Between five and fix in the morning of the eighteenth, it blew hard, and the *Pendulum* ftopped.

The

The following table is conftructed in every refpect the-
fame as that defcribed page 163, and differs from
it only in having an *additional column*, in which is given
the rate of acceleration of the Pendulum in twenty-four
hours, according to the time by the watch, corrected by
a mean of fixteen altitudes of the fun taken on the 15th,
and a mean of thirty-nine altitudes on the 18th of Auguft,
from which the watch appears to have loft, during the interval of the three days, at the rate of 23″,7 per day. The
rate of acceleration of the pendulum in twenty-four hours
being thus determined, agreeable to the acceleration obferved in each of the laft eight periods, being thofe of the
longeft duration; and thefe obfervations being already
corrected for the thermometer; a mean is taken from the
whole as the true rate of acceleration of the pendulum on
mean time in twenty-four hours.

T A B L E

T A B L E [B.]

Observations with the Pendulum from the 14th to the 16th of August, 1773, in Latitude 79° 44′ N.

1 Observations referred to	2 Duration in Time by the Watch.	3 Seconds gained by the *Pendulum* on the Watch.	4 Mean Height of the Thermometer.	5 Difference of the Thermometer at the Time of adjustment in London, and at the Time of Observation.	6 Contraction of the *Pendulum* rod by the cold, in parts of an Inch.	7 Time gained on the Watch by the contraction of the *Pendulum* rod.	8 Time gained by the *Pendulum* on the Watch, corrected for the Thermometer.	9 Time lost by the Watch according to its Rate of going, as determined by the Altitudes of the Sun.	10 Time gained by the *Pendulum* on the Mean Time, allowing for the Thermometer and rate of the Watch's losing.	11 Ratio of Acceleration *per* Hour.	12 Ratio of acceleration of the *Pendulum* on the Mean Time in Twenty-Four Hours.
	h ′ ″	″	°	°		″	″	″	″	″	
20——21	0 59 55	5	37	23	,0057	0,26	4,74	0,99	3,75	3,75	
1——2	1 30 00	6½	43⅓	16⅔	,0042	0,25	6,25	1,47	4,78	3,19	
40——41	2 20 47½	12½	40	20	,0050	0,54	11,96	2,31	9,65	4,11	
41——42	5 36 34	26	40	20	,0050	1,25	24,75	5,63	19,12	3,41	
1——3	6 13 30	29½	40¾	19¼	,0049	1,41	28,09	6,14	21,95	3,52	
5——6	8 9 22½	37½	36	24	,0060	2,26	35,24	8,04	27,20	3,34	
1——4	11 0 9	51	38¾	21¼	,0054	2,70	48,30	10,86	37,44	3,41	
5——7	14 59 49	60	36	24	,0060	4,17	55,83	14,79	41,04	2,73	″
25——42	22 59 22½	97½	38½	21½	,0054	5,75	91,75	22,71	69,04	3,00	. . 72,07
21——40	23 01 23	96½	38	22	,0055	5,86	90,64	22,73	67,91	2,95	. . 70,79
6——20	23 52 17	103	36	24	,0060	6,60	96,40	23,55	72,85	3,05	. . 73,24
20——40	24 01 18	101½	38¼	21¾	,0054	6,00	95,50	23,72	71,78	2,99	. . 71,71
6——21	24 52 12	108	36⅔	23⅓	,0057	6,75	101,25	24,59	76,66	3,08	. . 73,98
21——41	25 22 11	109	38	22	,0055	6,49	102,51	24,43	78,08	3,07	. . 73,86
6——40	47 53 35½	204½	38	22	,0055	12,20	192,30	45,49	146,81	3,06	. . 73,57
5——42	64 00 19½	280½	37½	22½	,0056	16,67	263,83	63,20	200,63	3,13	. . 75,23
											Mean 73,06
											Which gives the Acceleration of the Pendulum on true Time from the change of Latitude.

From

The material originally positioned here is too large for reproduction in this reissue. A PDF can be downloaded from the web address given on page iv of this book, by clicking on 'Resources Available'.

From the result of this table, the time gained by the pendulum in twenty-four hours of mean time, after deducting the acceleration on account of the contraction of its rod by the cold, is seventy-three seconds, and six hundredths of a second; which is one second, and two hundredths of a second more than by the result of the observations of the 16th and 17th of July. But although the rate of going of the watch from the 15th to the 18th days of Auguft, was ascertained by a mean of fifty-five altitudes of the sun, I am inclined to give the preference to the observations of July, where the exact period of twenty-four hours was determined by a revolution of the sun, observed with a telescope whose magnifying power was sixty. And notwithstanding that the height of the thermometer during the time of observation in August was remarkably uniform, and that the watch was found by the comparisons with the pendulum to have lost during the whole time as uniformly as could reasonably be expected; yet a small irregularity in its rate of going near the beginning or end of the observation, might occasion the difference of this result from the former.

As the time corrected by the mean of six altitudes of the sun taken on the 16th and 17th July, differed only one second and a half from that observed by the

E e   revolution

revolution of the fun, there is reafon to believe that the period of three days, determined by a mean of fifty-five altitudes, taken on the 15th and 18th of Auguft, might be relied on to one fecond at moft: and that, although the conclufion from the obfervations of Auguft are not fo decifive, on account of its depending in fome fmall degree on the regularity of the watch, it ftrongly corroborates the conclufion from the obfervations in July, as it proves that the acceleration of the pendulum proceeded from an uniform caufe, which produced equal effects in each cafe. This is yet further proved, by comparing the pendulum when it returned to London with the fame clock with which it had been compared before the voyage, the thermometer being at this time alfo at 60°, and the additional weight of a mufket bullet and a half being applied to the weight which kept it going; the pendulum and the clock were found to agree fo well, that no fenfible difference could be diftinguifhed in their beats for the fpace of twelve hours.

From all which circumftances it may fairly be concluded, that a pendulum which vibrates feconds at London, will gain from feventy-two to feventy-three feconds in twenty-four hours, in latitude 79° 50'; allowing the temperature of the air to be the fame at both places.

4   Thefe

Thefe obfervations give a figure of the earth nearer to Sir Ifaac Newton's computation than any others which have hitherto been made.

According to Sir Ifaac Newton the Pendulum gains in latitude 79° 50′,   66″,9 ;

In which cafe the equatorial diameter
would be to the polar as   -   -   230 to 229 :

According to Mr. Bradley's computation,
from Mr. Campbell's obfervations,   76,6 ;

Equatorial diameter to the polar as   -   201 to 200 :

According to Maupertuis,   -   -   86,5 ;

Equatorial diameter to the polar as   -   178 to 179 :

According to my obfervations,   - $\begin{cases} 72,28 \\ 73,06 \ ; \end{cases}$

Equatorial diameter to the polar as   - $\begin{cases} 212,9 \text{ to } 211,9 \\ 210,7 \text{ to } 209,7 : \end{cases}$

The mean of which is very nearly as   -   212 to 211.

R E F E R E N C E to P L A T E   XI.

Fig. 1. Is a general view of the apparatus when fitted up; the pendulum being locked by the trigger, and ready for an experiment.

Fig. 2. The upper part of fig. 1, on a larger fcale, in order to fhew the feveral parts more diftinctly.

Fig. 3. Reprefents the whole frame and apparatus when packed for carriage.

Fig. 4. Is the cap which covers the wheels and pallets, detached from fig. 3.

A.   Fig 1. The pendulum-ball.

B. B.   The pendulum-rod.

C. C. Fig. 2. The axis of the pendulum.

D.   -   An oblong hole in the axis, into which the end of the pendulum-rod is fitted, and fecured by means of the fteel pin d.

E. E.   -   The upper part of the wooden frame; to which the three legs are ftrongly fixed by hinges and table-joints, and on which is fcrewed

F. F. F. F. A ftrong brafs frame which fupports the pendulum and wheels.

G. G.

G. G. Fig. 1. A flat board that forms one of the fides of the box, fig. 3, and has two fmall mortifes near its ends, which receive the points of the fore-legs of the ftand; two fmall fteel rods, which are jointed near the lower end of the back-leg hook into the ends of this board, fo as to preferve the relative pofition of the three legs unalterable: and near the middle of it is fitted

H.   -   A piece of filvered glafs, with a diamond line on it from back to front, for adjufting the pofition of the ftand: and

I.   ⌐   The trigger for locking the pendulum.

K.   -   A wooden wedge which is occafionally put under either end of the board G. G. to adjuft the ftand to its proper pofition; and when packed, is put in its place, as reprefented in the figure.

L. L. L.   Pieces of wood fcrewed to the legs, having cavities in them which embrace the pendulum-ball when the legs of the ftand are brought together in order to be packed, as in fig. 3.

M.   -   A flat piece of wood, under the ends of which are confined the fteel rods that conneɛt the back leg of the ftands to the board G. G. when the ftand is packed.

N. A turn-

N.   -   A turn-button, under which the line which carries the weights is put when packed for carriage.

O.   -   A pin on which the weights are put when packed.

P.   -   The pulley and ratchet by means of which the machine is kept going whilſt it is winding up.

Q.   -   The weight that keeps the pendulum in motion.

R.   -   The counter-weight.

S.   -   The index which ſhows the ſeconds on a divided circle fixed on the axis of the ſwing-wheel.

T.   -   The thermometer ſuſpended on a hook immediately behind the pendulum wire.

W. W.   Two leather ſtraps that ſecure the whole when packed, as in fig. 3.

NATURAL

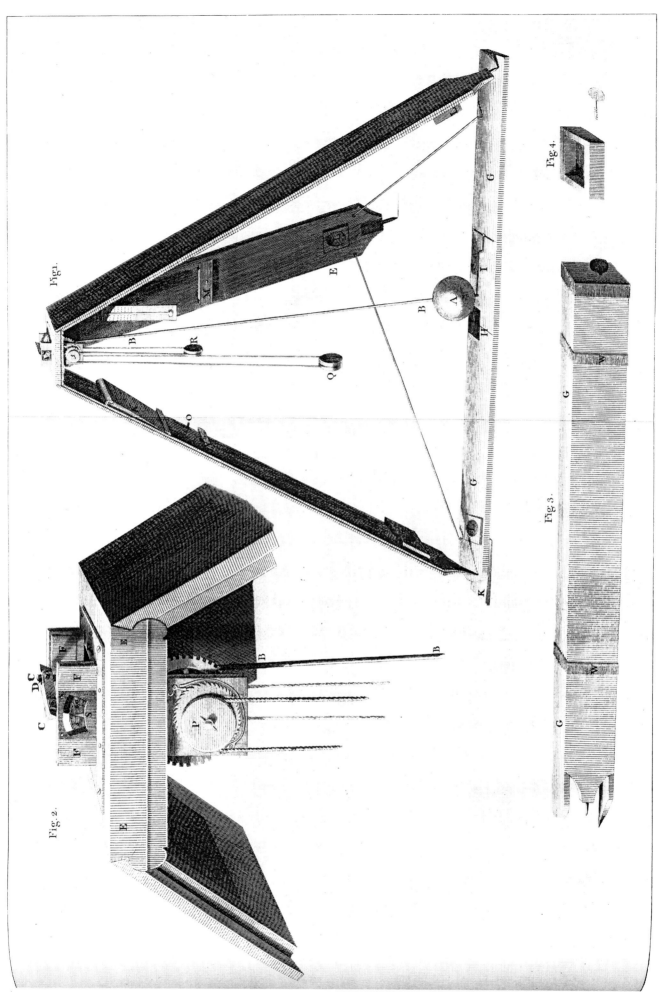

N A T U R A L   H I S T O R Y.

THOUGH the ſhortneſs of my ſtay at Spitſbergen, and the multiplicity of occupations, in which I was neceſſarily employed, during the greateſt part of that time, rendered it impoſſible for me to make many obſervations on its natural productions; yet as there are among thoſe few ſome which have not before been made public, I am in hopes that this article will not be found wholly unprofitable. The following catalogue, imperfect as it is, may ſerve to give a general idea of the ſparing productions of that inhoſpitable climate.

As modern naturaliſts have formed the technical terms of their ſcience out of the Latin, it becomes neceſſary to make ſome uſe of that language, in order to render the deſcriptions of ſuch things as are new, intelligible to thoſe for whoſe uſe they are intended : I ſhall always, however, annex Engliſh names to the ſcientifick ones, when ſuch are to be found.

MAMMALIA.

MAMMALIA.

TRICHECHUS *Rofmarus, Linn. Syft. Nat.* 49. 1.
Arctick Walrus. *Penn. Syn. Quadr.*
p. 335.

This animal, which is called by the Ruffians Morfe, from thence by our feamen corruptly Sea Horfe, and in the Gulph of St. Lawrence Sea Cow, is found every where about the coaft of Spitfbergen, and generally where-ever there is ice, though at a diftance from the land. It is a gregarious animal, not inclined to attack, but dangerous if attacked, as the whole herd join their forces to revenge any injury received by an individual.

PHOCA *Vitulina. Linn. Syft. Nat.* 56. 3.
Common Seal. *Penn. Syn. Quadr.* p. 339.

Found on the çoaft of Spitfbergen.

CANIS *Lagopus. Linn. Syft. Nat.* 95. 63.
Arctick Fox. *Penn. Syn. Quadr.* p. 155.

Found on the main land of Spitfbergen and iflands adjacent, though not in any abundance. It differs from our Fox, befides its colour, in having its ears much more rounded. It fmells very little. We ate of the flefh of one, and found it good meat.

5   URSUS

Ursus *Maritimus. Linn. Syft. Nat.* 70. 1.

Polar Bear. *Penn.Syn. Quadr.* p. 192. T. 20. F. 1.

Found in great numbers on the main land of Spitfbergen; as alfo on the iflands and ice fields adjacent. We killed feveral with our mufquets, and the feamen ate of their flefh, though exceeding coarfe. This animal is much larger than the black bear; the dimenfions of one were as follows:

	Feet.	Inches.
Length from the fnout to the tail, -	7	1
Length from the fnout to the fhoulder-bone,	2	3
Height at the fhoulder, - - -	4	3
Circumference near the fore legs, - -	7	0
Circumference of the neck clofe to the ear,	2	1
Breadth of the fore paw, - - -	0	7
Weight of the carcafs without head, fkin or entrails, - - -	610 lb.	

Cervus *Tarandus. Linn. Syft. Nat.* 93. 4.

Rein Deer. *Penn. Syn. Quadr.* p. 46. T. 8. F. 1.

Found every where on Spitfbergen.

We ate the flefh of one which we killed, and found it excellent venifon.

Balaena *Myfticetus. Linn. Syft. Nat.* 105. 1.

Common Whale. *Penn. Brit. Zool.* p. 85.

F f   This

This species, which is sought after by the fishermen in preference to all other whales, is found generally near the ice. We saw but few of them during our stay.

BALAENA *Physalus. Linn. Syst. Nat.* 106. 2.
Fin Fish. *Penn. Brit. Zool.* p. 41.
Found in the ocean near Spitsbergen.

A   V   E   S.

ANAS *mollissima. Linn. Syst. Nat.* 198. 15.
Eider Duck. *Penn. Brit. Zool.* p. 454.
Found on the coast of Spitsbergen.

ALCA *arctica. Linn. Syst. Nat.* 211. 4.
The Puffin. *Penn. Brit. Zool.* p. 405.
Found on the coast of Spitsbergen.

ALCA *Alle. Linn. Syst. Nat.* 211. 5.
Found on the coast of Spitsbergen in great abundance.

PROCELLARIA *glacialis. Linn. Syst. Nat.* 213. 3.
The Fulmar. *Penn. Brit. Zool.* p. 431.
Found on the coast of Spitsbergen.

COLYMBUS *Grylle. Linn. Syst. Nat.* 220. 1.
Found on the coast of Spitsbergen.

5

COLYMBUS *Troile. Linn. Syst. Nat.* 220. 2.
Found on the coast of Spitsbergen.

COLYMBUS *glacialis. Linn. Syst. Nat.* 221. 5.
　　　The great Northern Diver. *Penn. Brit.*
　　　Zool. p. 413.
Found on the coast of Spitsbergen.

LARUS *Rissa. Linn. Syst. Nat.* 224. 1.
Found on the coast of Spitsbergen.

LARUS *Parasiticus. Linn. Syst. Nat.* 226. 10.
　　　The Arctick Gull. *Penn. Brit. Zool.* p. 420.
Found on the coast of Spitsbergen.

LARUS *Eburneus*, niveus, immaculatus, pedibus
　　　plumbeo-cinereis.
Found on the coast of Spitsbergen.

This beautiful bird is not described by Linnæus, nor, I believe, by any other author; it is nearly related indeed to the Rathsher, described by Marten in his voyage to Spitsbergen, (See page 77 of the English translation) but, unless that author is much mistaken in his description, differs essentially from it. Its place in the *Systema Naturæ* seems to be next after the *Larus nævius*, where the specifick difference given above, which will distinguish

it

it from all the fpecies defcribed by Linnæus, may be inferted.

DESCRIPTION.

Tota avis (quoad pennas) nivea, immaculata.
Roftrum plumbeum.
Orbitæ oculorum croceæ.
Pedes cinereo-plumbei. *Ungues* nigri.
Digitus Pofticus articulatus, unguiculatus.
Alæ cauda longiores.
Cauda æqualis, pedibus longior.
Longitudo totius avis, ab apice roftri ad finem caudæ,   Uncias 16
Longitudo inter apices alarum expanfarum,   -   37
——— Roftri,   -   -   -   -   2

STERNA *Hirundo. Linn. Syft. Nat.* 227. 2.
The greater Tern. *Penn. Brit. Zool.* p. 428.
Found on the coaft of Spitfbergen.

EMBERIZA *nivalis. Linn. Syft. Nat.* 308. 1.
The greater Brambling. *Penn. Brit. Zool.* 321.
Found not only on the land of Spitfbergen, but alfo upon the ice adjacent to it, in large flocks: what its food can be is difficult to determine; to all appearance it is a
granivorous

granivorous bird, and the only one of that kind found in thefe climates, but how that one can procure food in a country which produces fo few vegetables, is not eafy to guefs.

AMPHIBIA.

CYCLOPTERUS *Liparis. Linn. Syſt. Nat.* 414. 3.
    Sea Snail. *Penn. Brit. Zool.* III. p. 105.

Two only of thefe were taken in a trawl near Seven Ifland Bay.

PISCES.

GADUS *carbonarius. Linn. Syſt. Nat.* 438. 9.
    The Coal Fifh. *Penn. Brit. Zool.* III. p. 152.

Though we trawled feveral times on the North fide of Spitfbergen, and the feamen frequently tried their hooks and lines, yet nothing was taken except a few individuals of this and the foregoing fpecies.

INSECTA.

CANCER *Squilla. Linn. Syſt. Nat.* 1051. 66.
    The Prawn. *Merr. Pin.* 192.

Found

Found in the ftomach of a feal, caught near the coaft of Spitfbergen.

Cancer *Boreas,* macrourus, thorace carinato aculeato, manibus lævibus, pollice fubulato incurvo.

Tab. XII. Fig. 1.

This fingular fpecies of Crab, which has not before been defcribed, was found with the former in the ftomach of a Seal; its place in the *Syftema Naturæ* feems to be next after *Cancer Norwegicus.*

DESCRIPTION.

Thorax ovatus, tricarinatus: *Carinæ laterales* tuberculofæ, antice fpina acuta terminatæ; *Carina dorfalis* fpinis tribus vel quatuor validis armata; antice producta in roftrum porrectum, acutum, breve, Thorace quintuplo brevius; præter fpinas carinarum, anguli laterales thoracis antice in fpinas terminantur.

Antennæ duæ, thorace fere triplo breviores, bifidæ: *Ramulus fuperior* craffiufculus, filiformis, obtufus; *Inferior* gracilis, fubulatus.

Palpi duo, duplicati; *Ramus fuperior* foliatus, feu explanatus in *laminam* ovalem, obtufam, longitudine antennarum, intus et antice villis ciliatam; *Ramus interior* antenniformis, fubulatus, multiarticulatus, antennis triplo longior.

Paraftatides

Paraſtatides decem, anteriores parvi; poſtremi magni, pediformes articulo ultimo explanato in laminam ovali-oblongam.

Pedes decem, duo primores cheliferi, carpis incraſſatis, reliqui ſimplices; pares ſecundi et tertii filiformes, graciles; quarti et quinti craſſiuſculi.

Cauda thorace longior, ſexarticulata; articulis quinque anterioribus carinatis, carinis ſpina antrorſum vergente armatis; articulus ſextus ſupra bicarinatus, muticus, terminatus *foliolis* quinque, articulis caudæ longioribus; intermedio lanceolato, acuto, porrecto, craſſo, ſupra planiuſculo, quadricarinato carinis interioribus obſoletis, ſubtus concavo; lateralibus ovali-oblongis, obtuſis.

Neuſteri decem (nulli ſub articulo ultimo) duplicati: Foliolis lanceolatis, ciliatis.

Obſ. Specimina magnitudine variant, alia triuncialia, alia ſeptem uncias longa.

CANCER *Ampulla*, macrourus, articularis, corpore ovali, pedibus quatuordecim ſimplicibus, laminis femorum poſtici paris ovato-ſubrotundis.

Tab. XII. Fig. 3.

This ſingular animal was alſo taken out of the ſtomach of the ſame ſeal in which the two former were found. Its place in the *Syſtema Naturæ* is next to *Cancer Pulex*.

DESCRIPTION.

DESCRIPTION.

Infectum ex ovali-oblongum, glabrum, punctulatum, articulis quatuordecim compositum, quorum primus capitis est, septem thoracem mentiuntur, et sex caudam tegunt.

Capitis clypeus antice inter antennas in processum conicum, acutum descendit.

Antennæ quatuor, subulatæ, articulatæ, simplices, corpore decuplo breviores.

Pedes quatuordecim, simplices, unguiculati; *femora* postremi paris postice acuta, lamina dimidiato-subrotunda, integra, magna, quatuor lineas longa.

Cauda foliata, foliolo unico brevi bifido: *Laciniæ* lanceolatæ, acutæ.

Neusteri duodecim, duplicati, subulati, pilis longis ciliati, posteriores retrorsum porrecti.

Obs. Specimina magnitudine variant, uncialia et biuncialia erant.

CANCER *nugax*, macrourus, articularis, pedibus quatuordecim simplicibus, laminis femorum sex posteriorum dilatatis subrotundo cordatis.

Tab. XII. Fig. 2.

This animal, which has not before been described, should be inferted in the *Syftema Naturæ* near *Cancer Pulex*; it was taken in the trawl near Moffen Ifland.

4 DESCRIPTION.

DESCRIPTION.

Infectum oblongum, compreſſum, dorſo rotundatum, glabrum, ſeſquiunciale, articulis quatuordecim compoſitum, quorum primus capitis eſt, ſeptem thoracem mentiuntur, et ſex caudam efficiunt.

Capitis Clypeus ſinu obtuſo antice pro antennis emarginatus.

Antennæ quatuor, ſubulatæ, multiarticulatæ; *ſuperiores* corpore ſextuplo breviores, bifidæ: articulo baſeos communi, magno; *Ramulus* interior exteriori duplo brevior.

Inferiores ſimplices, ſuperioribus duplo longiores.

Pedes quatuordecim, ſimplices, unguiculati, unguibus parum incurvis. *Femora* ſex poſteriora poſtice aucta.

Lamina foliacea, ſubrotundo-cordata, dimidiata, margine integra, magna, (tres lineas longa.)

Cauda apice foliata. *Foliolis* duobus, oblongis, obtuſis, parvis.

Neuſteri duodecim, duplicati, lineari-lanceolati, poſteriores retrorſum porrecti, ut facile pro appendicibus caudæ ſumantur.

CANCER *Pulex. Linn. Syſt. Nat.* p. 1055. 81.
Taken up in the trawl along with the former.

G g   VERMES.

V E R M E S.

Sipunculus *Lendix*, corpore nudo cylindraceo, apertura fubterminali. Tab. XIII. Fig. 1.

Found adhering, by its fmall fnout, to the infide of the inteftines of an Eider Duck. Mr. Hunter, who at my requeft diffected it, informed me that he had feen the fame fpecies of animal adhering to the inteftines of whales.

Description.

Corpus croceum, fubcylindraceum, tres lineas longum, craffitie pennæ pafferinæ, utraque extremitate parum attenuatum, apice terminatum in *Roftrum* anguftum corpore quintuplo brevius, quo tunicis internis inteftinorum fefe affigit ; prope alteram extremitatem *Apertura* fimplex, pro lubitu extenfibilis.

A. A piece of the inteftine, with the animals adhering thereto.

B. One of the animals magnified.

C. The fame cut open.

Ascidia *gelatinofa*. *Linn. Syft. Nat.* 1087. 2.

Taken

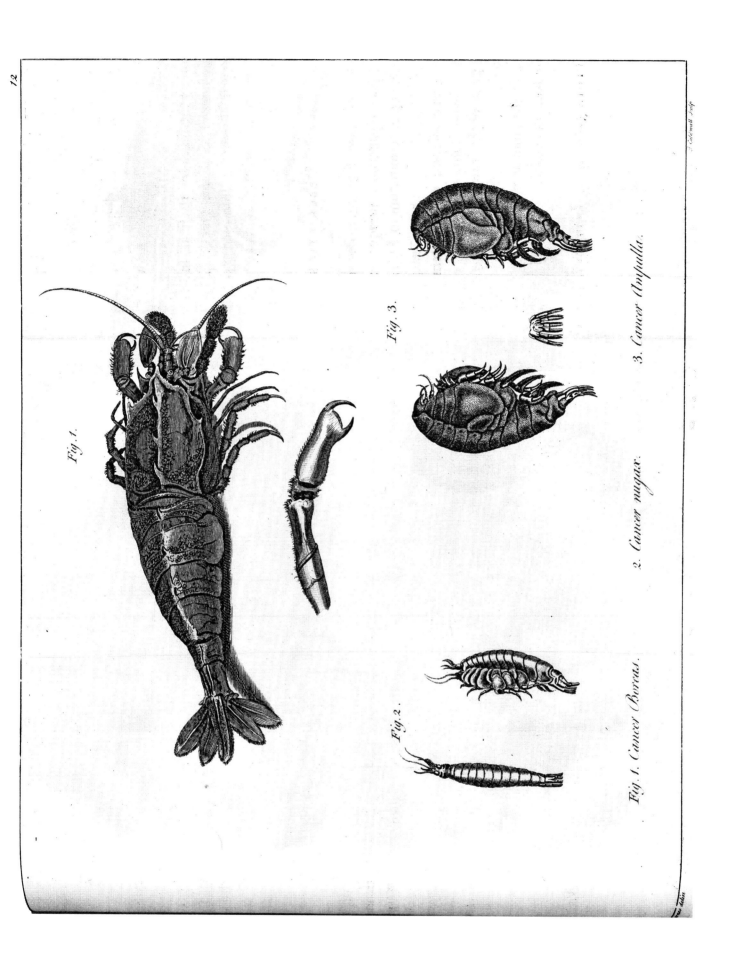

Fig. 1.

Fig. 2.

Fig. 3.

Fig. 1. Cancer Boreas.

2. Cancer nugax.

3. Cancer Ampulla.

Taken up in the trawl, on the North fide of Spitfbergen.

Ascidia *ruftica. Linn. Syft. Nat.* 1087. 5.
Taken up likewife in the trawl, on the North fide of Spitfbergen.

Lernea *branchialis. Linn. Syft. Nat.* 1092. 1.
Found in the gills of the Sea fnail mentioned before.

Clio *helicina* nuda corpore fpirali.
> *Marten's Spitfbergen Englifh*, p. 141. t. Q. fig. *e.* Snail flime fifh.

Found in innumerable quantities throughout the Arctick feas.

DESCRIPTION.

Corpus magnitudine pifi, in fpiram ad inftar helicis involutum.

Alæ ovatæ, obtufæ, expanfæ, corpore majores.

Clio *limacina* nuda, corpore obconico.
> The Sea May Fly. *Marten's Spitfbergen Englifh*, p. 169. Tab. P. f. 5.

This

This little animal is found where the laft is, in equal abundance, peopling as it were this almoft uninhabited ocean. Marten fays that they are the chief food of the whale-bone whale; and our fifhermen, who call them by the name of whale food, are of the fame opinion.

MEDUSA *capillata. Linn. Syft. Nat.* 1097. 6.
    Sea Blubber.

Taken up on the paffage home, about the latitude 65°

ASTERIAS *pappofa. Linn. Syft. Nat.* 1098. 2.
Taken up on the North fide of Spitfbergen.

ASTERIAS *rubens. Linn. Syft. Nat.* 1099. 3.
    Sea Star.

Alfo taken up in the trawl on the North fide of Spitfbergen.

ASTERIAS *Ophiura. Linn. Syft. Nat.* 1100. 11.

We likewife took this up in the trawl, on the North fide of Spitfbergen.

ASTERIAS *pectinata. Linn. Syft. Nat.* 1101. 14.

This, as well as all the reft of this genus, was taken up in the trawl on the North fide of Spitfbergen.

CHITON

CHITON *ruber*. *Linn*. *Syſt*. *Nat*. 1107. 7.
>Coat of Mail Shell.

Taken in the trawl, on the North ſide of Spitſbergen.

LEPAS *Tintinnabulum*. *Linn*. *Syſt*. *Nat*. 1168. 12.
>Acorn Shell.

Was picked up on the beach of Smeerenberg harbour; but as it is much worn and broken, it is impoſſible to be certain, whether it is a native of thoſe ſeas, or has been brought there by accident.

MYA *truncata*. *Linn*. *Syſt*. *Nat*. 1112. 26.
Likewiſe found on the beach in Smeerenberg harbour.

MYTILUS *rugoſus*. *Linn*. *Syſt*. *Nat*. 1156. 249.
Was found with the former on the beach at Smeerenberg.

BUCCINUM *carinatum*, teſta oblongo-conica tranſverſim ſtriata; anfractibus ſuperioribus oblique obtuſeque multangulis; inferioribus unicarinatis.
Tab. XIII. Fig. 2.
Found on the beach at Smeerenberg harbour.
N. B. The ſhell has been reverſed by a miſtake of the engraver.

TURBO

Turbo *helicinus*, tefta umbilicata convexa obtufa : an-fractibus quatuor lævibus.

Taken up in the trawl, on the North fide of Spitfbergen.

Serpula *fpirorbis. Syft. Nat.* 1265. 794.

Found in plenty fticking to the ftones and dead fhells in Smeerenberg harbour.

Serpula *triquetra. Linn. Syft. Nat.* 1265. 795.

Found with the laft adhering to dead fhells.

Sabella *fruftulofa*, tefta folitaria libera fimplici curvata : fragmentis conchaceis fabulofifque.

Taken up in the trawl on the North fide of Spitfbergen.

DESCRIPTION.

Vagina fpithamea vel longior, craffitie pennæ anferinæ, undique tecta *fragmentis conchaceis* fæpe magnitudine unguis, et fabulis magnitudine feminum cannabis.

Millepora *polymorpha. Linn. Syft. Nat.* 1285. 53.
Varietas rubra.

Found thrown up on the beach at Smeerenberg harbour.

CELLEPORA

CELLEPORA *pumicofa. Linn. Syft. Nat.* 1286. 56.
Found on the beach at Smeerenberg.

SYNOICUM *turgens.* Tab. XIII. Fig. 3.

Taken up in the trawl, on the North fide of Spitfbergen.

This animal is quite new to the Natural Hiftorians, and fo different from the Zoophytes which have been hitherto defcribed, that it may be confidered as a diftinct genus, whofe characters are the following:

Animalia nonnulla, ex apice finguli ftirpis fefe aperientia.

Stirpes plures, radicatæ, carnofo-ftupofæ, e bafi communi erectæ, cylindraceæ, apice regulariter pro animalibus pertufæ.

It fhould be inferted next to the Alcyonium, with which it in fome particulars agrees, but differs from it materially in having the openings for the animals only at the top, and the animals themfelves not exferted like polypes (Hydra) which is the cafe in the Alcyonium.

DESCRIPTION.

Stirpes plures, radicatæ, carnofo-ftupofæ, digitiformes, cylindraceæ, fuperne paulo craffiores, obtufæ, magnitudine digiti infantis, fuberectæ, apice orificiis nonnullis perforatæ, inferne dilatatæ feu explanatæ in bafin communem lapidibus adhærentem.

Orificia

Orificia fex ad novem, ordine circulari plerumque dif-
pofita ; fub fingulo orificio cavitas longitudinalis, forfitan
fingulo animali propria, in qua

1mo Faux angufta, brevis.

2do *Inteftinum* inftar ftomachi dilatatum, oblongo-
ovatum, inferne *foraminibus* duobus pertufum ; inter illa
foramina aliud defcendit inteftinum, valde anguftum,
filiforme, arcum brevem formans.

Cavitas, quæ per totam ftirpem longitudinaliter pro fingulo animali deorfum tendit, fuperne ab inteftinis vix dif-
tincta, infra illa autem cylindrum exhibet granulis parvis
(forfitan ovulis) repletam.

A. Shews the animals adhering to a ftone.

B. One of the animals feparate, a little magnified.

C. The fame cut open lengthways.

D. The fame cut open acrofs.

FLUSTRA *pilofa. Linn. Syft. Nat.* 1301. 3.
Found adhering to ftones in Smeerenberg harbour.

FLUSTRA *membranacea. Linn. Syft. Nat.* 1301. 5.
Found with the laft mentioned fpecies.

P L A N T Æ.

AGROSTIS *algida* panicula mutica contracta, calycibus
breviffimis inæqualibus.

2   This

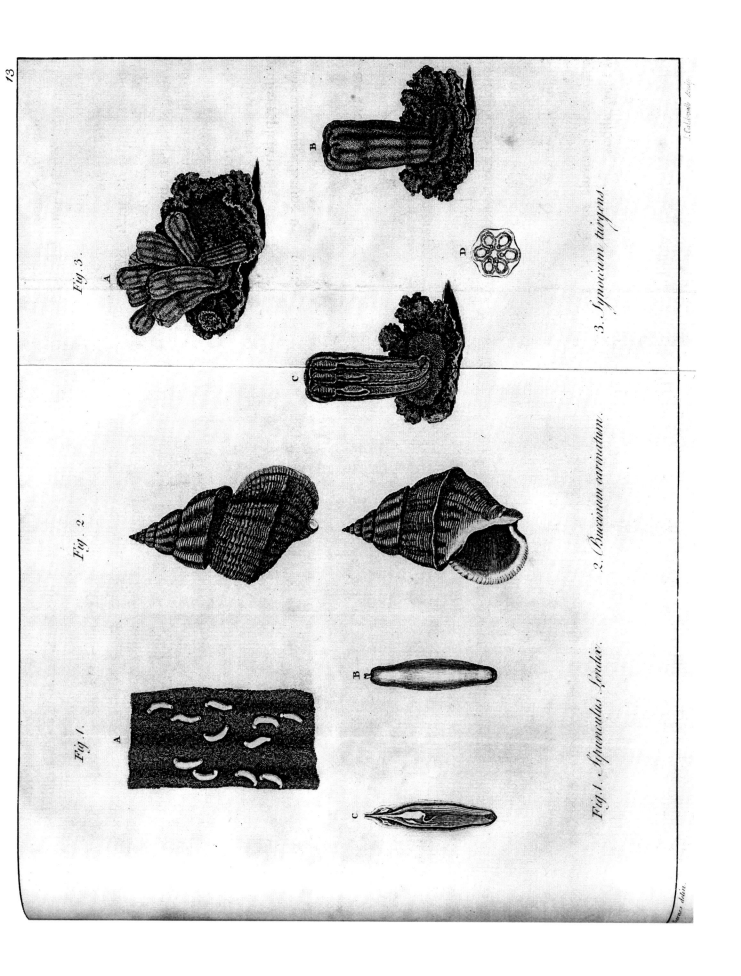

This fmall grafs, which has not before been known to botanifts, may be inferted among the fpecies of *Agroftis* next to the *minima*.

DESCRIPTION.

Gramen in cæfpitibus nafcens.

Radix fibrofa, perennis.

Folia plurima radicalia, pauciffima caulina, glabra, latiufcula, longitudine culmi, patula, bafi dilatata in vaginas laxas.

Culmi adfcendentes, glabri, fefquiunciales.

Panicula lineari-oblonga, contracta, ftricta, multiflora.

Calycis Glumæ membranaceæ, albidæ, glabræ, muticæ, inæquales: *exterior* minutiffima, ovata, obtufa; *interior* oblonga, acuta, corolla quintuplo brevior.

Corollæ Glumæ oblongæ, acutæ, carinatæ, muticæ, glabræ, femilineares: exterior paulo longior.

Stamina tria.

Stigmata duo.

Semen unicum, oblongum, utrinque acuminatum, a corolla liberum.

TILLÆA *aquatica. Linn. Spec. Plant.* 186..2.

JUNCUS *campeftris. Linn. Spec. Plant.* 468.17.

H h   SAXIFRAGA

SAXIFRAGA *oppofitifolia*. *Linn. Spec. Plant.* 575. 18.

SAXIFRAGA *cernua*. *Linn. Spec. Plant.* 577. 26.

SAXIFRAGA *rivularis*. *Linn. Spec. Plant.* 577. 28.

SAXIFRAGA *cæfpitofa*. *Linn. Spec. Plant.* 578. 34.

CERASTIUM *alpinum*. *Linn. Spec. Plant.* 628. 8.

RANUNCULUS *fulphureus*, calycibus hirfutis, caule fub-bifloro, petalis rotundatis, integerrimis, foliis inferioribus fublobatis, fupremis multipartitis.

Ranunculus quartus. *Mart. Spitz. Engl.* p. 58. T. T. F. *d*.

Obf. Primo intuitu *Ranunculo glaciali* fimillimus, differt autem, quod *Petala* rotundata, integerrima, intenfe lutea, fulgida; et *Folia* minus fubdivifa; *fuperiora* fiffa, laci-niis oblongo lanceolatis integerrimis; *inferiora caulina* lata, plana, leviter triloba vel quadriloba.

This new plant fhould be inferted next to *Ranunculus glacialis*.

COCHLEARIA *Danica*. *Linn. Spec. Plant.* 903. 3.

COCHLEARIA *Groenlandica*. *Linn. Spec. Plant.* 904. 4.

SALIX *herbacea*. *Linn. Spec. Plant.* 1445. 16.

POLYTRICHUM *commune*. *Linn. Spec. Plant.* 1573. 1.

BRYUM

BRYUM *Hypnoides. Linn. Spec. Plant.* 1584. 21.

Befides thefe, there were two other kinds of Bryum, the fpecies of which could not be determined, for want of the fructification; the one refembled Bryum trichoides læte virens, &c. *Dill. Mufc.* 391, t. 50, f. 61; and the other Bryum hypnoides pendulum, *Dill. Muf.* 394, t. 50, F. 64, C.

HYPNUM *aduncum. Linn. Spec. Plant.* 1592. 23.

JUNGERMANNIA *julacea. Linn. Spec. Plant.* 1601. 20.
Another fpecies of Jungermannia was alfo found, but without fructification; it is not much unlike Lichenaftrum ramofius foliis trifidis. *Dill. Mufc.* 489, t. 70, f. 15.

LICHEN *ericetorum. Linn. Spec. Plant.* 1608. 12.

LICHEN *Iflandicus. Linn. Spec. Plant.* 1611. 29.

LICHEN *nivalis. Linn. Spec. Plant.* 1612. 30.

LICHEN *caninus. Linn. Spec. Plant.* 1616. 48.

LICHEN *polyrrhizos. Linn. Spec. Plant.* 1618. 57.

LICHEN *pyxidatus. Linn. Spec. Plant.* 1619. 60.

LICHEN *cornutus. Linn. Spec. Plant.* 1620. 64.

Lichen *rangiferinus*. *Linn. Spec. Plant.* 1620, 66.

Lichen *globiferus*. *Linn. Mant.* 133.

Lichen *paschalis*. *Linn. Spec. Plant.* 1621. 69.

Lichen *chalybeiformis*. *Linn. Spec. Plant.* 1623. 77.

Account

Account of Doctor Irving's Method of obtaining fresh
Water from the Sea by Distillation.

AS the method of rendering salt water fresh, by
distillation, introduced by Doctor Irving into the
Royal Navy in the year 1770, and practised in this voyage,
is an object of the highest importance to all navigators,
and has not hitherto been generally known, I have added
the following very full account of its principles, apparatus,
and advantages, with which I was favoured by Doctor
Irving himself.

" Previous to an account of this method of rendering
" sea water fresh by distillation, it may not be improper
" to give a short detail of the experiments which have
" been formerly made by others on this subject; pointing
" out at the same time the several disadvantages attending
" their processes, and the general causes which obstructed
" the desired success.

" Without entering into an account of the earlier expe-
" riments, it will be sufficient to take a view of such as
" have been prosecuted with most attention, for the
" last forty years.

" The

" The firſt of theſe was the proceſs of Mr. Appleby,
" publiſhed by order of the Lords of the Admiralty, in the
" Gazette of June 22d, 1734. By the account of that
" proceſs it appears, that Mr. Appleby mixed with the
" ſea water to be diſtilled, a conſiderable quantity of the
" *Lapis Infernalis* and calcined bones. The highly un-
" palatable taſte of the water, however, excluſive of the
" extreme difficulty, if not impoſſibility, of reducing the
" proceſs into practice, prevented the further proſecution
" of this method.

" Another proceſs for procuring freſh water at ſea,
" was afterwards publiſhed by Doctor Butler. Inſtead of
" the *Lapis Infernalis* and calcined bones, he propoſed the
" uſe of ſoap leys; but though the ingredients were ſome-
" what varied, the water was liable to the ſame objections
" as in the preceding experiment. Doctor Stephen
" Hales uſed powdered chalk ; and introduced ventila-
" tion, by blowing ſhowers of air up through the diſtil-
" ling water, by means of a double pair of bellows. It
" was found by this method, that the quantity of freſh
" water obtained in a given time, was ſomewhat greater
" than what had been procured by the proceſs of Mr.
" Appleby. This invention, however, was ſubject to
" ſeveral diſadvantages. The air box which lay on the
" bottom of the ſtill, as well as the chalk, much ob-
" ſtructed the action of the fire upon the water, at the
" ſame time that the boiling heat of the latter was
                                        " diminiſhed

" diminiſhed by the ventilation : ſo that more than double
" the uſual quantity of fuel was neceſſary to produce the
" ſame effect. Beſides this method by no means improved
" the taſte of the water.

" The next who attempted any improvement was the
" learned Doctor Lind, of Portſmouth. He diſtilled ſea
" water without the addition of any ingredients ; but as
" the experiment he made was performed in a veſſel con-
" taining only two quarts, with a glaſs receiver, in his
" ſtudy, nothing concluſive can be drawn from it for
" the uſe of ſhipping. Indeed experiments of the like
" kind had been made by the chemiſts in their labora-
" tories, for at leaſt a century before.

" In the year 1765, Mr. Hoffman introduced a Still of a
" new conſtruction, with a *ſecret ingredient* ; but the large
" ſpace which this machine occupied, being ſeven feet
" five inches by five feet eight inches, and, with its ap-
" paratus, ſix feet ſeven inches high, made it extremely
" inconvenient : at the ſame time that, on account of its
" ſhallow form, the uſe of it was impracticable during
" any conſiderable motion of the ſhip. The water ob-
" tained, likewiſe, poſſeſſed all the diſadvantages common
" to the preceding methods.

" About

" About the fame time experiments were made with a
" ftill of the common conftruction, and Mr. Dove's *in-*
" *gredient.* This method was attended with no advan-
" tage over any that had been formerly ufed; the diftilled
" water was moft unpalatable; and the enormous fize of
" the apparatus, which occupied a fpace of thirteen feet
" feven inches by fix feet one inch, and fix feet five inches
" in height, rendered it impracticable on board fhips.
" An experiment was immediately afterwards made with
" the fame ftill without any ingredient; the refult, how-
" ever, was uniformly a moft unpalatable tafte of the
" water.

" About this period, alfo, M. Poiffonnier of Paris intro-
" duced into the French marine a ftill, three feet fix
" inches long, two feet wide, and eighteen inches deep.
" A portion of the chimney paffed through the upper
" part of the ftill, much in the fame manner as that of
" Mr. Hoffman: thefe gentlemen fuppofed that by this
" means they fhould fave fuel. The mouth of M.
" Poiffonnier's ftill was thirteen inches wide, on which he
" placed a tin plate, pierced like a cullender, with thirty-
" feven holes of fix lines diameter each; to thefe were
" fixed tin pipes, of the fame bore and feven inches long,
" terminating within the ftill-head. The intention of
" this contrivance is to prevent any of the water in the
" ftill from paffing over into the worm, while the fhip
" is in confiderable motion.

4   " In

" In every other refpect M. Poiffonnier employs
" a ftill-head, worm-pipe, and worm-tub, with all its
" ufual apparatus; and he directs fix ounces of *foffil*
" *alcali* to be mixed with the fea water at each diftilla-
" tion, to prevent the acid of the Magnefia falt from
" rifing with the vapour, when falt begins to form on the
" bottom of the ftill. It is probable that in M.
" Poiffonnier's ftill, which was even more fhallow in its
" form than Mr. Hoffman's, fome of the water might be
" thrown up toward the worm; in which cafe the pierced
" plate with pipes might be of fome fervice in breaking the
" direction of the water. But by Doctor Irving's tube
" this inconvenience is entirely prevented, as experience
" fully evinces, viz. in a voyage to Falkland's Iflands,
" where it has been ufed in diftillation every day; in
" feveral voyages to the Eaft Indies; and in this voyage, as
" is mentioned in the Journal.

" M. Poiffonnier, in correcting this error in the
" conftruction of his ftill, has introduced another of the
" moft capital nature in diftillation. For by means of
" the pipe-cullender, the vapour will meet with the
" greateft refiftance to its afcent, which will retard the
" progrefs of diftillation in a very high degree, and
" increafe the *Empyreuma*.

" From all the experiments abovementioned, it
" is evident, that no method had hitherto been
" invented of making fea-water frefh, which was

I i

" not

" not attended with fuch inconveniences as rendered
" the feveral proceffes of fcarce any utility. The defects
" of the various methods above enumerated, may be re-
" duced to the following heads:

" 1. The fmall quantity of water produced by the
" ordinary methods of diftillation with a ftill-head, and
" worm, could never be adequate to the purpofes of
" fhipping, though the apparatus fhould be kept in con-
" ftant ufe; and at the fame time, this mode of diftilla-
" tion required a quantity of fuel, which would occupy
" greater fpace than might be fufficient for the ftowage
" of water.

" 2. A *ftill-burnt* tafte, which always accompanies this
" method of diftillation, and renders the water extremely
" unpalatable, exciting heat and thirft, if drank when
" recently diftilled.

" 3. A total ignorance with refpect to the proper time
" of ftopping the diftillation, whereby falt was permitted
" to form on the bottom of the boiler; which burning,
" and corroding the copper, decompofed the felenitic and
" magnefia falts, caufing their acids to afcend with the
" vapour, and act on the ftill-head and worm pipe, im-
" pregnating the water with metallic falts of the moft per-
" nicious quality.

" 4. The fpace occupied by the ftill, ftill-head, and
" worm-tub, renders the ufe of them in moft cafes totally
" impracticable on board fhips. Add to this, their wearing
" out fo faft on account of the caufes above mentioned,

" the

" the great expence of the apparatus, with the hazard of
" the ftill-head being blown off, and the inconveniences
" thence arifing.

" 5. The ufe of ingredients, which though omitted in
" fome experiments in fmall, were neverthelefs erro-
" neoufly confidered as effential to the making fea-water
" fweet and palatable by diftillation.

" 6. The inconvenience of a cumberfome apparatus,
" calculated only to be eventually ufeful in unexpected
" diftrefs for water, but conftantly occupying a great deal
" of room in a fhip, too neceffary for the ordinary pur-
" pofes to be fpared for that object.

" Having fpecified the principal defects of the feveral
" methods hitherto propofed for making fea water frefh,
" it will be proper before ftating the advantages of Doctor
" Irving's method, to confider briefly the principles of
" diftillation in general, and the chemical analyfis of
" fea water.

" Water, in an exhaufted receiver, rifes in vapour more
" copioufly at 180° of Fahrenheit's thermometer, than in
" the open air at 212°, which may be confidered as its
" boiling point.

" It therefore follows, that any compreffion upon the
" boiling fluid checks the vapour in rifing, and confe-
" quently diminifhes the quantity of water obtained. This
" is clearly examplified in the fteam-engine, where the

I i 2   " confumption

" confumption of water in the boiler is very inconfider-
" able, in comparifon to what would happen if the
" compreffion arifing from the throat-pipe and valve of
" that machine was taken off, and the preffure of the
" atmofphere only admitted.   But by the reftraint of that
" valve, the vapour becomes hotter, and increafes in
" rarity and elafticity; qualities effential to the purpofes
" of the engine, although the reverfe of thofe which
" ought to take place in common diftillation.   For the
" columns of vapour fhould be removed from the boiling
" fluid as faft as they afcend, without fuffering any other
" refiftance than that of the atmofphere, which, in the
" ordinary bufinefs of diftillation, cannot be prevented.

" The impropriety of the common procefs of diftillation,
" will appear evident by comparing it with the above
" principles and facts.

" In the common method of diftillation, the whole
" column of vapour from a ftill of whatever fize, after
" afcending to the ftill-head, muft not only find its paffage
" through a pipe of fcarce an inch and half diameter ; but
" defcend contrary to its fpecific gravity through air
" which is fifteen times its weight, in fpiral convolutions :
" a courfe fo extremely ill adapted to the progrefs of an
" elaftic vapour, that frequently the ftill-head is blown off
" with incredible violence, owing to the increafed heat

3   " and ·

" and elafticity of the vapour confined by this conftruction.
" In the mean time, the external furface of the pipe
" communicates heat to the water in contact with it,
" which, inftead of being entirely carried off, mixes with
" the furrounding fluid, and heats the whole, rendering
" it unfit for condenfing the vapour within; efpecially
" when it is confidered that the fubftance of the pipe is at
" leaft a quarter of an inch thick.

" From what has been faid, it is plain, that the quan-
" tity of diftilled water will be leffened in proportion to
" the refiftance made to the afcent of the vapour, while
" the difficulty of condenfation will be greatly augmented,
" in confequence of the increafed heat and elafticity of
" the vapour. But thefe difadvantages, however great,
" refpecting the mode of diftillation, give rife to another
" evil of a ftill more important nature, as affecting the
" diftilled fluid with a noxious *burnt tafte* or *empyreuma*;
" occafioned by the vapour, highly heated, paffing over
" fo much furface of metal, viz. the ftill-head, crane-neck,
" and a pipe of fix or feven feet in length, before it reaches
" the water in the worm tub.

" Having difcuffed the fubject of diftillation, we come
" now to treat of the chemical analyfis of fea water.

" Sea-water

" Sea water contains chiefly a neutral falt, compofed of
" foffil alcali and marine acid. It likewife contains a falt
" which has magnefia for its bafis, and the fame acid.
" Thefe two falts are blended together in our common
" falt in England, which is prepared by quick boiling
" down fea water. But when the procefs is carried on by
" the fun, or a flow heat, they may be collected fepa-
" rately; that which has the foffil alcali for its bafis
" cryftallizing firft; and this is of a vaftly fuperior quality
" for preferving meat, and for the other culinary pur-
" pofes. The mother liquor now remaining, being
" evaporated, affords a vitriolic magnefia falt, which in
" England is manufactured in large quantities, under the
" name of Fpfom falt.

" Befides thefe falts, which are objects of trade, fea-
" water contains a felenitic falt, a little true Glauber's falt,
" often a little nitre, and always a quantity of gypfeous
" earth fufpended by means of fixed air.

" The fpecific gravity of fea-water to that of pure dif-
" tilled water, is at the Nore as 1000 to 1024,6; in the
" North fea as 1000 to 1028,02.

" The quantity of falt obtained by boiling fea-water in
" different latitudes, from 51° 30′ to 80°,43 N. L. is in-
" ferted in a table in the former part of this Appendix.

" Sea-water,

" Sea-water, when boiled down to a ftrong brine, admits
" with difficulty the feparation of frefh water from it; the
" diftillation becoming flower as the ftrength of the brine
" increafes, fo that a greater quantity of fuel is confumed
" in procuring a fmaller portion of water, and this like-
" wife of a bad quality. From this effential circumftance
" arifes the neceffity of letting out the brine by the cock
" of the boiler, when the diftillation is advanced to a
" certain degree; and of adding more fea-water to con-
" tinue the procefs if required.

" The defects of the feveral fchemes formerly propofed for
" rendering fea-water frefh being pointed out, the general
" principles of diftillation explained, and the component
" parts of fea-water analytically examined; the advan-
" tages of the method invented by Doctor Irving remain
" to be ftated, which may be reduced to the following:
" 1. The abolifhing all ftills, ftill heads, worm pipes,
" and their tubs, which occupy fo much fpace as to
" render them totally incompatible with the neceffary
" bufinefs of the fhip; and ufing in the room of thefe,
" the fhip's kettle or boiler, to the top whereof may oc-
" cafionally be applied a fimple tube, which can be eafily
" made on board a veffel at fea, of iron plate, ftove
" funnel, or tin fheet; fo that no fituation can prevent a
" fhip from being completely fupplied with the means of
" diftilling fea-water.

" 2. In

" 2. In confequence of the principles of diftillation
" being fully afcertained, the contrivance of the fimpleft
" means of obtaining the greateft quantity of diftilled
" water, by making the tube fufficiently large, to receive
" the whole column of vapour; and placing it nearly in a
" horozontal direction to prevent any compreffion of the
" fluid, which takes place fo much with the common
" worm.

" 3. The adopting the fimpleft and moft efficacious
" means of condenfing vapour; for nothing more is re-
" quired in the diftillation but keeping the furface of the
" tube always wet ; which is done by having fome fea-
" water at hand, and a perfon to dip a mop or fwab into
" this water, and pafs it along the upper furface of the
" tube. By this operation the vapour contained in the
" tube will be entirely condenfed with the greateft rapi-
" dity. imaginable ; for by the application of the wet mop
" thin fheets of water are uniformly fpread, and mechani-
" cally preffed upon the furface of the hot tube ; which
" being converted into vapour, make way for a fucceffion
" of frefh fheets; and thus both by the evaporation and
" clofe contact of the cold water conftantly repeated, the
" heat is carried off more effectually than by any other
" method yet known.

" 4. The carrying on the diftillation without any addi-
" tion, a correct chemical analyfis of fea water having
" evinced the futility of mixing ingredients with it, either
" to prevent an acid from rifing with the vapour, or to
" deftroy

" deſtroy any bituminous oil ſuppoſed to exiſt in ſea
" water, and to contaminate the diſtilled water, giving it
" that fiery unpalatable taſte inſeparable from the former
" proceſſes.

" 5. The aſcertaining the proper quantity of ſea water
" that ought to be diſtilled, whereby the freſh water is
" prevented from contracting a noxious impregnation of
" metallic ſalts, and the veſſel from being corroded and
" otherwiſe damaged by the ſalts caking on the bottom
" of it.

" 6. The producing a quantity of ſweet and wholeſome
" water, perfectly agreeable to the taſte, and ſufficient
" for all the purpoſes of ſhipping.

" 7. The taking advantage of the dreſſing the ſhip's
" proviſions, ſo as to diſtil a very conſiderable quantity
" of water from the vapour which would otherwiſe be
" loſt, without any addition of fuel.

" To ſum up the merits of this method in a few
" words :

" The uſe of a ſimple tube, of the moſt eaſy con
" ſtruction, applicable to any ſhip's kettle. The rejecting
" all ingredients. Aſcertaining the proportion of water to
" be diſtilled, with every advantage of quality, ſaving of
" fuel, and preſervation of boilers. The obtaining freſh
" water, wholeſome, palatable, and in ſufficient quantities.

K k

Taking

" Taking advantage of the vapour which afcends in the
" kettle while the fhips provifions are boiling.

" All thefe advantages are obtained by the abovemen-
" tioned fimple addition to the common fhip's kettles.
" But Doctor Irving propofes to introduce two further
" improvements.

" The firft is a hearth, or ftove, fo conftructed, that the
" fire which is kept up the whole day for the common
" bufinefs of the fhip, ferves likewife for diftillation;
" whereby a fufficient quantity of water for all the œcono-
" mical purpofes of the fhip may be obtained, with a very
" inconfiderable addition to the expence of fuel.

" The other improvement is that of fubftituting, even
" in the largeft fhips, caft-iron boilers, of a new con-
" ftruction, in the place of coppers."

DIRECTIONS for DISTILLING SEA-WATER.

" As foon as fea-water is put into the boiler, the tube
" is to be fitted either into the top or lid, round which,
" if neceffary, a bit of wet linen may be applied, to
" make it fit clofe to the mouth of the veffel; there will
" be

" be no occafion for luting, as the tube acts like a funnel
" in carrying off the vapour.

" When the water begins to boil, the vapour fhould
" be allowed to pafs freely for a minute, which will
" effectually clean the tube and upper part of the boiler.
" The tube is afterwards to be kept conftantly wet, by
" paffing a mop or fwab, dipped in fea-water, along its
" upper furface. The wafte water running from the mop,
" may be carried off by means of a board, made like a
" fpout, and placed beneath the tube.

" The diftillation may be continued till three fourths of
" the water be drawn off, and no further. This may be
" afcertained either by a gauge-rod put into the boiler,
" or by meafuring the water diftilled. The brine is then
" to be let out.

" Water may be diftilled in the fame manner while the
" provifions are boiling.

" When the tube is made on fhore, the beft fubftance
" for the purpofe is thin copper well tinned, this being
" more durable in long voyages than tin plates.

" Inftead of mopping, the tube, if required, may have
" a cafe made alfo of copper, fo much larger in diameter
" as to admit a thin fheet of water to circulate between
K k 2   " them

" them, by means of a fpiral copper thread, with a pipe
" of an inch diameter at each end of the cafe; the
" lower for receiving cold water, and the upper for
" carrying it off when heated.

" When only a very fmall portion of room can be
" conveniently allowed for diftillation, the machine
" (N° 2. in the Plate), which is only twenty-feven inches
" long, may be fubftituted, as was done in this voyage.
" The principal intention of this machine, however, is to
" diftil rum and other liquors; for which purpofe it has
" been employed with extraordinary fuccefs, in preventing
" an *empyreuma*, or *fiery* tafte."

Explanation of Plate XIV.

" Figure 1, reprefents in perfpective a fection of the
" two boilers taken out of the frame. In the back
" part at D, E, are feen openings for the cocks. On
" the top is a diftilling tube A, B, C, five inches dia-
" meter at A, and decreafing in fize to three inches at C;
" the length from B to C is five feet. Near C is a ring
" to prevent the water which is applied to the furface
" from mixing with the diftilled water. In the infide of
" the tube, below B, is a fmall lip or ledging, to hinder
" the diftilled water from returning into the boiler by the
" rolling of the fhip.

" In

" In figure 2, A, B, C, D, reprefent a vertical fection
" of a copper box, twenty-feven inches long, feven inches
" wide, and eleven in height, tinned on the infide.   In
" the bottom F, is an aperture about fix inches in diameter,
" having a ring to fit on the ftill or boiler.   The dotted
" lines which run nearly horizontal, are veffels of thin
" copper, tinned on the outfide, two feet long, feven
" inches wide, and three quarters of an inch deep.   At
" G is a funnel to receive cold water, which is conveyed
" into the veffels by communicating pipes, contrived in
" fuch a manner as to form a complete and quick circu-
" lation of the water through their whole extent.   When
" the water is become hot by the action of the fteam, it
" is difcharged by the horizontal pipe at A.   E is a pipe
" from which the diftilled water or fpirits run, and is bent
" in fuch a form, that the liquor, running from it, acts
" as a valve, and hinders any fteam from efcaping that
" way.   On the top of the box, at H, is a fafety-valve,
" which prevents any danger from a great accumulation
" of vapour, not condenfed for want of a proper fupply
" of cold water."

ACCOUNT

Account of the Astronomical Observations and Time-Keepers, by Mr. Lyons.

" THE obfervations for finding the time at fea, were
" taken with a brafs Hadley's Sextant of eighteen
" inches radius, made by Dollond; and fometimes by
" Captain Phipps, with a fmaller of four inches radius,
" made by Ramfden, which commonly agreed with the
" other within a minute. The error of the fextant
" was generally found by obferving the diameter of the
" Sun; which if the fame as double the femidiameter
" fet down in the Nautical Almanac, fhewed that the
" inftrument was perfectly adjufted; if it differed, the
" difference was the error of the fextant. It was necef-
" fary to know this error of adjuftment very exactly,
" and therefore I generally repeated the obfervation of
" the Sun's diameter feveral times, and from the mean
" of the refult found the error of the fextant. This error
" will equally affect all the obfervations taken near
" the fame time, and therefore cannot be difcovered
" from the comparifon of feveral obfervations. Under
" the equator, an error of one minute in altitude, near
" the prime vertical, will only produce an error of
" four feconds in the apparent time; but in the latitude

of

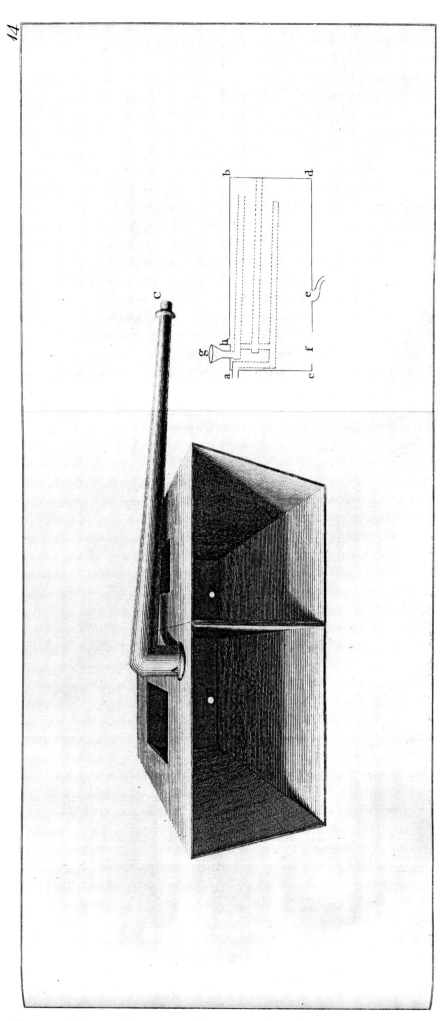

" of eighty degrees it will caufe an error of twenty-three
" feconds. As we generally took feveral fucceffive ob-
" fervations, any error in the obfervation itfelf will be
" generally independent of the reft; and as I have calcu-
" lated each feparately, the conclufions will fhew which
" are erroneous, by their differing much from the mean
" of all, which cannot but be very near the truth.

" In calculating thefe obfervations, I found by the
" logboard how much we had altered our latitude fince
" the laft obfervation; and fometimes, when we had
" an obfervation the noon following the obfervation
" for the time, the latitude of the fhip at the time
" the altitudes were taken was inferred from it. As moft
" of our altitudes were obferved when the fun was near
" the prime vertical, a fmall error in the latitude will
" not produce any confiderable change in the time;
" indeed, if it is exactly in the prime vertical, it will not
" make any change at all.

" To find the Longitude from thefe obfervations: to
" the apparent time found by calculation, apply the
" equation of time according to its fign, which will
" give the mean time; the difference between which and
" that marked by the watch, will fhew how much it is
" too flow or too faft for mean time.

" Captain

" Captain Phipps's pocket watch, made by Mr.
" Arnold, when compared with the regulator at Green-
" wich, May 26th, was twenty-four feconds too flow;
" it was there found to lofe twelve feconds and a quarter
" a day on mean time. From this it is eafy to find
" what time it is at Greenwich at any moment fhewn by
" the watch.

" The watch was compared every day about noon
" with the two time-keepers made by Meff. Arnold and
" Kendal; and from this comparifon, and their rates of
" going previoufly fettled at Greenwich, together with
" knowing how much they differed from mean time at
" Greenwich before we fet out, was calculated the table
" which fhews what the mean time is at Greenwich
" according to each time-keeper, when the watch is at
" twelve hours.

" By the help of this table, we may eafily find the
" longitude of the fhip, as deduced from the going
" of each time-keeper. Having found how much the
" watch is too faft or too flow for mean time at the
" fhip, we know what the mean time is at the fhip
" when the watch is at twelve hours; and by the table
" we can find what is the mean time at Greenwich at
" the fame time, fuppofing each time-keeper had kept
" the fame rate of going as it had before our departure:

4   the

" the difference of thefe mean times will give the longi-
" tude of the fhip.

" For example, June 19th, in the afternoon, the
" watch was 1' 24" too flow for mean time at the place
" where we obferved; therefore, when the watch fhews
" twelve hours, the mean time at this place was 12^h 1' 24".
" At this time I find by the table, that according to
" Kendal's time-keeper, the mean time at Greenwich was
" 12^h 2' 7": from this fubtracting 12^h 1' 24", the mean
" time at the fhip, the remainder, 0' 43" is the difference
" of meridians; which, converted into parts of a degree,
" gives 0° 10' 45" for the longitude of the fhip according
" to Kendal, which is to the Weftward, becaufe the mean
" time at the fhip is lefs than that at Greenwich.

" When we were on fhore, the obfervations were
" made with an Aftronomical Quadrant, divided by Mr.
" Ramfden, of eighteen inches radius, which was
" placed on a folid rock of marble; the error of the line
" of collimation was found by inverting the quadrant,
" which was adjufted by a fpirit level. The weather did
" not permit us to take correfponding altitudes of the
" Sun, fo that we determined the apparent time by com-
" putation from altitudes of the Sun's limb; having before
" fettled the latitude of the place of obfervation, from
" meridian altitudes of the Sun's limbs taken with
" the fame inftrument.

L l   " The

" The Latitudes of the ſhip were determined moſt com-
" monly by the meridian altitude of the Sun's lower limb;
" in a few inſtances, by that of his upper limb, when the
" lower was not ſo diſtinct, or was hid by clouds. The
" height of the eye above the level of the ſea, in all theſe
" obſervations, was ſixteen feet. When we could not get
" a meridian obſervation, we made uſe of the method
" deſcribed in the Nautical Almanac for 1771, from two
" altitudes taken about noon, and at a little diſtance from it.

" It ſometimes happens that we can only take ſome
" altitudes very near the time of noon. If we have
" obſerved any altitudes of the Sun near the prime vertical,
" we may thence determine how much the watch is too
" faſt or too ſlow for apparent time; and conſequently,
" how much the time when the altitudes were taken, is
" diſtant from noon; it therefore remains to find how
" much theſe altitudes are different from the meridian
" altitude. This may eaſily be found by the following
" Rule:

" To the logarithm of the riſing, taken out of the
" tables in the Nautical Almanac for 1771, add the com-
" plement arithmetical of the logarithmic coſine of the
" ſuppoſed meridian altitude; from the ſum (the index
" being increaſed by five) ſubtract the logarithm ratio
" (found by the rules in the abovementioned Ephemeris)
" the remainder is the logarithmic ſine of the change in
" altitude.

" E X A M P L E.

"E X A M P L E. I.

" June the twenty-firſt, the altitude of the Sun's center
" was obſerved to be 46° 6' at 16' 45" after apparent noon;
" the latitude by account was 67° 17'; the Sun's declination
" being then 23° 28' N, the ſuppoſed meridian altitude
" 46° 11'.

" Suppoſed Latitude 67° 17' Co. Ar. Cof. 0,41322. Riſing 16' 45" 5. 2,42643
" Sun's declination 23 28 Co. Ar. Cof. 0,03749. Suppoſed Mer. Alt. Ar. Co. Cof. 0,15967

7,58610

" Log. Ratio 0,45071 0,45071

" The change in Altitude is +0° 5' Sine 7,13539
" Obſerved Altitude 46 6

" Meridian Altitude 46 11
" Declination 23 28

" Altitude of the Equator 22 43
" Latitude 67 17 N

" As the altitudes for determining how much the watch
" differs from apparent time were taken near the prime
" vertical, a great error in the ſuppoſed latitude will make
" a very inſenſible change in the apparent time; nor will
" it create any great difference in the variation of altitude
" near noon in a given time, as will appear by the following
" computation:

" Suppoſe

" Suppofe the latitude by account was 68° 17′, a degree
" greater than before.

5.
" Suppofed Latitude 68° 17′ Cof. Co. Ar. 0,43178 Rifing 16′ 45″ - 2,42643
" Declination 23 28 ——— 0,03749 Suppofed Mer. Alt. 45. 11. Cof.Co.Ar. 0,15191

7,57834
" Log. Ratio 0,46927 - - 0,46927

" The change in the Sun's Altitude is 0° 4′ 25″ - - Sine 7,10907
" Obferved Altitude 46 6

" Meridian Altitude 46 10 25
" Declination 23 28

" Altitude of the Equator 22 42 25
" Latitude 67 17 35 which only differs thirty-five feconds
" from the true latitude we found before.

" E X A M P L E II.

" June the twentieth, the altitude of the Sun's center
" was obferved 0ʰ 28′ 38″ after midnight, to be 1° 13′, the
" latitude by account being 67° 40′ N.

5.
" Suppofed Latitude 67° 40′ Cof. Co. Ar. 0,42022 Rifing 28′ 38″ 2,89380
" Declination 23 28 ——— 0,03749 Suppofed Mer. Alt. 1° 8′ Cof. Co. Ar. 0,00001

7,89381
" Log. Ratio 0,45771 - - - 0,45771

" Change in the Altitude — 0° 9′ - - - Sine 7,43610
" Obferved Altitude 1 13

" Meridian Altitude 1 4
" Co-Declination 66 32

" Latitude 67 36 N

" There

" There were two time-keepers fent out for trial by the
" Board of Longitude; one made by Mr. Kendal after Mr.
" Harrifon's principles; the other, by Mr. Arnold: this
" laft was fufpended in gimmals, but Mr. Kendal's was
" laid between two cufhions which quite filled up the box.
" They were both kept in boxes fcrewed down to the
" fhelves of the cabin, and had each three locks; the key
" of one of which was kept by the captain, of another by
" the firft lieutenant, and of the third by myfelf; they
" were wound up each day foon after noon, and compared
" with each other and with Captain Phipps's watch. They
" ftopped twice in the voyage, owing to their being run
" down; they were fet a-going again, and as they had been
" daily compared together, it was eafy to know how
" long each had ftopped, from the others that were ftill
" going; this time is allowed for in the table of the mean
" time at Greenwich by each time-keeper.

" When we were on fhore at the ifland where we ob-
" ferved July 15th, we found how much the watch was too
" flow for mean time. When we returned from the ice to
" Smeerenberg, and again compared the watch with the
" mean time, allowing the fmall difference of longitude
" between the ifland and Smeerenberg, we found that it
" went very nearly at the fame rate, as it did when tried
" at Greenwich: fo that its rate of going was nearly the
" fame in our run from England to the ifland, from thence
" to the ice and back again to Smeerenberg, and in our
3   " voyage

" voyage from thence to England, as we found on our
" return.   By this means we were induced to give the
" preference to the watch, and to conclude that the
" longitude found by it was not very different from the
" truth.

" The principles on which this watch is conſtructed, as
" I am informed by the maker, Mr. Arnold, are theſe: the
" balance is unconnected with the wheel-work, except at
" the time it receives.the impulſe to make it continue its
" motion, which is only while it vibrates 10° out of 380°,
" which is the whole vibration ; and during this ſmall
" interval it has little or no friction, but what is on the
" pivots, which work in ruby holes on diamonds : it has
" but one pallet, which is a plane ſurface formed out of
" a ruby, and has no oil on it.

" Watches of this conſtruction go whilſt they are wound
" up ; they keep the ſame rate of going in every poſition,
" and are not affected by the different forces of the ſpring :
" the compenſation for heat and cold is abſolutely ad-
" juſtable.

" Time-keepers of this ſize are more convenient than
" larger, on ſeveral accounts; they are equally portable
" with a pocket watch, and by being kept nearly in the
" ſame degree of heat, ſuffer very little or no change from
" the viciſſitudes of the weather.

                                        " This

" This watch was exceedingly ufeful to us in our obfer-
" vations on land, as the other time-keepers could not
" fafely be moved: and indeed, in the prefent voyage,
" where they were on trial, it was contrary to the intent
" for which they were put on board, and might have been
" attended with accidents by which the rate of their going
" might have been greatly affected.

" The longitudes by Mr. Arnold's larger time-keeper
" are very different from thofe by the watch in our voyage
" back from Spitfbergen to England; owing, probably, to
" the balance-fpring being rufted, as we found when it
" was opened at the Royal Obfervatory at Greenwich,
" on our return.

" The longitudes found by the Moon are deduced from
" diftances of the Moon from the Sun's limbs, or from
" Stars, taken with the fextant; whilft the altitudes of
" the Moon and Sun, or Star, were taken by two other
" obfervers.

" In one inftance (June 26th) the obfervations were all
" made by Captain Phipps with the fmall fextant fuc-
" ceffively; and the altitudes of the Moon and Sun at the
" very inftant the diftances were obferved, are deduced
" from the changes in thefe altitudes during the interval
" of obfervation.

" I have

" I have calculated the longitude from each fet of
" obfervations feparately, to fhew how near they agree
" with each other, and what degree of precifion one
" may expect in fimilar cafes.

" Obfervations of the diftances of the Moon and Sun, or
" Stars, may be ufeful to inform us if the time-keepers
" have fuffered any confiderable change in their rate of
" going.   For if the longitude deduced from the moon
" differs above two degrees from that found by the
" watches, it is reafonable to imagine, that this difference
" is owing to fome fault in the watch, as the longitude
" found by lunar obfervations can   hardly   vary this
" quantity from the truth: but if the difference is much
" lefs, as about half a degree, it is more probable that the
" watch is right, fince a fmall error in the diftance will
" produce this difference.

" The diftances of the Moon from Jupiter were ob-
" ferved, becaufe Jupiter is a very bright object; and the
" obfervations are eafier and lefs fallacious, particularly
" that of the altitude, than thofe of a fixed ftar, whofe
" light is much fainter. This method, however, requires
" a different form of calculation, from that of the obferved
" diftance of the Moon from a fixed ftar, whofe diftances
" are computed for every three hours, in the Nautical
" Almanac. The principal difficulty in the calculation
" is to find the Moon's longitude from the obfervation of
　　　　　　　　　　　　　　　　　　　　　　　　" the

" the diftance. This I have endeavoured to facilitate by
" the following problem, which may be applied to any
" zodiacal ftar, and will be of ufe when the ftar fet down
" in the Ephemeris cannot be obferved.

"P R O B L E M.

" Having given the diftance of two objects near the
" ecliptic, with their latitudes, to find their difference of
" longitude.

"S O L U T I O N.

" Find an arc A, whofe logarithmic fine is the fum of
" the logarithms of the fines of the two latitudes and the
" logarithmic tangent of half the diftance, rejecting twenty
" from the index of the fum.

" Find an arc B, whofe logarithmic fine is the fum of
" the logarithmic verfed fine of the difference of latitude,
" and the logarithmic cotangent of the diftance, rejecting
" ten from the index of the fum.

" Then A added to the obferved diftance, and B fub-
" tracted from the fum, leaves the difference of longitude.

" If one of the latitudes is South, and the other North,
" the fum of the two arcs A and B fubtracted from the
" diftance, leaves the difference of longitude.

M m   " EXAMPLE.

"E X A M P L E.

" Auguſt the thirty-firſt, the obſerved diſtance of the
" Moon's center from Jupiter, cleared of refraction and
" parallax, was 32° 35' 52", the Moon's latitude being
" 1° 47' N, and that of Jupiter 1° 36' S.

" Latitude ☽ 1° 47' Sine 8,4930 Difference of Latitude, 3° 23' Vers. Sin. 7,2413.
" Lat. ♃ - 1 36   Sine 8,4459
" Half diſtance 16 18 Tang. 9,4660   Diſtance 32 36 Cotang. 10,1941

" Arc A. 0' 52" - - Sine 26,4049   Arc B. 9' 25" - - - Sine 17,4354
" The ſum of theſe Arcs — 10' 17" Subtracted from
" the diſtance - 32° 35 52

      " leaves 32 25 35 the difference of Longitude between the Moon and Jupiter.

" Knowing the longitude of Jupiter from the Ephe-
" meris, and the difference between it and that of the
" Moon, we may infer the longitude of the Moon by
" obſervation: and from the longitudes ſet down for
" noon and midnight of each day in the Nautical
" Almanac, find the apparent time at Greenwich when
" the Moon had that longitude, which compared with
" the apparent time at the Ship, will give the difference
" of meridians.

A Table

A Table shewing what the Mean Time is at Greenwich, by each Time-keeper, when the Pocket Watch made by Arnold is at 12ʰ.

Day of the Month.	Arnold.			Kendal.			Watch.			Day of the Month.	Arnold.			Kendal.			Watch.		
	h	′	″	h	′	″	h	′	″		h	′	″	h	′	″	h	′	″
June 2	12	0	38	11	59	56	12	1	49	July 27	11	50	34	12	5	27	12	13	5
3	12	1	1	12	0	14	12	2.	2	28	11	49	59	12	5	48	12	13	17
4	12	1	16	12	0	25	12	2	15	29	11	49	31	12	6	12	12	13	29
5	12	1	36	12	0	45	12	2	27	30	11	48	57	12	6	40	12	13	42
6	12	1	50	12	0	55	12	2	39	31	11	48	9	12	6	52	12	13	54
7	12	2	6	12	1	10	12	2	51	Aug. 1	11	47	24	12	7	0	12	14	6
8	12	2	8	12	1	10	12	3	4	2	11	46	34	12	7	12	12	14	19
9	12	1	50	12	0	53	12	3	16	3	11	45	50	12	7	32	12	14	31
10	12	2	3	12	1	5	12	3	28	4	11	44	39	12	7	34	12	14	43
11	12	2	11	12	1	28	12	3	40	5	11	43	43	12	7	38	12	14	55
12	12	2	16	12	1	34	12	3	53	6	11	42	36	12	7	31	12	15	8
13	12	2	4	12	1	28	12	4	5	12	11	58	7	.	.	.	.	.	.
14	12	2	10	12	1	38	12	4	17	13	11	56	32	.	.	.	.	.	.
15	12	2	16	12	1	48	12	4	29	14	11	55	16	12	5	21	12	16	45
16	12	1	59	12	1	35	12	4	42	15	11	54	3	12	5	38	12	16	58
17	12	2	6	12	1	48	12	4	54	16	11	52	46	12	5	53	12	17	10
18	12	2	5	12	1	51	12	5	6	17	11	51	27	12	6	10	12	17	23
19	12	2	14	12	2	7	12	5	18	18	11	50	8	12	6	33	12	17	35
20	12	2	2	12	2	3	12	5	31	19	11	48	41	12	6	38	12	17	47
21	12	1	57	12	2	5	12	5	43	20	11	47	7	12	6	52	12	18	0
22	12	1	43	12	2	3	12	5	55	21	11	45	23	12	6	58	12	18	12
23	12	1	13	12	1	30	12	6	8	22	11	43	34	12	6	47	12	18	24
24	12	1	2	12	1	39	12	6	20	23	11	41	51	12	6	55	12	18	36
25	12	0	24	12	1	17	12	6	32	24	11	39	51	12	6	58	12	18	49
26	11	59	52	12	0	59	12	6	44	25	11	37	56	12	6	56	12	19	1
27	11	59	44	12	1	4	12	6	57	26	11	35	56	12	6	58	12	19	13
28	11	59	26	12	1	2	12	7	9	27	11	34	7	12	7	15	12	19	25
29	11	59	11	12	1	3	12	7	21	28	11	32	17	12	7	32	12	19	38
30	11	58	55	12	0	59	12	7	34	29	11	30	17	12	7	32	12	19	50
July 1	11	58	45	12	1	7	12	7	46	30	11	28	9	12	7	43	12	20	2
2	11	58	29	12	1	10	12	7	58	31	11	26	14	12	7	57	12	20	15
3	11	58	20	12	1	21	12	8	10	Sept. 1	11	24	5	12	8	13	12	20	27
4	11	58	14	12	1	31	12	8	23	2	11	21	46	12	8	13	12	20	39
5	11	58	2	12	1	39	12	8	35	3	11	19	43	12	8	38	12	20	51
6	11	57	50	12	1	47	12	8	47	4	11	17	29	12	8	53	12	21	4
7	11	57	42	12	1	59	12	8	59	5	11	14	59	12	9	4	12	21	16
8	11	57	26	12	2	10	12	9	12	6	11	12	22	12	9	22	12	21	28
9	11	57	20	12	2	25	12	9	24	7	11	9	38	12	9	22	12	21	40
10	11	56	59	12	2	33	12	9	36	9	11	3	53	12	9	44	12	22	5
11	11	56	47	12	2	45	12	9	49	11	10	57	16	12	9	46	12	22	30
12	11	56	25	12	2	45	12	10	1	13	10	50	45	12	10	16	12	22	54
13	11	56	13	12	2	58	12	10	13	14	10	35	0	12	10	31	12	23	6
14	11	55	33	12	2	44	12	10	25	15	10	42	31	12	10	47	12	23	19
15	.	.	.	.	.	.	12	10	38	16	10	39	36	12	11	4	12	23	31
16	11	55	20	12	2	34	12	10	50	17	10	35	59	12	11	31	12	23	43
17	11	55	5	12	2	52	12	11	2	18	10	31	53	12	11	47	12	23	56
18	11	54	56	12	3	18	12	11	14	19	10	27	11	12	11	52	2	24	8
19	11	54	21	12	3	22	12	11	27	20	10	23	0	12	12	15	12	24	20
20	11	54	1	12	3	32	12	11	39	21	10	18	38	12	12	40	12	24	32
21	11	53	39	12	3	59	12	11	51	23	10	8	54	12	13	39	12	24	57
22	11	53	15	12	4	18	12	12	4	24	10	4	13	12	14	10	12	25	9
23	11	52	50	12	4	38	12	12	16	25	9	58	52	12	14	37	12	25	21
24	11	52	15	12	4	47	12	12	28	26	9	53	54	12	14	59	12	25	34
25	11	51	48	12	5	9	12	12	40	27	9	48	8	12	15	35	12	25	46
26	11	51	10	12	5	16	12	12	53										

Observations

Obfervations for finding the Longitude by the Time-keepers.

May 30, P. M. off Sheernefs.

Time by the Watch.	Alt. of the Sun's lower Limb.	Alt. of the Sun's Center.	Apparent Time.	Mean Time.	Watch too flow.		
h ′ ″	o ′ ″	o ′ ″	h ′ ″	h ′ ″	′ ″		
5 48 46	17 46 0	17 55 0	5 53 47	5 50 57	2 11	Mean of the	Eq. Time 2′—50″
5 51 12	17 14 0	17 23 0	5 57 25	5 54 35	3 23	two laft,	
5 53 12	16 57 0	17 6 0	5 59 10	5 56 20	3 8	3′ 15″	

	h ′ ″	h ′ ″	h ′ ″
At 12ʰ by the Watch, mean Time at the Ship,	12 3 15	12 3 15	12 3 15
At Greenwich, by the Watch,	12 1 13	by Arnold, 12 0 27	by Kendal, 11 59 49
Difference of Meridians,	0 2 2	0 2 48	0 3 26
Longitude of the Ship,	0° 30′ 30″ E	0° 42′ 0″	0° 51′ 30″

June 4, A. M.

Time by the Watch.	Alt. of the Sun's lower Limb.	Alt. of the Sun's Center.	Apparent Time.	Mean Time.	Watch too flow.		
h ′ ″	o ′ ″	o ′ ″	h ′ ″	h ′ ″	′ ″		
9 44 15	51 47 30	51 56 30	9 52 44	9 50 37	6 22		Eq. Time 2′—7″
9 47 30	52 8 0	52 17 0	9 55 32	9 53 25	5 55	Mean 6′ 9″	
9 50 0	52 27 30	52 36 30	9 58 16	9 56 9	6 9		

	h ′ ″	h ′ ″	h ′ ″
At 12ʰ by the Watch, mean Time at the Ship,	12 6 9	12 6 9	12 6 9
At Greenwich, by the Watch,	12 2 15	by Arnold, 12 1 16	by Kendal, 12 0 25
Difference of Meridians,	0 3 54	0 4 53	0 5 44
Longitude of the Ship,	0° 58′ 30″ E	1° 13′ 15″	1° 26′ 0″

June 6, A. M.

Time by the Watch.	Alt. of the Sun's lower Limb.	Alt. of the Sun's Center.	Apparent Time.	Mean Time.	Watch too flow.		
h ′ ″	o ′ ″	o ′ ″	h ′ ″	h ′ ″	′ ″		
9 49 15	52 25 0	52 33 50	9 59 43	9 57 15	8 40		Eq. Time. 1′—48″
9 51 10	52 38 45	52 46 35	10 1 41	9 59 53	8 43	Mean 8′ 51″	
9 52 45	52 51 30	53 0 20	10 3 43	10 1 55	9 10		

	h ′ ″	h ′ ″	h ′ ″
At 12ʰ by the Watch, mean Time at the Ship,	12 8 51	12 8 51	12 8 51
At Greenwich, by the Watch,	12 2 39	by Arnold, 12 1 50	by Kendal, 12 0 55
Difference of Meridians,	0 6 12	0 7 1	0 7 56
Longitude of the Ship,	1° 33′ 0″ E	1° 45′ 15″	1° 59′ 0″

Obfervations

Obfervations for finding the Longitude by the Time-keepers.

June 8, A. M.

Time by the Watch.	Alt. of the Sun's lower Limb.	Alt. of the Sun's Center.	Apparent Time.	Mean Time.	Watch too flow.		
h ′ ″	∘ ′ ″	∘ ′ ″	h ′ ″	h ′ ″	′ ″	Mean 5′ 49″	Eq. Time 1′—26″
9 28 0	48 48 0	48 56 45	9 35 11	9 33 45	5 45		1′—25″
10 54 0	57 10 0	57 19 0	11 1 19	10 59 54	5 54		

At 12ʰ by the Watch, mean Time at the Ship,   12 5 49 . . . . 12 5 49 . . . . 12 5 49

At Greenwich, by the Watch,   12 3 4 by Arnold, 12 2 8 by Kendal, 12 1 10

Difference of Meridians,   0 2 45   0 3 41   0 4 39

Longitude of the Ship,   0° 41′ 15″ E   0° 55′ 15″   1° 9′ 45″

June 8, P. M.

Time by the Watch.	Alt. of the Sun's lower Limb.	Alt. of the Sun's Center.	Apparent Time.	Mean Time.	Watch too flow.		
h ′ ″	∘ ′ ″	∘ ′ ″	h ′ ″	h ′ ″	′ ″	Mean 4′ 51″	Eq. Time 1′—16″
5 42 0	19 53 0	20 0 0	5 48 12	5 46 56	4 56		
5 44 35	19 32 0	19 38 50	5 50 38	5 49 22	4 47		
5 46 50	19 12 0	19 18 50	5 52 56	5 51 40	4 50		

At 12ʰ by the Watch, mean Time at the Ship,   12 4 51 . . . . 12 4 51 . . . . 12 4 51

At Greenwich, by the Watch,   12 3 4 by Arnold, 12 2 8 by Kendal, 12 1 10

Difference of Meridians,   0 1 47   0 2 43   0 3 41

Longitude of the Ship,   0° 26′ 45″ E   0° 40′ 45″   0° 55′ 15″

June 11, A. M.

Time by the Watch.	Alt. of the Sun's lower Limb.	Alt. of the Sun's Center.	Apparent Time.	Mean Time.	Watch too fait.		
h ′ ″	∘ ′ ″	∘ ′ ″	h ′ ″	h ′ ″	′ ″		Eq. Time 0′—51″
9 4 35	44 41 0	44 49 40	9 1 17	9 0 26	4 9	} Mean 4′ 2″	
9 6 10	44 55 0	45 3 40	9 3 1	9 2 10	4 0		
9 7 50	45 9 0	45 17 40	9 4 45	9 3 54	3 56		
10 12 49	52 36 0	52 44 50	10 5 19	10 4 28	8 21		

At 12ʰ by the Watch, mean Time at the Ship,   11 55 58 . . . . 11 55 58 . . . . 11 55 58

At Greenwich, by the Watch,   12 3 40 by Arnold, 12 2 11 by Kendal, 12 1 28

Difference of Meridians,   0 7 42   0 6 13   0 5 30

Longitude of the Ship,   1° 55′ 30″ W   1° 33′ 15″   1° 22′ 30″

Obfervations.

Observations for finding the Longitude by the Time-keepers.

June 13, A. M.

Time by Arnold.	Alt. of the Sun's lower Limb.	Alt. of the Sun's Center.	Apparent Time.	Mean Time.	Arnold too flow.		
h ′ ″	o ′ ″	o ′ ″	h ′ ″	h ′ ″	′ ″		Lat. 59° 24′
10 16 17	49 39 0	49 50 10	10 20 37	10 20 11	3 54	} Mean	Eq. Time 0—26″
10 20 17	49 55 0	50 6 10	10 24 8	10 23 42	3 25	} 3′ 26″	
10 25 35	50 18 0	50 29 10	10 29 27	10 29 1	3 26		

	h ′ ″		h ′ ″		h ′ ″
At 10ʰ by Arnold, mean Time at the Ship,	10 3 26		10 3 26 . . .		10 3 26
At Greenwich, by the Watch,	10 3 50	by Arnold,	10 1 49	by Kendal,	10 1 13
Difference of Meridians,	0 0 24		0 1 37		0 2 13
Longitude of the Ship,	0° 6′ 0″ W		0° 24′ 15″ E		0° 33′ 15″ E

June 13, P. M.

Time by Arnold.	Alt. of the Sun's lower Limb.	Alt. of the Sun's Center.	Apparent Time.	Mean Time.	Arnold too flow.		
h ′ ″	o ′ ″	o ′ ″	h ′ ″	h ′ ″	′ ″		Lat. 59° 46′ 0″
5 36 22	22 10 30	22 18 0	5 41 6	5 40 44	4 22	*	Eq. Time 0—22
5 38 55	21 52 0	21 59 30	5 43 18	5 42 56	4 1	*	
5 39 57	21 44 30	21 54 10	5 44 20	5 43 58	4 1	* Mean of	
5 41 17	21 35 0	21 42 30	5 46 25	5 46 3	4 46	the five	
5 43 3	21 20 0	21 27 30	5 48 8	5 47 46	4 43	marked *	
5 45 9	21 6 30	21 13 50	5 49 43	5 49 21	4 12	4′ 8″	
5 47 40 {	20 46 30	20 56 0	5 52 7	5 51 45	4 5	*	
	20 47 0	20 54 20	5 52 53	5 52 31	4 51	*	

	h ′ ″		h ′ ″		h ′ ″
At 6ʰ by Arnold, mean Time at the Ship,	6 4 8		6 4 8		6 4 8
At Greenwich, by the Watch,	6 3 52	by Arnold,	6 1 49	by Kendal,	6 1 14
Difference of Meridians,	0 0 16		0 2 19		0 2 54
Longitude of the Ship,	0° 4′ 0″ E		0° 34′ 45″		0° 43′ 30″

June 14, A. M.

Time by Arnold.	Alt. of the Sun's lower Limb.	Alt. of the Sun's Center.	Apparent Time.	Mean Time.	Arnold too faſt.		
h ′ ″	o ′ ″	o ′ ″	h ′ ″	h ′ ″	′ ″		Lat. 60° 17′
9 44 32	45 57 0	46 8 0	9 43 56	9 43 43	0 49		Eq. Time 0′—13″
9 48 41	46 21 0	46 32 0	9 48 20	9 48 7	0 34	Mean 0′ 48″	
9 52 53	46 41 0	46 52 0	9 52 4	9 51 51	1 2		

	h ′ ″		h ′ ″		h ′ ″
At 10ʰ by Arnold, mean Time at the Ship,	9 59 12		9 59 12		9 59 12
At Greenwich, by the Watch,	10 3 59	by Arnold,	10 1 52	by Kendal,	10 1 20
Difference of Meridians,	0 4 47		0 2 40		0 2 8
Longitude of the Ship,	1° 11′ 45″ W		0° 40′ 0″		0° 32′ 0″

Obſervations

Observations for finding the Longitude by the Time-keepers.

June 15, A. M.

Time by Arnold.	Alt. of the Sun's lower Limb.	Alt. of the Sun's Center.	Apparent Time.	Mean Time.	Arnold too flow.		
h ′ ″	o ′ ″	o ′ ″	h ′ ″	h ′ ″	′ ″		
8 26 48	38 3 0	38 13 40	8 28 16	8 28 13	1 35		Lat. 60° 17′
8 28 5	38 11 30	38 22 10	8 29 40	8 29 37	1 32	Mean 1′ 33″	Eq. Time 0—3″
8 29 8	38 20 0	38 30 40	8 30 53	8 30 50	1 42		

	h ′ ″	h ′ ″	h ′ ″
At 8ʰ by Arnold, mean Time at the Ship,	8 1 33	8 1 33	8 1 33
At Greenwich, by the Watch,	8 4 9 by Arnold,	8 1 56 by Kendal,	8 1 28
Difference of Meridians,	0 2 36	0 0 23	0 0 5
Longitude of the Ship,	0° 39′ 0″ W	0° 5′ 45″ W	0° 1′ 15″ E

June 17, A. M.

Time by Arnold.	Alt. of the Sun's lower Limb.	Alt. of the Sun's Center.	Apparent Time.	Mean Time.	Arnold too flow.		
h ′ ″	o ′ ″	o ′ ″	h ′ ″	h ′ ″	′ ″		
9 33 11	43 41 0	43 52 0	9 35 29	9 35 53	2 42		Lat. 62° 43′ 30″
9 34 58	43 51 0	44 2 0	9 38 36	9 39 0	4 2		Decl. 23 25 20
9 36 45	44 2 0	44 13 0	9 39 36	9 40 0	3 15	Mean 3′ 31″	Eq. Time 0+24
9 37 40	44 6 30	44 17 30	9 40 31	9 41 55	4 15		
9 42 4	44 30 0	44 41 0	9 45 13	9 45 37	3 33		

	h ′ ″	h ′ ″	h ′ ″
At 10ʰ by Arnold, mean Time at the Ship,	10 3 31	10 3 31	10 3 31
At Greenwich, by the Watch,	10 4 50 by Arnold,	10 2 2 by Kendal,	10 1 44
Difference of Meridians,	0 1 19	0 1 29	0 1 47
Longitude of the Ship,	0° 19′ 45″ W	0° 22′ 15″ E	0° 26′ 45″ E

June 18, P. M.

Time by the Watch.	Alt. of the Sun's lower Limb.	Alt. of the Sun's Center.	Apparent Time.	Mean Time.	Watch too flow.		
h ′ ″	o ′ ″	o ′ ″	h ′ ″	h ′ ″	′ ″		
3 32 41	35 58 30	36 9 10	3 33 5	3 33 45	1 4		Lat. 65° 25′ 0′
3 34 24	35 50 0	36 0 40	3 34 35	3 35 15	0 51	Mean 1′ 4″	Decl. 23 26 10
3 37 38	35 29 0	35 39 40	3 38 15	3 38 55	1 17		Eq. Time 0+40

	h ′ ″	h ′ ″	h ′ ″
At 12ʰ by the Watch, mean Time at the Ship,	12 1 4	12 1 4	12 1 4
At Greenwich, by the Watch,	12 5 6 by Arnold,	12 2 5 by Kendal,	12 1 5
Difference of Meridians,	0 4 2	0 1 1	0 0 4
Longitude of the Ship,	1° 0′ 30″ W	0° 15′ 15″	0° 11′ 45

Observations

Observations for finding the Longitude by the Time-keepers.

June 19, P. M.

Time by the Watch.	Alt. of the Sun's lower Limb.	Alt. of the Sun's Center.	Apparent Time.	Mean Time.	Watch too slow.		
h ' "	o ' "	o ' "	h ' "	h ' "	' "		
3 55 38	33 33 0	33 43 30	3 54 51	3 55 45	0 7	*	Lat. 66° 27' 0"
3 56 39	33 20 0	33 30 30	3 57 9	3 58 3	1 24		Decl. 23 27 10
3 58 8	33 12 0	33 22 30	3 58 33	3 59 27	1 19		Eq. Time 0+54
4 5 28	32 30 0	32 40 30	4 5 55	4 6 49	1 21	Mean of all	
4 6 8	32 25 0	32 35 30	4 6 47	4 7 41	1 33	but the two	
4 7 57	32 16 0	32 26 30	4 8 20	4 9 14	1 17	marked *	
4 8 30	32 12 30	32 23 0	4 8 57	4 9 51	1 21	1' 24"	
6 4 34	20 44 30	20 54 0	6 5 19	6 6 14	1 40		Lat. 66° 35' 0"
6 5 27	20 41 0	20 50 30	6 5 54	6 6 49	1 22		Decl. 23 27 0
6 9 9	20 9 0	20 18 20	6 11 25	6 12 20	3 11	*	Eq. Time 0+55

	h ' "	h ' "	h ' "
At 12ʰ by the Watch, mean Time at the Ship,	12 1 24	12 1 24	12 1 24
At Greenwich, by the Watch,	12 5 19 by Arnold,	12 2 14 by Kendal,	12 3 7
Difference of Meridians,	0 3 55	0 0 50	0 0 43
Longitude of the Ship,	0° 58' 45" W	0° 12' 30"	0° 10' 45"

June 21, A. M.

Time by the Watch.	Alt. of the Sun's lower Limb.	Alt. of the Sun's Center.	Apparent Time.	Mean Time.	Watch too slow.		
h ' "	o ' "	o ' "	h ' "	h ' "	' "		
8 50 33	37 14 0	37 24 40	8 52 41	8 53 56	3 23	} Mean	Lat. 67° 35' 0"
8 54 0	37 30 30	37 41 10	8 56 12	8 57 27	3 27	} 3' 25"	Decl. 23 27 55
8 59 22	37 53 0	38 3 40	9 0 57	9 2 12	2 50		Eq. Time 1+15

	h ' "	h ' "	h ' "
At 12ʰ by the Watch, mean Time at the Ship,	12 3 25	12 3 25	12 3 25
At Greenwich, by the Watch,	12 5 43 by Arnold,	12 1 57 by Kendal,	12 2 5
Difference of Meridians,	0 2 18	0 1 28	0 1 20
Longitude of the Ship,	0° 34' 30" W	0° 22' 0" E	0° 20' 0" E

Observations

Observations for finding the Longitude by the Time-keepers.

June 25, A. M.

Time by Arnold.	Alt. of the Sun's lower Limb.	Alt. of the Sun's Center.	Apparent Time.	Mean Time.	Arnold too flow.		
h ' "	o ' "	o ' "	h ' "	h ' "	' "		
7 58 27	32 31 0	32 41 30	8 34 25	8 36 32	38 5		Lat. 73° 57' 0"
8 0 40	32 36 15	32 46 45	8 35 56	8 38 3	37 23		Decl. 23 24 25
8 2 58	32 42 30	32 53 0	8 37 41	8 39 48	36 50	Mean	Eq. Time 2+7
8 3 52	32 46 15	32 56 45	8 39 28	8 41 35	37 43	37' 36"	
8 4 58	32 50 30	33 1 0	8 40 0	8 42 7	37 9		
8 5 42	32 54 0	33 4 30	8 41 0	8 43 7	37 25		

	h ' "	h ' "	h ' "
At 8ʰ by Arnold, mean Time at the Ship,	8 37 36	8 37 36	8 37 36
At Greenwich, by the Watch,	8 8 36 by Arnold,	8 2 28 by Kendal,	8 3 2

	o ' "	o ' "	o ' "
Difference of Meridians,	0 29 0	0 35 8	0 34 15
Longitude of the Ship,	7° 15' 0" E	8° 47' 0"	8° 33' 45"

June 26, P. M.

Time by the Watch.	Alt. of the Sun's lower Limb.	Alt. of the Sun's Center.	Apparent Time.	Mean Time.	Watch too flow.		
h ' "	o ' "	o ' "	h ' "	h ' "	' "		
3 31 36	29 17 0	29 27 15	4 10 25	4 12 49	41 13		Lat. 74° 25' 0"
3 34 59	29 3 0	29 13 15	4 14 10	4 16 34	41 35		Decl. 23 21 50
3 35 31	28 58 30	29 8 45	4 15 21	4 17 45	42 14		Eq. Time 2+24
3 36 55	28 55 0	29 5 15	4 16 52	4 19 16	42 21	} Mean	
3 38 14	28 49 0	28 59 15	4 17 52	4 20 16	42 2	42' 14"	
3 39 10	28 44 30	28 54 45	4 19 6	4 21 30	42 20		

	h ' "	h ' "	h ' "
At 12ʰ by the Watch, mean Time at the Ship,	12 42 14	12 42 14	12 42 14
At Greenwich, by the Watch,	12 6 44 by Arnold,	11 59 52 by Kendal,	12 0 59

	o ' "	o ' "	o ' "
Difference of Meridians,	0 35 30	0 42 22	0 41 15
Longitude of the Ship,	8° 52' 30" E	10° 35' 30"	10° 18' 45"

N n   Observations

Observations for finding the Longitude by the Time-keepers.

June 28, P. M.

Time by the Watch.	Alt. of the Sun's lower Limb.	Alt. of the Sun's Center.	Apparent Time.	Mean Time.	Watch too flow.			
h ' ''	o ' ''	o ' ''	h ' ''	h ' ''	' ''			
5 56 50	20 45 0	20 54 30	6 33 21	6 36 5	39 15	} Mean 38' 29"	Lat.	77° 30' 0"
5 58 40	20 42 0	20 51 30	6 34 18	6 37 2	38 22		Decl.	23 16·10
5 59 2	20 40 0	20 49 30	6 34 55	6 37 39	38 37		Eq. Time	2 + 44

	h ' ''	h ' ''	h ' ''
At 12ʰ by the Watch, mean Time at the Ship,	12 38 29	12 38 29	12 38 29
At Greenwich, by the Watch,	12 7 9	12 59 26	12 1 2
Difference of Meridians,	0 31 20	0 39 3	0 37 27
Longitude of the Ship,	7° 50' 0" E	9° 45' 45"	9° 21' 45"

June 29, P. M.

Time by the Watch.	Alt. of the Sun's lower Limb.	Alt. of the Sun's Center.	Apparent Time.	Mean Time.	Watch too flow.			
h ' ''	o ' ''	o ' ''	h ' ''	h ' ''	' ''			
3 41 37	27 29 0	27 39 10	4 22 41	4 25 41	44 4		Lat.	78° 1' 40"
3 43 25	27 20 0	27 30 10	4 25 1	4 28 1	44 36		Decl.	23 13 15
3 46 30	27 11 0	27 21 10	4 28 47	4 31 47	45 17	Mean 45' 25"	Eq. Time	3 + 0
3 47 44	27 6 0	27 16 10	4 30 28	4 33 28	45 44			
3 48 53	27 0 0	27 10 10	4 32 36	4 35 36	46 43			
3 50 24	26 57 0	27 7 10	4 33 29	4 36 29	46 5			

	h ' ''	h ' ''	h ' ''
At 12ʰ by the Watch, mean Time at the Ship,	12·45 25	12 45 25	12 45 25
At Greenwich, by the Watch,	12 7 21 by Arnold,	11 59 11 by Kendal,	12 1 3
Difference of Meridians,	0 38 4	0 46 14	0 44 22
Longitude of the Ship,	9° 31' 0" E	11° 33' 30"	11° 5' 30"

June 30, P. M.

Time by the Watch.	Alt. of the Sun's lower Limb.	Alt. of the Sun's Center.	Apparent Time.	Mean Time.	Watch too flow.			
h ' ''	o ' ''	o ' ''	h ' ''	h ' ''	' ''			
5 58 43	20 27 0	20 36 25	6 40 1	6 43 14	44 31	} Mean 45' 29"	Lat.	78° 7' 15"
6 0 4	20 20 0	20 29 25	6 42 21	6 45 34	45 30		Decl.	23 9 20
6 1 37	20 15 30	20 24 55	6 43 52	6 47 5	45 28		Eq. Time	3 + 13
6 2 28	20 14 15	20 23 40	6 44 17	6 47 30	45 2			

	h ' ''	h ' ''	h ' ''
At 12ʰ by the Watch, mean Time at the Ship,	12 45 29	12 45 29	12 45 29
At Greenwich, by the Watch,	12 7 34 by Arnold,	11 58 55 by Kendal,	12 0 59
Difference of Meridians,	0 37 55	0 46 34	0 44 30
Longitude of the Ship,	9° 28' 45" E	11° 38' 30"	11° 7' 30"

Observations

Obſervations for finding the Longitude by the Time-keepers.

July 2, P. M.

Time by the Watch.	Alt. of the Sun's lower Limb.	Alt. of the Sun's Center.	Apparent Time.	Mean Time.	Watch too flow.		
h ′ ″	° ′ ″	° ′ ″	h ′ ″	h ′ ″	′ ″		
5 46 4	20 55 0	21 4 30	6 28 59	6 32 34	46 30		Lat. 78° 23′ 50″
5 47 44	20 52 0	21 1 30	6 29 59	6 33 34	45 50	Mean 44′ 58″	Decl. 23 0 50
5 49 59	20 47 0	20 56 30	6 31 41	6 35 16	45 17		Eq. Time 3 + 35
5 52 57	20 41 0	20 50 30	6 33 47	6 37 22	44 25		
5 53 55	20 37 0	20 46 30	6 35 11	6 38 46	44 51	of the four	
5 54 49	20 35 0	20 44 30	6 35 47	6 39 22	44 33	laſt 44′ 32″	
5 56 35	20 30 30	20 40 0	6 37 20	6 40 55	44 20		

	h ′ ″	h ′ ″	h ′ ″
At 12ʰ by the Watch, mean Time at the Ship,	12 44 32	12 44 32	12 44 32
At Greenwich, by the Watch,	12 7 58 by Arnold,	11 58 29 by Kendal,	12 1 10

	° ′ ″	° ′ ″	° ′ ″
Difference of Meridians,	0 36 34	0 46 3	0 43 22
Longitude of the Ship, .	9° 8′ 30″ E	11° 30′ 45″	10° 50′ 30″

July 6, P. M.

Time by the Watch.	Alt. of the Sun's lower Limb.	Alt. of the Sun's Center.	Apparent Time.	Mean Time.	Watch too flow.		
h ′ ″	° ′ ″	° ′ ″	h ′ ″	h ′ ″	′ ″		
6 32 12	19 26 0	19 3 40	7 15 59	7 20 16	48 4		Lat. 79° 57′ 0″
6 36 0	19 18 0	18 55 40	7 19 19	7 23 36	47 36	Mean 47′ 41″	Decl. 22 28 20
6 38 35	19 13 0	18 50 40	7 21 24	7 25 41	47 6		Eq. Time 4 + 17
6 39 23	19 9 0	18 46 40	7 23 4	7 27 21	47 58		
6 40 57	19 5 30	18 43 10	7 24 20	7 28 37	47 40		

	h ′ ″	h ′ ″	h ′ ″
At 12ʰ by the Watch, mean Time at the Ship,	12 47 41	12 47 41	12 47 41
At Greenwich, by the Watch,	12 8 47 by Arnold,	11 57 50 by Kendal,	12 1 47

	° ′ ″	° ′ ″	° ′ ″
Difference of Meridians,	0 38 54	0 49 51	0 45 54
Longitude of the Ship,	9° 43′ 30″ E	12° 27′ 45″	11° 28′ 30″

July 11, A. M.

Time by Arnold.	Alt. of the Sun's lower Limb.	Alt. of the Sun's Center.	Apparent Time.	Mean Time.	Arnold too flow.		
h ′ ″	° ′ ″	° ′ ″	h ′ ″	h ′ ″	′ ″		
3 32 22	. . . . .	17 39 20	4 19 49	4 24 45	52 23	Mean 52′ 31″	Lat. 80° 4′ 0″
3 38 48	. . . . .	17 54 30	4 26 31	4 31 27	52 39		Decl. 22 7 20
							Eq. Time 4 + 56

	h ′ ″	h ′ ″	h ′ ″
At 3ʰ by Arnold, mean Time at the Ship,	3 52 31	3 52 3	3 52 31
At Greenwich, by the Watch,	3 16 23 by Arnold,	3 3 21 by Kendal,	3 9 19

	° ′ ″	° ′ ″	° ′ ″
Difference of Meridians,	0 36 8	0 49 10	0 43 12
Longitude of the Ship,	9° 2′ 0″ E	12° 17′ 30″	10° 48′ 0″

Obſervations

Observations for finding the Longitude by the Time-keepers.

July 12, P. M.

Correction for Error of Sextant, —4' 30"

Time by the Watch.	Alt. of the Sun's lower Limb.	Alt. of the Sun's Center.	Apparent Time.	Mean Time.	Watch too slow.		
h ' '	o ' "	o ' "	h ' "	h ' "	' "		Lat. 80° 4' 0"
7 26 25	16 5 0	16 9 10	8 15 9	8 20 18	53 53		Lat. 80° 4' 0"
7 27 58	16 3 0	16 7 10	8 16 8	8 21 17	53 19	Mean	Decl. 21 53 10
7 28 44	16 2 15	16 6 25	8 16 30	8 21 39	52 55	53' 38"	Eq. Time 5 +9
7 29 48	15 59 0	16 3 10	8 19 3	8 24 12	54 24		

	h ' "		h ' "		h ' "
At 12h by the Watch, mean Time at the Ship,	12 53 38	. . . . .	12 53 38	. . . . .	12 53 38
At Greenwich, by the Watch,	12 10 1 by Arnold,		11 56 25 by Kendal,		12 2 45
Difference of Meridians,	0 43 37		0 57 13		0 50 53
Longitude of the Ship,	10° 54' 15" E		14° 18' 15"		12° 43' 15"

On Shore on an Island near Vogel Sang, Latitude 79° 50'

Correction for Error of the Astronomical Quadrant, + 7"

Day of the Month.	Time by the Watch.	Alt. of the Sun's lower Limb.	Alt. of the Sun's Center.	Apparent Time.	Eq. Time.	Mean Time.	Watch too slow.	Means.	Co. Decl.
	h ' "	o ' "	o ' "	h ' "	' "	h ' "	' "	' "	o ' "
July 15 P. M.	3 30 53	25 21 50	25 35 29	4 16 31	5+29	4 22 0	51 7	} 51 0	68 33 2
	3 32 57	25 17 0	25 30 39	4 18 23		4 23 52	50 55	}	
	3 34 22	25 13 20	25 26 59	4 19 52		4 25 21	50 59	}	
A. M.	3 9 50	15 39 47	15 52 6	3 54 59	5+31	4 0 30	50 40		68 37 39
16 P. M.	5 55 25	18 55 12	19 8 8	6 41 1	5+35	6 46 36	51 11	} 51 5½	68 43 44
	5 59 0	18 46 10	18 59 6	6 44 25		6 50 0	51 0	}	
17 P. M.	5 31 45	19 46 40	19 59 43	6 17 17	5+40	6 22 57	51 12		68 54 0
18 A. M.	8 28 3	13 8 20	13 20 0	8 52 53	5+41	8 58 34	50 31		68 55 0

	h ' "		h ' "		h ' "
July 16, at 12h by the Watch, mean Time at the Island,	12 51 0	. . . . .	12 51 0	. . . . .	12 51 0
At Greenwich, by the Watch,	12 10 50 by Arnold,		11 55 20 by Kendal,		12 2 34
Difference of Meridians,	0 40 10		0 55 40		0 48 26
Longitude of the Island,	10° 2' 30" E		13° 55' 0"		12° 6' 30"

Observations for finding the Longitude by the Time-keepers.

July 26, P. M.

Time by the Watch.	Alt. of the Sun's lower Limb.	Alt. of the Sun's Center.	Apparent Time.	Mean Time.	Watch too slow.		
h ′ ″	° ′ ″	° ′ ″	h ′ ″	h ′ ″	h ′ ″		
3 29 25	22 46 0	22 55 40	4 25 41	4 31 43	1 2 18	} Mean 1ʰ 2′ 16″	Lat. 80° 20′ 0″
3 31 14	22 42 0	22 51 40	4 27 23	4 33 25	1 2 11		Co. Decl. 70 40 40
3 33 35	22 36 0	22 45 40	4 29 53	4 35 55	1 2 20		Eq. Time 6+2
3 35 34	22 33 30	22 43 10	4 31 4	4 37 6	1 1 32		
3 36 50	22 31 0	22 40 40	4 31 59	4 38 1	1 1 11		
3 38 47	22 29 0	22 38 40	4 32 51	4 38 53	1 0 6		

	h ′ ″	h ′ ″	h ′ ″
At 12ʰ by the Watch, mean Time at the Ship,	1 2 16	1 2 16	1 2 16
At Greenwich, by the Watch,	12 12 53 by Arnold,	11 51 10 by Kendal,	12 5 16
Difference of Meridians,	0 49 23	1 11 6	0 57 0
Longitude of the Ship,	12° 20′ 45″ E	17° 46′ 30″	14° 15′ 0″

July 27, P. M.

Time by the Watch.	Alt. of the Sun's lower Limb.	Alt. of the Sun's Center.	Apparent Time.	Mean Time.	Watch too slow.		
h ′ ″	° ′ ″	° ′ ″	h ′ ″	h ′ ″	h ′ ″		
5 51 16	16 15 0	16 23 45	6 58 31	7 4 32	1 13 16		Lat. 80° 23′ 0″
5 53 22	16 10 30	16 19 15	7 0 24	7 6 25	1 13 3		Co. Decl. 70 55 45
5 55 26	16 5 45	16 14 30	7 2 24	7 8 25	1 12 59	Mean 1ʰ 13′ 3″	Eq. Time 6+1
5 58 35	15 58 0	16 6 45	7 5 40	7 11 41	1 13 6		
6 0 56	15 53 0	16 1 45	7 7 47	7 13 48	1 12 52		

	h ′ ″	h ′ ″	h ′ ″
At 12ʰ by the Watch, mean Time at the Ship,	1 13 3	1 13 3	1 13 3
At Greenwich, by the Watch,	12 13 5 by Arnold,	11 50 34 by Kendal,	12 5 27
Difference of Meridians,	0 59 58	1 22 29	1 7 36
Longitude of the Ship,	14° 59′ 30″ E	20° 37′ 15″	16° 54′ 0″

July 28, P. M.

Time by the Watch.	Alt. of the Sun's lower Limb.	Alt. of the Sun's Center.	Apparent Time.	Mean Time.	Watch too slow.		
h ′ ″	° ′ ″	° ′ ″	h ′ ″	h ′ ″	h ′ ″		
5 22 34	17 10 0	17 18 50	6 30 46	6 36 46	1 14 12	Mean 1ʰ 14′ 24″	Lat. 80° 28′ 10″
5 28 58	16 54 30	17 3 20	6 37 34	6 43 34	1 14 36		Co. Decl. 71 9 10
							Eq. Time 6+0

	h ′ ″	h ′ ″
At 12ʰ by the Watch, mean Time at the Ship,	1 14 24	1 14 24
At Greenwich, by the Watch,	12 13 17 by Kendal,	12 5 48
Difference of Meridians,	1 1 7	1 8 36
Longitude of the Ship,	15° 16′ 45″ E	17° 9′ 0″

Observations

Obfervations for finding the Longitude by the Time keepers.

July 30, P. M.

Time by the Watch.	Alt. of the Sun's lower Limb.	Alt. of the Sun's Center.	Apparent Time.	Mean Time.	Watch too flow.		
h ′ ″	o ′ ″	o ′ ″	h ′ ″	h ′ ″	h ′ ″		
3 14 40	21 17 0	21 26 30	4 37 24	4 43 20	1 28 40		Lat. 80° 33′ 0″
3 22 6	20 59 0	21 8 30	4 45 1	4 50 57	1 28 51		Co. Decl. 71 38 50
3 26 34	20 48 45	20 58 15	4 49 21	4 55 17	1 28 43		Eq. Time 5 + 56
3 29 11	20 41 30	20 51 0	4 52 21	4 58 17	1 29 6	Mean	
3 30 54	20 37 30	20 47 0	4 54 1	4 59 57	1 29 3	1ʰ 28′ 54″	
3 32 45	20 33 30	20 43 0	4 55 33	5 1 29	1 28 44		
3 34 43	20 28 0	20 37 30	4 57 59	5 3 55	1 29 12		

		h ′ ′		h ′ ″
At 12ʰ by the Watch, mean Time at the Ship,		1 28 54	. . . .	1 28 54
At Greenwich, by the Watch,		12 13 42	by Kendal,	12 6 40
Difference of Meridians,		1 15 12		1 22 14
Longitude of the Ship,		18° 48′ 0″ E		20° 33′ 30″

July 31 P. M.

Time by the Watch.	Alt. of the Sun's lower Limb.	Alt. of the Sun's Center.	Apparent Time.	Mean Time.	Watch too flow.		
h ′ ″	o ′ ″	o ′ ″	h ′ ″	h ′ ″	h ′ ″		
3 53 30	19 26 0	19 35 10	5 18 7	5 24 1	1 30 31		Lat. 80° 37′ 0″
3 55 46	19 21 30	19 30 40	5 19 55	5 25 49	1 30 3		Co. Decl. 71 52 10
3 58 30	19 17 0	19 26 10	5 21 45	5 27 39	1 29 9		Eq. Time 5 + 54
4 0 2	19 12 30	19 21 40	5 23 29	5 29 23	1 29 21		
4 0 50	19 8 0	19 17 10	5 25 28	5 31 22	1 30 32		
4 1 57	19 7 0	19 16 10	5 26 29	5 32 23	1 30 26		
4 2 50	19 6 30	19 15 40	5 26 56	5 32 50	1 30 0	Mean	
4 4 19	19 3 0	19 12 10	5 27 31	5 33 25	1 29 6	1ʰ 29′ 55″	
4 5 36	18 59 0	19 8 10	5 29 9	5 35 3	1 29 27		
4 6 35	18 56 0	19 5 10	5 30 23	5 36 17	1 29 42		
4 7 26	18 52 0	19 1 10	5 32 1	5 37 55	1 30 29		
4 8 14	18 50 30	18 59 40	5 32 39	5 38 33	1 30 19		
4 9 23	18 49 0	18 58 10	5 33 13	5 39 9	1 29 46		

		h ′ ″		h ′ ″
At 12ʰ by the Watch, mean Time at the Ship,		1 29 55	. . . .	1 29 55
At Greenwich, by the Watch,		12 13 54	by Kendal,	12 6 52
Difference of Meridians,		1 16 1		1 23 3
Longitude of the Ship,		19° 0′ 15″ E		20° 45′ 45″

Obfervations

Observations for finding the Longitude by the Time-keepers.

At Smeerenberg, Lat. 79° 44′
By the Astronomical Quadrant, Correction for Error of Quadrant — 32″

Day of the Month.	Time by the Watch.			Alt. of the Sun's lower Limb.			Alt. of the Sun's Center.			Apparent Time.			Mean Time.			Watch too slow.		Eq. Time.		Co. Decl.		
	h	′	″	o	′	″	o	′	″	h	′	″	h	′	″	′	″	′	″	o	′	″
August 14 P. M.	5	38	30	12	24	0	12	35	0	6	30	21	6	34	31	56	1	4+10		75	50	30
	5	47	37	12	0	0	12	11	0	6	39	31	6	43	41	56	4					
	6	1	15	11	24	0	11	34	40	6	53	24	6	57	34	56	19					
	6	2	39	11	21	0	11	31	40	6	54	59	6	59	9	56	30			75	50	50
	6	5	2	11	15	0	11	25	40	6	56	54	7	1	4	56	2					
	6	6	8	11	12	0	11	22	40	6	58	4	7	2	14	56	6					
	6	7	24	11	9	0	11	19	40	6	59	15	7	3	25	56	1					
	6	8	39	11	6	0	11	16	40	7	0	0	7	4	9	55	30	4+ 9				
	6	9	45	11	3	0	11	13	40	7	1	31	7	5	40	55	55					
	6	11	3	11	0	0	11	10	40	7	2	42	7	6	51	55	48					
	6	15	44	10	48	0	10	58	30	7	7	23	7	11	32	55	48			75	51	0
	6	16	41	10	45	0	10	55	30	7	8	41	7	12	50	56	9					
	6	17	51	10	42	0	10	52	30	7	9	54	7	14	3	56	12					
	6	19	10	10	39	0	10	49	20	7	11	8	7	15	17	56	7					
	6	20	22	10	36	0	10	46	20	7	12	20	7	16	29	56	7					
15, A. M.	4	56	57	13	6	0	13	17	20	5	48	53	5	52	50	55	53	3+57		75	59	20
	4	59	20	13	12	0	13	23	20	5	51	9	5	55	6	55	46					
	5	2	26	13	21	0	13	32	20	5	54	32	5	58	29	56	3					
	5	3	35	13	24	0	13	35	20	5	55	43	5	59	40	56	5					
	5	4	46	13	27	0	13	38	20	5	56	55	6	0	52	56	6			75	59	30
	5	7	6	13	33	0	13	44	20	5	59	5	6	3	2	55	56					
	5	8	19	13	36	0	13	47	20	6	0	12	6	4	9	55	50					
	5	9	12	13	39	0	13	50	30	6	1	24	6	5	21	56	9					
	5	10	23	13	42	0	13	53	30	6	2	31	6	6	28	56	5					
	5	11	34	13	45	0	13	56	30	6	3	41	6	7	38	56	4					
	5	12	43	13	48	0	13	59	30	6	4	49	6	8	46	56	3					
	5	13	49	13	51	0	14	2	30	6	5	56	6	9	53	56	4					
	5	20	42	14	9	0	14	20	40	6	12	44	6	16	41	55	59			75	59	40
	5	22	56	14	15	0	14	26	40	6	14	59	6	18	56	56	0					
	5	24	2	14	18	0	14	29	40	6	16	5	6	20	2	56	0					
	5	27	25	14	27	0	14	38	40	6	19	28	6	23	25	56	0					
18, A. M.	4	57	8	12	15	0	12	26	0	5	50	51	5	54	19	57	11	3+28		76	56	50
	5	0	31	12	24	0	12	35	0	5	54	13	5	57	41	57	10					
	5	1	46	12	27	0	12	38	0	5	55	21	5	58	49	57	3					
	5	2	51	12	30	0	12	41	0	5	56	29	5	59	57	57	6					
	5	3	57	12	33	0	12	44	0	5	57	35	6	1	3	57	6					
	5	6	11	12	39	0	12	50	10	5	59	51	6	3	19	57	8					
	5	7	20	12	42	0	12	53	10	6	1	2	6	4	30	57	10					
	5	11	52	12	54	0	13	5	10	6	5	35	6	9	3	57	11			76	57	0
	5	13	6	12·57		0	13	8	10	6	6	42	6	10	10	57	4					
	5	15	15	13	3	0	13	14	20	6	9	0	6	12	28	57	13					
	5	16	32	13	6	0	13	17	20	6	10	8	6	13	36	57	4					
	5	17	39	13	9	0	13	20	20	6	11	15	6	14	43	57	4					
	5	19	50	13	15	0	13	26	20	6	13	29	6	16	57	57	7					
	5	20	55	13	18	0	13	29	20	6	14	37	6	18	5	57	10					
	5	22	4	13	21	0	13	32	20	6	15	48	6	19	16	57	12			76	57	10
	5	24	24	13	27	0	13	38	20	6	18	3	6	21	31	57	7					
	5	25	35	13	30	0	13	41	20	6	19	11	6	22	39	57	4					
	5	27	43	13	36	0	13	47	30	6	21	20	6	24	57	57	14					
	5	28	55	13	39	0	13	50	30	6	22	30	6	26	4	57	9					

Obfervations for finding the Longitude by the Time-keepers.

Day of the Month.	Time by the Watch.	Alt. of the Sun's lower Limb.	Alt. of the Sun's Center.	Apparent Time.	Mean Time.	Watch too flow.	Eq. Time.	Co. Decl.
	h ′ ″	o ′ ″	o ′ ″	h ′ ″	h ′ ″	′ ″	′ ″	o ′ ″
Auguft 18 A. M.	5 37 58	14 3 0	14 14 40	6 31 44	6 35 11	57 13	3+2	76 57 20
	5 41 23	14 12 0	14 23 40	6 35 44	6 39 11	57 48		
	5 42 28	14 15 0	14 26 40	6 36 19	6 39 46	57 18		
	5 43 39	14 18 0	14 29 40	6 37 27	6 40 54	57 15		76 57 30
	5 45 49	14 24 0	14 35 40	6 39 1	6 42 28	56 39		
	5 47 4	14 27 0	14 38 40	6 40 49	6 44 16	57 12		
	5 48 13	14 30 0	14 41 40	6 42 1	6 45 28	57 15		
	5 49 21	14 33 0	14 44 40	6 43 9	6 46 36	57 15		76 57 40
	5 59 59	15 0 0	15 11 50	6 53 27	6 56 54	57 15		
	6 0 53	15 3 0	15 14 50	6 54 37	6 58 4	57 11		
	6 1 58	15 6 0	15 17 50	6 55 45	6 59 12	57 14		
	6 3 8	15 9 0	15 20 50	6 56 53	7 0 20	57 12		
	6 4 17	15 12 0	15 23 50	6 58 3	7 1 30	57 13		
	6 5 29	15 15 0	15 26 50	6 59 12	7 2 39	57 10		76 57 50
	6 6 36	15 18 0	15 29 50	7 0 24	7 3 51	57 15		
	6 7 42	15 21 0	15 32 50	7 1 33	7 5 0	57 18		
	6 11 19	15 30 0	15 41 50	7 5 1	7 8 28	57 9		
	6 13 32	15 36 0	15 47 50	7 7 19	7 10 46	57 14		
	6 14 49	15 39 0	15 51 0	7 8 33	7 12 0	57 11		
	6 16 1	15 42 0	15 54 0	7 9 43	7 13 10	57 9		
18, P. M.	5 10 49	12 18 0	12 29 0	6 4 21	6 7 42	56 53	3+21	77 6 50
	5 12 55	12 12 0	12 23 0	6 6 35	6 9 56	57 1		
	5 14 6	12 9 0	12 20 0	6 7 43	6 11 4	56 58		
	5 15 14	12 6 0	12 17 0	6 8 51	6 12 12	56 58		
	5 16 16	12 3 0	12 14 0	6 9 58	6 13 19	57 3		
	5 17 22	12 0 0	12 11 0	6 11 5	6 14 26	57 4		
	5 18 40	11 57 0	12 8 0	6 12 13	6 15 34	56 54		
	5 19 35	11 54 0	12 5 0	6 13 21	6 16 42	57 7		
	5 20 48	11 51 0	12 1 50	6 14 27	6 17 48	57 0		
	5 21 51	11 48 0	11 58 50	6 15 40	6 19 1	57 10		

	I. Aug. 14, P. M.	II. Aug. 15, A. M.	III. Aug. 18, A. M.	IV. Aug. 18, P. M.
At 12ʰ by the Watch, mean Time at Smeerenberg,	12ʰ 56′ 2″	12ʰ 56′ 0″	12ʰ 57′ 11′	12ʰ 57′ 1
At Greenwich, by the Watch,	12 16 45	12 16 45	12 17 35	12 17 35
Difference of Meridians,	0 39 17	0 39 15	0 39 36	0 39 26
Longitude of Smeerenberg,	9° 49′ 15″	9° 48′ 45″	9° 54′ 0″	9° 51′ 30″

Mean of the firft, fecond, and fourth, 9° 49′ 40″; of all, 9° 50′ 45″ E.

At 12ʰ by the Watch, mean Time at Smeerenberg,	12ʰ 56′ 2″	12ʰ 56′ 0″	12ʰ 57′ 11″	12ʰ 57′ 1
At Greenwich, by Kendal,	12 5 21	12 5 21	12 6 31	12 6 33
Difference of Meridians,	0 50 41	0 50 39	0 50 40	0 50 28
Longitude of Smeerenberg,	12° 40′ 15″	12° 39′ 45″	12° 40′ 0″	12° 37′ 0″

Mean 12° 39′ 15″ E.

From comparing the 1ft with the 3d, the Watch lofes in a Day, 19,7
            4th, ... 14,8
      2d . . 3d, ... 23,7
           4th, ... 17,4

Mean of all four, ... 18,9

Obfervations

Obfervations for finding the Longitude by the Time-keepers.

Auguſt 31, P. M.

Time by the Watch.	Alt. of the Sun's lower Limb.	Alt. of the Sun's Center.	Apparent Time.	Mean Time.	Watch too flow.			
h ' ''	o ' ''	o ' ''	h ' ''	h ' ''	' ''			
6 1 54	4 35 0	4 36 10	6 35 43	6 35 31	33 37		Lat.	68° 46' 0''
6 4 31	4 23 0	4 23 50	6 38 1	6 37 49	33 18		Co. Decl.	81 37 10
6 6 20	4 10 0	4 10 30	6 40 33	6 40 21	34 1	Mean	Eq. Time	0—12
6 7 40	4 2 0	4 2 10	6 42 7	6 41 55	34 15	33' 51''		
6 10 1	3 51 0	3 50 50	6 44 16	6 44 4	34 3			
6 11 33	3 44 0	3 43 30	6 45 39	6 45 27	33 54			

h ' ''   h ' ''

At 12ʰ by the Watch, mean Time at the Ship,   12 33 51 . . . . 12 33 51
At Greenwich, by the Watch,   12 20 15 by Kendal, 12 7 57

Difference of Meridians,   0 13 36   0 25 54
Longitude of the Ship,   3° 24' 0'' E   6° 28' 30''

Sept. 3, P. M.

Time by the Watch.	Alt. of the Sun's lower Limb.	Alt. of the Sun's Center.	Apparent Time.	Mean Time.	Watch too flow.			
h ' ''	o ' ''	o ' ''	h ' ''	h ' ''	' ''			
5 14 0	7 50 0	7 55 30	5 46 31	5 45 25	31 25		Lat.	65° 31' 0''
5 16 30	7 30 0	7 35 20	5 48 52	5 47 46	31 16		Co. Decl.	82 41 20
5 17 7	7 24 30	7 29 30	5 49 34	5 48 28	31 21		Eq. Time	1— 6
5 18 20	7 20 0	7 25 0	5 50 5	5 48 59	30 39	Mean		
5 18 55	7 16 30	7 21 30	5 50 30	5 49 24	30 29	30' 41''		
5 19 40	7 13 0	7 18 0	5 50 55	5 49 49	30 9			
5 20 50	7 4 30	7 9 20	5 52 16	5 51 10	30 20			
5 21 50	6 58 0	7 2 50	5 52 43	5 51 37	29 47			

h ' ''   h ' ''

At 12ʰ by the Watch, mean Time at the Ship,   12 30 41 . . . . 12 30 41
At Greenwich, by the Watch,   12 20 51 by Kendal, 12 8 38

Difference of Meridians,   0 9 50   0 22 3
Longitude of the Ship,   2° 27' 30'' E   5° 30' 45''

Sept. 6, A. M.

Time by the Watch.	Alt. of the Sun's lower Limb.	Alt. of the Sun's Center.	Apparent Time.	Mean Time.	Watch too flow.			
h ' ''	o ' ''	o ' ''	h ' ''	h ' ''	' ''			
8 56 25	26 50 0	27 0 10	9 22 57	9 20 59	24 34		Lat.	62° 50' 0''
8 58 27	26 58 0	27 8 10	9 24 35	9 22 38	24 11	Mean	Co. Decl.	83 41 30
						24' 22''	Eq. Time	1—58

h ' ''   h ' ''

At 12ʰ by the Watch, mean Time at the Ship,   12 24 22 . . . . 12 24 22
At Greenwich, by the Watch,   12 21 28 by Kendal, 12 9 22

Difference of Meridians,   0 2 54   0 15 0
Longitude of the Ship,   0° 43' 30'' E   3° 45' 0''

O o   Obſervations

Observations for finding the Longitude by the Time-keepers.								
Sept. 6, P. M.								
Time by the Watch.	Alt. of the Sun's lower Limb.	Alt. of the Sun's Center.	Apparent Time.	Mean Time.	Watch too slow.			
h ′ ″	o ′ ″	o ′ ″	h ′ ″	h ′ ″	′ ″		Lat. 61° 57′ 0″	
4 44 14	10 35 0	10 42 10	5 15 17	5 13 14	29 0		Co. Decl. 83 49 0	
4 45 54	10 26 0	10 33 0	5 16 35	5 14 32	28 38		Eq. Time 2—3	
4 47 29	10 13 0	10 20 0	5 18 27	5 16 24	28 55	Mean		
4 48 59	10 4 0	10 10 50	5 19 45	5 17 42	28 43	28′ 49″		
4 50 0	9 56 0	10 1 50	5 21 2	5 18 59	28 59			
4 52 36	9 39 0	9 45 40	5 23 20	5 21 17	28 41			

At 12ʰ by the Watch, mean Time at the Ship,   12 28 49 . . . . 12 28 49
At Greenwich, by the Watch,   12 21 28 by Kendal, 12 9 22

Difference of Meridians,   0 7 21   0 19 27
Longitude of the Ship,   1° 50′ 15″ E   4° 51′ 45″

Sept. 14, P. M.								
Time by the Watch.	Alt. of the Sun's lower Limb.	Alt. of the Sun's Center.	Apparent Time.	Mean Time.	Watch too slow.			
h ′ ″	o ′ ″	o ′ ″	h ′ ″	h ′ ″	′ ″		Lat. 55° 32′ 0″	
2 54 41	22 39 0	22 48 50	3 30 55	3 26 8	31 27		Co. Decl. 86 50 0	
2 55 40	22 36 0	22 45 50	3 31 21	3 26 34	30 54		Eq. Time 4—47	
2 56 34	22 29 0	22 38 50	3 32 17	3 27 30	30 56	Mean		
2 57 41	22 18 0	22 27 50	3 33 48	3 29 1	31 20	31′ 12″		
2 58 52	22 10 0	22 19 50	3 34 52	3 30 5	31 13			
3 2 24	21 43 0	22 52 50	3 38 31	3 33 44	31 20			

At 12ʰ by the Watch, mean Time at the Ship,   12 31 12 . . . . 12 31 12
At Greenwich, by the Watch,   12 23 6 by Kendal, 12 10 31

Difference of Meridians,   0 8 6   0 20 41
Longitude of the Ship,   2° 1′ 30″ E   5° 10′ 15″

Sept. 25, A. M. in Hosely Bay.								
Time by the Watch.	Alt. of the Sun's lower Limb.	Alt. of the Sun's Center.	Apparent Time.	Mean Time.	Watch too slow.			
h ′ ″	o ′ ″	o ′ ″	h ′ ″	h ′ ″	′ ″		Lat. 52° 6′ 0″	
9 22 47	30 54 0	31 4 40	9 58 47	9 50 17	28 30	Mean	N. Pol. dist. 91 1 10	
9 24 17	31 5 0	31 15 40	10 0 49	9 52 19	28 2	28′ 16″	Eq. Time 8—30	

At 12ʰ by the Watch, mean Time at the Ship,   12 28 16 . . . . 12 28 16
At Greenwich, by the Watch,   12 25 21 by Kendal, 12 14 37

Difference of Meridians,   0 2 55   0 13 39
Longitude of the Ship,   0° 43′ 45″ E   3° 24′ 45″

Observations

Observations for finding the Longitude by the Moon.

June 13, A. M.

Time by Arnold.	Alt. of the Sun's lower Limb.	Alt. of the Moon's lower Limb.	Distance of the Sun and Moon's nearest Limbs.	True Distance of the Centers.	Apparent Time at Greenwich.	Apparent Time at the Ship.	Diff. of Meridians.	Longitude of the Ship.
h ′ ″	° ′ ″	° ′ ″	° ′ ″	° ′ ″	h ′ ″	h ′ ″	′ ″	° ′ ″
10 16 17	49 39 0	21 17 0	74 37 0	74 30 53	22 17 17	22 20 37	3 20	0 50 0 E
10 20 17	49 55 0	20 54 0	74 37 0	74 30 39	22 17 47	22 24 8	6 21	1 35 15
10 25 35	50 13 0	20 20 0	74 37 0	74 30 22	22 18 23	22 29 27	11 4	2 46 0
							Mean	1 43 45

June 14, A. M.

Correction for Error of the Sextant, — 3′ 46″

Time by Arnold.	Alt. of the Sun's lower Limb.	Alt. of the Moon's lower Limb.	Distance of the Sun and Moon's nearest Limbs.	True Distance of the Centers.	Apparent Time at Greenwich.	Apparent Time at the Ship.	Diff. of Meridians.	Longitude of the Ship.
h ′ ″	° ′ ″	° ′ ″	° ′ ″	° ′ ″	h ′ ″	h ′ ″	′ ″	° ′ ″
9 44 32	45 57 0	30 42 0	63 47 30	63 45 45	21 52 12	21 43 56	8 16	2 4 0 W
9 48 41	40 21 0	30 26 0	63 44 0	63 41 54	22 0 42	21 48 20	12 22	3 5 30
9 52 53	46 41 0	30 10 0	63 41 30	63 39 3	22 6 59	21 52 4	14 55	3 43 45
							Mean	2 57 45 W

June 15, A. M.

Time by Arnold.	Alt. of the Sun's lower Limb.	Alt. of the Moon's lower Limb.	Distance of the Sun and Moon's nearest Limbs.	True Distance of the Centers.	Apparent Time at Greenwich.	Apparent Time at the Ship.	Diff. of Meridians.	Longitude of the Ship.
h ′ ″	° ′ ″	° ′ ″	° ′ ″	° ′ ″	h ′ ″	h ′ ″	′ ″	° ′ ″
10 30 36	49 50 0	34 10 0	52 35 0	52 37 41	22 32 3	22 32 12	0 9	0 2 15 E
10 32 4	49 54 0	34 20 0	52 34 45	52 37 23	22 34 56	22 33 40	1 16	0 19 30 W
10 34 33	50 3 0	34 10 0	52 32 0	52 34 26	22 39 17	22 30 0	3 8	0 47 0
10 36 23	50 9 0	34 4 0	52 32 0	52 34 18	22 39 35	22 37 59	1 36	0 24 0
10 39 54	50 18 0	33 51 0	52 31 15	52 33 20	22 41 44	22 41 30	0 14	0 3 30
10 41 34	50 28 0	33 40 0	52 31 0	52 32 51	22 42 47	22 42 10	0 37	0 9 15
							Mean	0 17 0 W

June 25, P. M.

Time by the Watch.	Alt. of the Sun's lower Limb.	Alt. of the Moon's lower Limb.	Distance of the Sun and Moon's nearest Limbs.	True Distance of the Centers.	Apparent Time at Greenwich.	Apparent Time at the Ship.	Diff. of Meridians.	Longitude of the Ship.
h ′ ″	° ′ ″	° ′ ″	° ′ ″	° ′ ″	h ′ ″	h ′ ″	′ ″	° ′ ″
7 49 2	12 54 0	11 40 0	65 58 0	66 21 55	7 30 23	8 22 13	51 50	12 57 30 E

Observations

Observations for finding the Longitude by the Moon.

June 26, P. M.

Time by the Watch.	Alt. of the Sun's lower Limb.	Center.	Alt. of the Moon's lower Limb.	Center.	Distance of the Sun and Moon's nearest Limbs.	True Distance of the Centers.	Apparent Time at Greenwich.	Apparent Time at the Ship.	Diff. of Meridians.	Longitude of the Ship.
h ' "	o '	o '	o ' "	o ' "	o ' "	o ' "	h ' "	h ' "	' "	o ' "
1 24 25	. .	36 18	. . .	12 51	75 39 30	75 41 30	1 25 1	2 4 15	39 50	9 57 30 E
1 28 14	35 58	. . .								
1 29 48	. .	. . .	12 50 0							
1 32 5	. .	36 1	. . .	13 6	.75 43 0	75 45 13	1 32 5	2 11 55	39 50	9 57 30
1 34 3	. .	. . .	12 58 30							
1 36 9	35 41									

July 11, A. M.

Arnold too slow for Apparent Time 47' 35".   Correction for Error of the Sextant, + 4' 24"

Time by Arnold.	Alt. of the Sun's lower Limb.	Center.	Alt. of the Moon's lower Limb.	Distance of the Sun and Moon's nearest Limbs.	True Distance of the Centers.	Apparent Time at Greenwich.	Apparent Time at the Ship.	Diff. of Meridians.	Longitude of the Ship.
h ' "	o '	o ' "	o ' "	o ' "	o ' "	h ' "	h ' "	' "	o ' "
3 28 15		17 20 10	13 6 0	95 44 0	96 3 35	15 32 47	6 15 50	45 3	10 45 45
3 30 12	17 25								
3 32 22		17 39 20	13 9 0	95 40 0	95 59 20	15 41 58	16 19 57	37 59	9 29 45
3 34 7	17 33								
3 38 48		17 54 30	13 13 0	95 36 0	95 55 8	15 51 3	16 26 23	35 20	8 50 0
3 40 24	17 50								
								Mean	9 42 0 E

Sept. 1, P. M. Moon's Distance observed from Aldebaran.

Time by the Watch.	Computed Alt. of Aldebaran.	Alt. of the Moon's lower Limb.	Distance of the Moon from Aldebaran.	True Distance of the Centers.	Apparent Time at Greenwich.	Apparent Time at the Ship.	Diff. of Meridians.	Longitude of the Ship.
h ' "	o ' "	o ' "	o "	o ' "	h ' "	h ' "	' "	o ' "
11 45 15	17 49 0	17 3 0	76 57 nearest Limb	77 0 59	11 56 7	12 22 44	26 37	6 39 15 E
12 7 43	20 45 0	17 10 0	77 18 farthest Limb	76 48 53	12 19 29	12 45 12	25 43	6 25 30
12 22 44	22 8 0	17 6 0	76 44 nearest Limb	76 44 15	12 27 33	13 0 13	32 40	8 10 0

Sept. 3, P. M. Moon's Distance observed from Aldebaran.

Time by the Watch.	Computed Alt. of Aldebaran.	Alt. of the Moon's lower Limb.	Distance of the Moon's W. limb from Aldeb.	True Diff. of the Moon's Cent. from Aldeb.	Apparent Time at Greenwich.	Apparent Time at the Ship.	Diff. of Meridians.	Longitude of the Ship.
h ' "	o ' "	o ' "	o ' "	o ' "	h ' "	h ' "	' "	o ' "
11 20 35	17 47 0	24 47 0	39 39 0	39 57 5	11 30 43	11 55 47	25 4	6 16 0 E

Observations

APPENDIX.

Observations of the Moon and Jupiter.

August 31, P.M.

Time by the Watch	Alt. of Jupiter	Alt. of the Moon's lower Limb	Distance of Jupiter and the Moon's farther Limb	True Distance of the Centers	Difference of Longitude	Difference between the Distance and Difference of Longitude	Longitude of Jupiter	Latitude of Jupiter	Latitude of the Moon	Longitude of the Moon by Observation	Longitude of the Moon by Ephemeris	Difference from Longitude	Apparent Time at Greenwich	Apparent Time at the Ship	Difference of Meridians	Longitude of the Ship
h ´ ´´	° ´ ´´	° ´ ´´	° ´ ´´	° ´ ´´	° ´ ´´	´ ´´	° ´ ´´	° ´	° ´	s ° ´ ´´	s ° ´ ´´	° ´ ´´	h ´ ´´	h ´ ´´	´ ´´	° ´ ´´
8 51 33	10 25 0	9 0 0	32 55 0	32 35 52	1 25 35	— 10 17	0 7 29	1 36 S	1 47 N	11 5 3 25	at 6ʰ 11 3 39 54	at 6ʰ 1 23 29	8 33 22	9 25 37	52 15	13 3 45
9 3 27	10 59 0	9 36 0	32 47 0	32 27 47	2 17 37	— 10 10	. . .	. .	. .	11 5 11 23		1 31 29	8 48 10	9 37 31	49 21	12 20 15
9 32 45	13 19 0	10 55 0	32 29 0	32 7 33	1 57 23	— 10 10	. . .	. .	1 43	11 5 31 37	at 9ʰ 11 5 17 57	at 9ʰ 0 13 40	9 25 7	10 6 49	41 42	10 25 30
9 51 54	14 40 0	11 36 0	32 22 0	31 59 18	1 49 8	— 10 10	. . .	. .	. .	11 5 39 52		0 21 55	9 40 17	10 25 58	45 41	11 25 15
10 38 25	17 45 0	12 49 0	31 58 0	31 31 27	1 21 17	— 10 10	0 7 30	. .	. .	11 5 49 46		0 49 46	10 31 29	11 21 29	41 0	10 15 0
10 43 18	20 52 0	13 6 0	31 28 0	30 57 24	0 47 14	— 10 10	. . .	. .	. .	11 6 41 46	at 12ʰ	at 12ʰ 1 23 49	11 30 34	12 17 22	46 48	11 42 0
1 35 37	22 45 0	9 55 0	30 33 0	29 54 38	0 29 44 28	— 10 10	. . .	1 38		11 7 44 32	11 6 55 45	0 48 17	13 29 40	14 9 41	40 1	10 0 15

Mean 11° 13′ E.

September 1, P.M.

Time by the Watch	Alt. of Jupiter	Alt. of the Moon's lower Limb	Distance of Jupiter and the Moon's farther Limb	True Distance of the Centers	Difference of Longitude	Difference between the Distance and Difference of Longitude	Longitude of Jupiter	Latitude of Jupiter	Latitude of the Moon	Longitude of the Moon by Observation	Longitude of the Moon by Ephemeris, at Midnight.	Difference of Longitude by Ephemeris from Longitude at Midnight.	Apparent Time at Greenwich	Apparent Time at the Ship	Difference of Meridians	Longitude of the Ship
h ´ ´´	° ´ ´´	° ´ ´´	° ´ ´´	° ´ ´´	´ ´´	´ ´´	° ´ ´´	° ´	° ´	s ° ´ ´´	s ° ´ ´´	° ´ ´´	h ´ ´´	h ´ ´´	´ ´´	° ´ ´´
11 59 20	21 55 0	17 8 0	18 8 0	17 38 22	0 17 26 21	— 12 1	0 7 23 30	1 36 S	1 4 N	11 19 57 9	11 19 48 53	0 8 16	12 15 39	12 36 49	21 10	5 17 30
16 14	22 8 17 0		18 4 0	17 33 56	0 17 21 55	. . .	. . .	. .	. .	11 20 1 35		0 13	12 24 40	12 53 43	29 3	7 15 45

September 3, P.M. with the Megameter, Correction for Error of Adjustment, + 2′ 52″.

Time by the Watch	Alt. of the Moon's lower Limb	Alt. of Jupiter	Distance of Jupiter and the Moon's Western Limb	True Difference of the Centers	Parallax in Latitude	Parallax in Altitude	Parallax in Longitude	Apparent Latitude of the Moon	Latitude of the Moon	Longitude of Jupiter	Difference between the Distance and Difference of Longitude	Difference of Longitude	Apparent Longitude of the Moon	Longitude of the Moon corrected by Parallax	Apparent Longitude of the Moon	Apparent Time at the Ship	Apparent Time at Greenwich	Difference of Meridians
h ´ ´´	° ´ ´´	° ´ ´´	° ´ ´´	° ´ ´´	´ ´´	´ ´´	´ ´´	° ´	° ´	s ° ´ ´´	´ ´´	s ° ´ ´´	s ° ´ ´´	s ° ´ ´´	s ° ´ ´´	h ´ ´´	h ´ ´´	´ ´´
9 30 53	15 33 0	15 27 0	6 40 0	6 57 58	+ 10 37	52 9	— 10 37	1 59 S	1 7	6 57 36	— 22	0 14 1 36	0 13 53 59	10 6 5	10 8 43	2 38 W		
9 45 20	16 47 0	16 50 0	6 52 44	7 10 42	+ 11 48	52 51	— 14 2	1 59	1 8	7 10 20	— 22	0 14 14 20	0 14 2 32	10 20 32	10 31 14	10 42		
10 1 4	18 6 0	18 7 0	7 1 10	7 19 8	+ 13 9	52 28	— 14 9	1 59	1 8	7 18 47	— 21	0 14 22 47	0 14 9 38	10 36 16	10 45 4	8 48		
10 25 7	20 12 0	20 14 0	7 8 4	7 26 2	+ 15 16	51 47	— 14 29	1 58	1 9	7 25 41	— 21	0 14 29 41	0 14 14 29	11 1 19	10 54 24	6 55		
10 40 54	21 30 0	21 54 0	7 16 10	7 34 8	+ 16 51	51 21	— 14 48	1 58	1 9	7 33 47	— 21	0 14 37 47	0 14 20 50	11 16 0	11 7 13	8 53		

The Elements of the above Calculation.

Apparent Time	Right Ascension of Mid-heaven	Longitude of Mid-heaven	Declination of Mid-heaven	Alt. of culminating Point	Apparent Latitude of the Moon	Latitude of the Moon	Parallax in Altitude	Longitude of the Moon corrected by Parallax	Apparent Longitude of the Moon	Alt. of the Nonagesimal	Angle between the Meridian and the Secondary to the Ecliptic	Longitude of the Nonagesimal	Longitude of the Moon	Distance of the Moon and the Nonagesimal
h ´ ´´	° ´	s ° ´	° ´	° ´	° ´		° ´ ´´	s ° ´ ´´	s ° ´ ´´	° ´	° ´	s ° ´	s ° ´	° ´ ´´
10 0 0	313 2	10 10 35	17 36 S	7 4	1 7		6 57 36	0 13 53 59	0 14 1 36	15 46	17 4	8 5 4	13 47	4 8 43
11 0 0	328 4	10 25 48	12 56	11 44	1 8		7 10 20	0 14 2 32	0 14 14 20	19 45	22 5	8 27 22	14 17	4 16 55
12 0 0	343 6	11 11 40	7 12	17 28	1 9		7 18 47	0 14 9 38	0 14 22 47	22 23	28 7	9 21 14	14 48	4 23 34

Latitude of Jupiter, 1° 37′ S
Longitude, 0ˢ 0° 0 4′
Watch too flow for } 35′ 12″
Apparent Time, }

F I N I S.

P p

DIRECTIONS to the BOOKBINDER.

Q q